PAH PUBLISHING

Salvage Yard Buyers Guide Series

PONTIAC MUSCLE CARS
Mechanical Parts 1964-1972

by
John R. Miller

First Published in 2002 by PAH Publishing International
711 Hillcrest , Monett, Missouri 65708 USA

Salvage Yard Buyers Guide Pontiac Muscle Cars: Mechanical Parts
ISBN: 978-0-9716459-6-7
Volume No 1 Salvage Yard Buyer Guide Series: Pontiac Muscle Car Mechanical Parts Second Printing 2003

Cover 1967 GTO owned by Eugene and Judi Anderson of Green Forest, Ark. **Back** 1969 Firebird 400 convertible at CST Auto Salvage Aroura, Mo

Printed and bound in the United States of America

PAH
Publishing

ACKNOWLEDGMENTS

This book would have not been possible if it were not for the assistance of the individuals. All those at R& R Auto salvage in Aurora, MO, and very special thank you to Ed Witte for letting me photograph parts at his salvage yard CST also in Aurora, MO. Ed has a large section of Pontiac parts and can be reached by phone at 417-678-6994 or fax him a list of your wanted parts at 417-678-7305.

On a personal note I would like to thank all those at PAH Publishing, for believing in this project. Also I would like to thank my family ,my lovely wife would didn't see me for days on end, because I was hidden behind a pile of GM part catalogs. Also to mom and dad, and the rest of my extended family. And finally to the Pontiac fans, it is your belief in this brand that keeps it running strong. -J.R. Miller

CONTENTS

Chapter 1: Engines

Engine

One of, if not the most, popular interchanges is an engine. Swapping in a big block for a small cube is still the best method of adding quick horsepower. But before you go jumping in you should take some time to familiarize yourself with the identification and inspection of used engines.

Identification

Engines can be identified by several different methods. If you're truly well grounded in Pontiac lore you may be able to distinguish one from the other by their appearance. Yet you may still need the casting number and or engine identification codes to help you discern one block from another.

CASTING NUMBERS

Actually referred to as a block part number by Pontiac, this number will appear near the top rear of the block. For 1967 and later blocks the casting number location was moved to the rear of the block, just behind the number 8 cylinder bore. Another quick method of identifying a 1967 or later block is that they have three freeze plugs, while earlier feature two freeze plugs.

The casting date is also key to identifying the block. It is stamped on the distributor hole and consists of a code letter for the month of casting, followed by the day of the month and the year, January-A through L-December. For example the code C117 would translate to March 11, 1967.

Some blocks, like the 1970 455-ci, 350-ci and 1968-69 428-ci have the displacement cast into the block, and this can be used. However never rely on this as the only method of identifying a block.

Engine Block Casting Numbers

Casting Number	Ram Air	Model Year Usage	Casting Number	Ram Air	Model Year Usage	Notes
326-ci Displacement						
9773153		1964	9778840		1966	
9778840		1965	9786339		1967	
350-ci Displacement						
9790079		1968-69	481990		1971-72	
9799916		1970			1972	
389-ci Displacement						
9773155		1964	9778789		1966	
9778789		1965				
400-ci Displacement						
9786133		1967	9799915	Yes	1970	
9792506	Yes	1968-69	979914	No	1970	
9790071	No	1968-69	481988		1971-72	
421-ci Displacement						
9773157		1964	9778791		1966*	*-early
9778791		1965	9782611		1966**	**-late
428-ci Displacement						
9786135		1967	9792968		1968	
455-ci Displacement						
9799140		1970	483677		1971#	#-H.O.
485428		1971*	485428		1972	*-except H.O.

Block casting number appears at the back of block. This number indicates a 400-ci block. The clock at the left indicates that the block was cast at, 2:00 o'clock.

Some blocks have the displacement cast in the sides.

ENGINE IDENTIFICATION NUMBERS

Because certain blocks may have the same casting (part) number, yet have different internal components, the best method for identifying an engine assembly is decoding the engine identification number. On V-8s this number is located on a machined pad on the passenger's side of the block, just under the engine production code. On the Sprint six-cylinder the number appears on the cylinder head to block contact surface behind the oil filler pipe. Engine identifications vary according to model and model year, yet there is a great deal of interchange available. Use the following charts to help you identify the engine.

Testing

It is best to run tests on a running engine. That way you can perform a series of tests, which include compression, leak down, vacuum, and you can listen for mechanical noises and look for signs of wear like smoke. However, in most cases finding a running engine is impractical. Yet there are tests that you can still run that will help you evaluate the engines condition.

First, you should give the block and its components an overall inspection. Look for signs of damage such as cracks and breaks; take extra time inspecting the area around mating areas. If possible, remove the cylinder heads, intake and exhaust manifolds. Take extra care in looking at these areas as cracks have a tendency to occur here. A cracked block is not worth the trouble.

Engine identification is found at the front of the block. The Y4 code indicates a 1973 400-ci block.

Next, check to see if the engine is frozen. Pour a small amount of oil down each of the bores to prevent cylinder ring scoring. Then use a large break over wrench, not under ½-inch drive, and a socket to attach to the front of the crankshaft and check to see if the engine is free moving. A engine that will not move indicates a frozen block, which can indicate rusted parts and require a complete rebuild. The engine should offer some resistance, as a free moving engine indicates the rings are worn. An engine that moves, then suddenly stops can indicate broken engine parts.

Pulling the spark plugs and inspecting them can give you an indication of the engines condition. Wet black deposits on the plugs indicate that oil is blowing past the rings, or the intake-valves. Black dry fluffy deposits on the plugs indicate a rich mixture and is not much of a consideration in determining an engines overall condition. If you find damage to a plug's electrode tip, be wary of misalign engine parts. Another simple test is to pull the oil dipstick and look for signs of water, which will show up as droplets. This can indicate a cracked block.

326-ci V-8 Engine Identification Codes

Code	Horsepower	Compression	Carburetor 2-BBL	4-BBL	Transmission MAN.	AUTO.	Model Year	Model
WP	250	8.6	X		X		1965-67	TEMPEST
WR	285	10.5		X	X		1965-67	TEMPEST
YN	250	8.6	X			X	1965	TEMPEST
YP	285	10.5		X		X	1965	TEMPEST
WX	250	9.2	X		X		1966-67	TEMPEST
XF	250	9.2	X			T.H.	1966-67	TEMPEST
XG	285	10.5		X		T.H.	1966-67	TEMPEST
YN	250	9.2	X			T.H.	1966-67	TEMPEST
YP	285	10.5		X		T.H.	1966-67	TEMPEST
WC	250	9.2	X		X		1967	FIREBIRD
WH	250	9.2	X		X		1967	FIREBIRD
WK	285	10.5		X	X		1967	FIREBIRD
WO	285	10.5		X	X		1967	FIREBIRD
XI	250	9.2	X			X	1967	FIREBIRD
XO	285	10.5		X		X	1967	FIREBIRD
YJ	250	9.2	X			X	1967	FIREBIRD
YM	285	10.5		X		X	1967	FIREBIRD
925	250	8.6	X		X		1964	TEMPEST
945	280	10.5		X	X		1964	TEMPEST
960	250	8.6	X			X	1964	TEMPEST
971	280	10.5		X		X	1964	TEMPEST

T.H. Turbo-Hydra-Matic

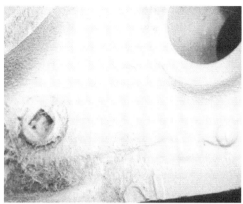

Some blocks have the last two digits of the model year

This mark indicates the day shift.

350-ci V-8 Engine Identification Codes

Code	Horsepower	Compression	Carburetor 2-BBL	4-BBL	Transmission MAN.	AUTO.	Model Year	Model
WP	265	9.2	X		X		1968-EARLY 1969	TEMPEST
WR	320	10.5		X	X		1968 — EARLY 1969	TEMPEST
YN	265	9.2	X			X	1968-EARLY 1969	TEMPEST
YP	320	10.5		X		X	1968, 1971	TEMPEST (Firebird 1971 only)
WU	265/255	9.2	X		X		LATE 1969-70	TEMPEST, FIREBIRD
WV	330	10.5		X	X		LATE 1969	TEMPEST
XR	265	9.2	X			X	EARLY 1969, 1971	TEMPEST, (Firebird 1971 ONLY)
XS	265	9.2	X			X	1969	TEMPEST
XT	330	10.5		X		X	EARLY 1969	TEMPEST
XU	330	10.5		X		X	LATE 1969	TEMPEST
YN	265	9.2	X			X	EARLY 1969, 1971	TEMPEST, (Firebird 1971 only)
YU	265/255/160	9.2/8.0	X			X	LATE 1969-72	TEMPEST, FIREBIRD
WN	250	8.0	X		3-SPD		1971	TEMPEST, FIREBIRD
WP	250	8.0	X		4-SPD.		1971	TEMPEST, FIREBIRD
WR	250/160	8.0	X		3-SPD.		1971-72	TEMPEST, FIREBIRD
WU	250	8.0	X		4-SPD.		1971	TEMPEST, FIREBIRD
YR	160	8.0	X			X	1972	TEMPEST
WC	265	9.2	X		X		1968-EARLY 1968	FIREBIRD
WK	320	10.5		X	X		1968-EARLY 1969	FIREBIRD
YJ	265	9.2	X			X	1968	FIREBIRD
YM	320	10.5		X		X	1968	FIREBIRD
WM	265	9.2	X		X		LATE 1969	FIREBIRD
WN	325	10.5		X	X		LATE 1969	FIREBIRD
XB	265	9.2	X			X	LATE 1969	FIREBIRD
XC	325	10.5		X		X	LATE 1969	FIREBIRD
XD	325	10.5		X		X	EARLY 1969	FIREBIRD
XL	265	9.2	X			X	EARLY 1969	FIREBIRD
YE	265	9.2	X			X	LATE 1969	FIREBIRD

389-ci Engine Identification Codes

Code	Horsepower	Compression	Carburetor 2-BBL	4-BBL	Transmission MAN.	AUTO.	Model Year	Model
76X	348	10.75	3x2		X		1964	Tempest
77J	348	10.75	3x2			X	1964	Tempest
78X	325	10.75		X	X		1964	Tempest
79J	325	10.75		X		X	1964	Tempest
O1A	215	8.6	X		X		1964	Catalina
O2B	215	8.6	X		X		1964	Catalina
23B	306	10.5		X	X		1964	Catalina
32B	330	10.75	3x2		X		1964	Catalina
10A	283	10.5	X			x	1964	Catalina
04L	230	8.6	X			X	1964	Catalina
05L	230	8.6	X			X	1964	Catalina
25K	303	105		X		X	1964	Catalina
26K	303	10.5		X		X	1964	Catalina
11H	267	10.5	X			X	1964	Catalina
12H	267	10.5	X			X	1964	Catalina
13H	240	7.9	X			X	1964	Catalina
33G	330	10.75	3x2			X	1964	Catalina
WS	360	10.75	3x2		X		1965-66	Tempest
WT	335	10.75		X	X		1965 -66	Tempest
YR	360	10.75	3x2			X	1965 -66	Tempest
YS	335	10.75		X		X	1965 -66	Tempest
WA	256	8.6	X		X		1965-66	Catalina
WB	256	8.6	X		X		1965 -66	Catalina
XA	260	7.9	X		X		1965 -66	Catalina
WC	290	10.5	X		X		1965 -66	Catalina
WE	333	10.5		X	X		1965 -66	Catalina
WF	338	10.75	3x2		X		1965	Catalina
YA	256	8.6	X			X	1965-66	Catalina
YB	256	8.6	X			X	1965 -66	Catalina
YC	290	10.5	X			X	1965 -66	Catalina
YD	290	10.5	X			X	1965 –66	Catalina
YE	325	10.5		X		X	1965 -66	Catalina
YF	325	10.5		X		X	1965 -66	Catalina
XB	260	7.9	X			X	1965 -66	Catalina
YG	338	10.75	3x2			X	1965	Catalina
WV	360	10.75	3x2		X		1966	Tempest
WW	360	10.75		X	X		1966	Tempest
XS	360	10.75	3x2		X		1966	Tempest
XE	335	10.75		X		X	1966	Tempest
YU	290	10.5	X			X	1966	Catalina
YV	290	10.5	X			X	1966	Catalina
YL	325	10.5		X		X	1966	Catalina
YW	325	10.5		X		X	1966	Catalina
YX	325	10.5		X		X	1966	Catalina

400-ci Engine Identification Codes

Code	Horsepower	Compression	2-BBL	4-BBL	MAN.	AUTO.	Model Year	Model
WA	265	8.6	X		X		1967 -68	Catalina
WA	290	10.5	X		X		1969	Catalina
WB	265	8.6	X		X		1967 -68	Catalina
WB	290	10.5	X		X		1969	Catalina
WD	333	10.5		X	X		1967	Catalina
WD	290	10.5	X		X		1969	Catalina
WE	290	10.0	X		3-spd		1970	All
WE	333	10.5		X	X		1967 -68	Catalina
WE	290	10.5	X		X		1969	Catalina
WH	345	10.75		X	X		1969	Firebird
WI	325/335	10.75		X	X		1967-68	Firebird
WK	300/200	8.2		X	x		1971	All
WL	325	10.75		Q-Jet	X		1967	Firebird
WQ	325/335	10.75		Q-Jet	X		1967-69	Firebird
WS	265/200	8.2	X		3-spd		1971-72	All
WS	366	10.25		X	X		1970	Tempest, Firebird
WS	360/366	10.75		X	X		1967-69	GTO
WT	300	8.2		X	3-spd		1971	All
WT	330/350	10.25		X	3-spd		1970	Firebird
WT	335/350	10.75		X	X		1967-69	GTO
WU	325	10.75		Q-Jet	X		1967	Firebird
WV	360	10.75		X	X		1967	GTO
WW	335/366	10.75		X	X		1967-69	GTO
WX	265	8.2	X		3-spd		1971	All
WX	350	10.0		X	3-spd		1970	Grand Prix
WX	350	10.5		X	X		1969	Grand Prix
WZ	325/330	10.75		X	X		1967-69	Firebird
XB	260	7.9	X			X	1967	Catlaina
XC	260	7.9	X			X	1967	Catlaina
XH	350	10.0		X		X	1970	Grand Prix
XH	333-350	10.5		X		X	1967-68	Catlaina
XH	350	10.5		X		X	1969	Grand Prix
XL	255	8.6	X			X	1967	GTO
XM	255/265	8.6	X			X	1967-69	GTO
XN	370	10.5		X		X	1970	Tempest, Firebird
XN	325/336=5	10.75		Q-Jet		X	1967-68	Firebird
XN	345	10.75		X		X	1969	Firebird
XP	370	10.5		X		X	1970	Tempest, Firebird
XP	360	10.75		X		X	1967-69	GTO
XS	360	10.75		X	X		1967-68	GTO
XV	330	10.25		X		X	1970	All
XX	265	8.2	X			X	1971	All
XX	265	8.6	X			X	1969-70	GTO- 69 all 1970
XY	333	10.5		X	X		1967	Catlaina
XZ	330	10.25		X		X	1970	All
XZ	333/350	10.5		X	X		1967-68	Catlaina
YA	265	8.6	X			X	1967-68	Catlaina
YA	265	10.5	X			X	1969	Catalina
YB	265	8.6	X			X	1967	Catalina
YB	265	8.8	X			X	1970	All
YB	290	10.5	X			X	1969	Catalina
YC	290	10.5	X			X	1967-68	Catalina
YD	290	10.0	X			X	1970	All
YD	290	10.5	X			X	1967, 1969	Catlaina
YE	325	10.5		X		X	1967-68	Catlaina
YF	325	10.5		X		X	1967	Catlaina
YF	265	10.5	X			X	1969	Grand Prix
YR	360	10.75		X	X		1967	GTO
YS	300/200	8.2		X		X	1971-72	All
YS	330/350	10.25		X		X	1970	All
YS	335/350	10.75		X		X	1967-69	GTO
YT	325/330	10.75		Q-Jet		X	1967-69	Firebird
YW	335	10.75		Q-Jet		X	1968-69	Firebird
YX	265/180	8.2	X			X	1971-72	All
YZ	345	10.5		X		X	1970	Firebird
YZ	360	10.75		X		X	1967-68	GTO
ZS	200/250	8.2		X		X	1972	All
ZX	180	8.2	X			X	1972	All

421-ci Engine Identification Codes

Code	Horsepower	Compression	Carburetor		Transmission		Model Year	Model
			2-BBL	4-BBL	MAN.	AUTO.		
35B	320	10.5		X	X		1964	Catalina, Grand Prix
44B	350	10.75	3x2		X		1964	Catalina, Grand Prix
45B	370	10.75	3x2		X		1964	Catalina, Grand Prix
46G	370	10.75	3x2			X	1964	Catalina, Grand Prix
47S	350	10.75	3x2			X	1964	Catalina, Grand Prix
38S	320	10.5		X		X	1964	Catalina, Grand Prix
43N	320	10.5		X		X	1964	Starchief, Bonneville
50Q	370	10.75	3x2			X	1964	Starchief
49N	350	10.75	3x2			X	1964	Starchief
WG	338	10.5		X	X		1965	full-size Pontiac
WH	356	10.75	3x2		X		1965-66	full-size Pontiac
WJ	376	10.75	3x2		X		1965-66	full-size Pontiac
YH	338	10.5		X		X	1965	full-size Pontiac
YJ	356	10.75	3X2			X	1965-66	full-size Pontiac
YK	376	10.75	3X2			X	1965-66	full-size Pontiac
WK	338	10.5		X	X		1966	full-size Pontiac
YT	338	10.5		X		X	1966	full-size Pontiac

428-ci Engine Identification Codes

Code	Horsepower	Compression	Carburetor		Transmission		Model Year	Model
			2-BBL	4-BBL	MAN.	AUTO.		
WG	360/375	10.5		X	X		1967-68	full-size Pontiac
YY(1)	360	10.5		X	X		1967	full-size Pontiac
YJ	376	10.75		X	X		1967	full-size Pontiac
XK(1)	376	10.75		X	X		1967	full-size Pontiac
YH	360	10.5		X		X	1967-68	full-size Pontiac
XD(1)	360	10.5		X		X	1967	full-size Pontiac
YK	376	10.75		X		X	1967-68	full-size Pontiac
Y2	360	10.5		X		X	1967	full-size Pontiac
Y3	376	10.75		X		X	1967	full-size Pontiac
WJ	390	10.75		X	X		1968	full-size Pontiac
WF	370	10.5		X	X		1969	Grand Prix
WL	390	10.75		X	X		1969	Grand Prix
XF	370	10.5		X	X		1969	Grand Prix
XG	390	10.75		X	X		1969	Grand Prix

455-ci Engine Identification Codes

Code	Horsepower	Compression	Carburetor		Transmission		Model Year	Model
			2-BBL	4-BBL	MAN.	AUTO.		
WA	370	10.25		X	X		1970	Tempest
WG	370	10.25		X	X		1970	G.P, full-size Pontiac
YH	360	10.0		X	X		1970	full-size Pontiac
YC	325	8.2		X		X	1971	all
YA	370	10.25		X		X	1970	Tempest
XF	370	10.25		X		X	1970	G.P, full-size Pontiac
WC	335	8.4		X	X		1971	Tempest
WJ	325	8.0		X	X		1971	all
YE	335/300	8.4		X		X	1971-72	Tempest, Firebird
WG	260	8.0	x		X		1971	full-size Pontiac
YA	325/250	8.2		X		X	1971-72	G.P. full-size Pontiac
YG	280	8.2	X			X	1971	full-size Pontiac
WL	325	8.4		X	X		1971	Tempest
WM	300	8.4		X	X		1972	Tempest, Firebird
YB	300	8.4		X		X	1972	Tempest, Firebird
WD	300	8.4		X	X		1972	Firebird
YE	300	8.4		X		X	1972	Firebird

G.P. -Grand Prix

Cylinder Block Interchange

Firebird

1967	
326-ci	1
400-ci	
Without Ram-Air	2
With Ram-Air	3
1968	
350-ci	4
400-ci	
Without Ram-Air	5
With Ram-Air	
Ram Air III	3
Ram Air IV	6
1969	
350-ci	4
400-ci	
Without Ram Air	5
With Ram Air	6
1970	
350-ci	7
400-ci	
Without Ram Air	10
With Ram Air	9
1971	
350-ci	7
400-ci	10
455-ci	
Without High Performance	8
With High Performance	11
1972	
350-ci	12
400-ci	13
455-ci	14

Grand Prix

1969	
400-ci	5
428-ci	19
1970	
400-ci	10
455-ci	8
1971	
400-ci	10
455-ci	8
1972	
400-ci	13
455-ci	14

Tempest/LeMans/GTO

1964	
326-ci	20
389-ci	15
1965	
326-ci	21
389-ci	16
1966	
326-ci	1
389-ci	17
1967	
400-ci	
2-bbl	18
4-bbl	
Without Ram-Air	2
With Ram-Air	3
350-ci	4
400-ci	
Without Ram-Air	5

With Ram-Air	
Ram Air III	3
Ram Air IV	6
1969	
350-ci	4
400-ci	
Without Ram Air	5
With Ram Air	6
1970	
350-ci	7
400-ci	
Without Ram Air	10
With Ram Air	9
1971	
350-ci	7
400-ci	10
455-ci	
Without High Performance	8
With High Performance	11

1972	
350-ci	12
400-ci	13
455-ci	14

2+2

1964	
389-ci	15
421-ci	22
1965	
389-ci	16
421-ci	23
1966	
389-ci	17
421-ci	
Early	23
Late	24
1967	
428-ci	25

Interchange Number: 1
Part Number: 9786339
Cubic Displacement: 326-ci
Usage: 1967 Firebird, 1966-67
Tempest

Interchange Number: 2
Part Number:
Cubic Displacement: 400--ci
Usage: 1967 Firebird, GTO , late 1967
full-size Pontiac. Without Ram-Air

Interchange Number: 3
Part Number:
Cubic Displacement: 400-ci
Usage: 1967-68 Firebird, GTO. With
Ram Air, except Ram Air IV.

Interchange Number: 4
Part Number:
Cubic Displacement: 350-ci
Usage: 1968-72 Firebird; 1970-1972
Pontiac full-size; 1968-1972
Tempest/LeMans 350-ci V-8.

Interchange Number: 5
Part Number:
Cubic Displacement: 400-ci
Usage: 1968-69 Firebird, Tempest;
1968-69 Pontiac full-size; 1969 Grand
Prix. With 400-ci except Ram Air.

Interchange Number: 6
Part Number:
Cubic Displacement: 400-ci
Usage: 1968-69 Firebird, Tempest. \
With 400-ci Ram Air IV.

Interchange Number: 7
Part Number:
Cubic Displacement: 350-ci
Usage: 1970-71 Firebird, Tempest, full-
size Pontiac. With 350-ci V-8.

Interchange Number: 8
Part Number:
Cubic Displacement: 455-ci
Usage: 1971 Firebird; 1970-1971, GTO,
Grand Prix. With 455-ci V-8

Interchange Number: 9
Part Number:
Cubic Displacement: 400-ci
Usage: 1970 Firebird, LeMans with Ram Air III.

Interchange Number: 10
Part Number:
Cubic Displacement: 400-ci
Usage: 1970 Firebird; 1970 LeMans without Ram Air.

Interchange Number: 11
Part Number:
Cubic Displacement: 455-ci
Usage: 1971 Firebird; 1970-1971, GTO, Grand Prix. With 455-ci High Performance V-8
Notes: Rated 370-hp in 1970, 335-hp in 1971

Interchange Number: 12
Part Number:
Cubic Displacement: 350-ci
Usage: 1972 Firebird; 1972 LeMans, full-size Pontiac, Ventura II. With 350-ci V-8.

Interchange Number: 13
Part Number:
Cubic Displacement: 400-ci
Usage: 1972-74 Firebird; LeMans, Grand Prix, full-size Pontiac. With 400-ci V-8

Interchange Number: 14
Part Number:
Cubic Displacement: 455-ci
Usage: 1971-74 Firebird, LeMans, Grand Prix full-size Pontiac With 455-ci V-8 except Super Duty.

Interchange Number: 15
Part Number:
Cubic Displacement: 389-ci
Usage: 1964 GTO, full-size Pontiac with 389-ci V-8.

Interchange Number: 16
Part Number:
Cubic Displacement: 389-ci
Usage: 1965 GTO, full-size Pontiac with 389-ci V-8.

Interchange Number: 17
Part Number:
Cubic Displacement: 389-ci
Usage: 1966 GTO, full-size Pontiac with 389-ci V-8.

Interchange Number: 18
Part Number:
Cubic Displacement: 400-ci
Usage: 1967 GTO, full-size Pontiac with 400-ci 2-bbl V-8.

Interchange Number: 19
Part Number:
Cubic Displacement: 428-ci
Usage: 1969 Grand Prix, 1968-69 full-size Pontiac with 428-ci V-8.

Interchange Number: 20
Part Number:
Cubic Displacement: 326-ci
Usage: 1964 Tempest with 326-ci V-8.

Interchange Number: 21
Part Number:
Cubic Displacement: 326-ci
Usage: 1965 Tempest with 326-ci V-8.

Interchange Number: 22
Part Number:
Cubic Displacement: 421-ci
Usage: 1964 Pontiac with 421-ci V-8.

Interchange Number: 23
Part Number:
Cubic Displacement: 421-ci
Usage: 1965-early 1966 Pontiac with 421-ci V-8.
Notes: Early models have a arrow to indicate front of piston.

Interchange Number: 24
Part Number:
Cubic Displacement: 421-ci
Usage: Late 1966 Pontiac with 421-ci V-8.
Notes: Has a notch to indicate front of pistons.

Interchange Number: 25
Part Number:
Cubic Displacement: 428-ci
Usage: 1967 Pontiac with 428-ci V-8.

Cylinder Heads

Many times it is the cylinder heads that make that Special High Performance powerplant special. Cylinder heads on models like the GTO used free flowing ports and larger valves. When interchanging heads, make sure you have the right ones. Cylinder heads can usually be identified by their casting number, which is located on the runners.

You should carefully inspect cylinder heads for cracks and signs of damage. You should also use a straight edge by cris-crossing from corner to corner on the sealing surface of the head. If the ruler does not lay flat, this is an indication of a warped head. Unless you have need for a large paper weight, reject this head. For expensive performance heads you may want to have the head Magnaflexed, which is a process that can discover hidden cracks.

Casting numbers will not always appear on cylinder head. The casting date is shown here H is the month (Aug) 08 is the 8th day of the month, 2 is the casting year or 1972. While the arrow indicates the night shift cast it.

Cylinder Head Interchange

Firebird

1967	
326-ci	
2-bbl	1
4-bbl	2
400-ci	
Without Ram Air	3
With Ram Air	
Early	3
Late	4
1968	
350-ci	
2-bbl	5
4-bbl	6
400-ci	
Without Ram Air	7
With Ram Air	8

1969	
350-ci	
2-bbl	
Early	5
Late	11
4-bbl	
Early	6
Late	10
400-ci	
Without Ram Air	14
With Ram Air III	
Manual Transmission	10
Automatic transmission	14
With Ram Air IV	12
1970	
350-ci	13
400-ci	

4-bbl	
Without Ram Air	14
With Ram Air III	
Manual Transmission	10
Automatic transmission	14
With Ram Air IV	12
1970	
350-ci	13
400-ci	
2-bbl	13
4-bbl	
Without Ram Air	
Manual transmission	18
Automatic transmission	15
455-ci	35
1971	
350-ci	13
400-ci	
2-bbl	16
4-bbl	17
455-ci	
Without Ram Air	19
With Ram Air	20
1972	
350	21
400-ci	
2-bbl	22
4-bbl	23
455-ci	
Without Ram Air	24
With Ram Air	25

Grand Prix

1969	
400-ci	
2-bbl	
Early	33
Late	34
4-bbl	14
428-ci	
Manual Transmission	10
Automatic transmission	14
With Ram Air IV	12
400-ci	
2-bbl	13
4-bbl	15
455-ci	35
1971	
400-ci	
2-bbl	16
4-bbl	17
455-ci	19
1972	
400-ci	
2-bbl	22
4-bbl	23
455-ci	24

2+2

389-ci	
389-ci	
10.5 c.r.	26
10.6 c.r.	28
421-ci	28
1965	
421-ci	
10.5 c.r.	36
10.6 c.r.	31

1966

4-bbl	36
3x2-bbl	31

1967

428-ci

360-hp or 370-hp	37
390-hp	3

Interchange Number: 1
Part Number: 9788065
Cubic Displacement: 326-ci
Usage: 1966-67 Tempest; 1967
Firebird. With 326-ci 2-bbl V-8.
Notes: 094 for 1966 and 140 for 1967

Interchange Number: 2
Part Number: 9788063
Cubic Displacement: 326-ci
Usage: 1966-67 Tempest; 1967
Firebird. With 326-ci 4-bbl V-8.
Notes: Casting Numbers 9782229 for
1966 and 9778693 for 1967

Interchange Number: 3
Part Number: 9788067
Cubic Displacement: 400-ci
Usage: 1967 Tempest, Firebird with
400-ci without Ram Air; Early 1967
Firebird, Tempest with Ram Air; 1967
2+2 with 428-ci V-8.
Notes: Ram Air used up to service
number 646615

Interchange Number: 4
Part Number: 9783657
Cubic Displacement: 400-ci
Usage: Late 1967 Firebird, Tempest
with 400-ci and Ram Air.
Notes: Used beginning and after
service number 646616

Interchange Number: 5
Part Number: 9792263
Cubic Displacement: 350-ci
Usage: 1968- early 1969 Tempest,
Firebird. With 350-ci 2-bbl V-8.

Interchange Number: 6
Part Number: 9792264
Cubic Displacement: 350-ci
Usage: 1968-Early 1969 Tempest,
Firebird. With 350-ci 4-bbl V-8.

Interchange Number: 7
Part Number: 9790118
Cubic Displacement: 400-ci
Usage: 1968 Tempest, Firebird with
400-ci without Ram Air; 1969 Firebird,
Tempest 400-ci Ram Air III with
automatic transmission.

Interchange Number: 8
Part Number: 9792700
Cubic Displacement: 400-ci
Usage: 1968 Tempest, Firebird. With
400-ci with Ram Air III

Interchange Number: 9
Part Number: 9794040
Cubic Displacement: 400-ci
Usage: 1968-69 Tempest, Firebird.
With 400-ci with Ram Air H.O.

Interchange Number: 10
Part Number: 9795043
Cubic Displacement: 350-ci/400-ci
Usage: Late 1969 Tempest, Firebird.
With 350-ci 4-bbl V-8; 1969 Firebird,
Tempest 400-ci with Ram Air II and
Manual transmission.; 1969 Grand
Prix, full-size Pontiac with 428-ci V-8
and manual transmission.
Notes: Has 45-degree intake valves.

Interchange Number: 11
Part Number: 9798599
Cubic Displacement: 350-ci
Usage: Late 1969 Tempest, Firebird.
With 350-ci 2-bbl V-8.
Notes: Has 45-degree intake valves.

Interchange Number: 12
Part Number: 9796721
Cubic Displacement: 400-ci
Usage: 1969 Tempest, Firebird. With
400-ci with Ram Air IV.

Interchange Number: 13
Part Number: 483713
Cubic Displacement: 350-/ 400-ci
Usage: 1970-71 Firebird, Tempest, full-
size Pontiac with 350-ci V-8; 1970
Firebird, Grand Prix, Tempest, Full-size
Pontiac with 400-ci 2-bbl V-8.

Interchange Number: 14
Part Number: 9799496
Cubic Displacement: 400-ci
Usage: 1969 Tempest, Firebird with
400-ci with Ram Air III with automatic
transmission; 1969 Firebird,
Tempest without 400-ci and Ram Air.;
1969 Grand Prix, 1968-69 full-size
Pontiac with 428-ci V-8 with auto. trans.

Interchange Number: 15
Part Number: 9799497
Cubic Displacement: 400-ci
Usage: 1970 Firebird, Grand Prix, Tempest with 400-ci V-8 with automatic transmission. Without Ram Air.

Interchange Number: 16
Part Number: 483714
Cubic Displacement: 400-ci
Usage: 1971 Firebird, full-size Pontiac, Tempest with 400-ci 2-bbl V-8.

Interchange Number: 17
Part Number: 481760
Cubic Displacement: 400-ci
Usage: 1971 Firebird, full-size Pontiac, Grand Prix, Tempest with 400-ci 4-bbl V-8.

Interchange Number: 18
Part Number: 9799496
Cubic Displacement: 400-ci
Usage: 1970 Firebird, Tempest with 400-ci 4-bbl V-8 without Ram Air and manual transmission; 1970 Firebird, Tempest 400-ci with Ram Air.

Interchange Number: 19
Part Number: 483714
Cubic Displacement: 455-ci
Usage: 1971 Firebird, full-size Pontiac, Grand Prix, Tempest with 455-ci 4-bbl V-8 without Ram Air.

Interchange Number: 20
Part Number: 481758
Cubic Displacement: 455-ci
Usage: 1971 Firebird, Tempest with 455-ci 4-bbl V-8 with Ram Air.

Interchange Number: 21
Part Number: 487076
Cubic Displacement: 350-ci
Usage: 1972 Firebird, full-size Pontiac, Grand Prix, Tempest and Ventura II with 350-ci V-8.

Interchange Number: 22
Part Number: 487075
Cubic Displacement: 400-ci
Usage: 1972 Firebird, full-size Pontiac Tempest with 400-ci 2-bbl V-8.

Interchange Number: 23
Part Number: 485316
Cubic Displacement: 400-ci
Usage: 1972 Firebird, full-size Pontiac, Grand Prix and Tempest with 400-ci 4-bbl.

Interchange Number: 24
Part Number: 487072
Cubic Displacement: 455-ci
Usage: 1972 Firebird, full-size Pontiac, Grand Prix and Tempest with 455-ci 4-bbl V-8 without Ram Air.

Interchange Number: 25
Part Number: 485319
Cubic Displacement: 455-ci
Usage: 1972 Firebird, Tempest with 455-ci 4-bbl V-8 with Ram Air.

Interchange Number: 26
Part Number: 9774766
Cubic Displacement: 326-ci
Usage: 1964 Tempest with 326-ci 2-bbl V-8; 1964 Bonneville and Grand Prix with 389-ci with 10.5 c.r.

Interchange Number: 27
Part Number: 9774768
Cubic Displacement: 326-ci
Usage: 1964 Tempest with 326-ci 4-bbl V-8.

Interchange Number: 28
Part Number: 9770716 (casting number)
Cubic Displacement: 389-ci
Usage: 1964 GTO; 1963-1964 Full-size Pontiac 421-ci V-8.

Interchange Number: 29
Part Number: 9781082
Cubic Displacement: 326-ci
Usage: 1965 Tempest with 326-ci 2-bbl V-8
Notes: Casting number 62

Interchange Number: 30
Part Number: 9781080
Cubic Displacement: 326-ci
Usage: 1965 Tempest with 326-ci 4-bbl V-8
Notes: Casting number 22

Interchange Number: 31
Part Number: 9784212
Cubic Displacement: 389-ci
Usage: 1965 GTO; 1965 Full-size Pontiac 421-ci V-8; 1966 full size Pontiac with 421-ci 3x2-bbl V-8.
Notes: Engines have 10.75 c.r.

Interchange Number: 32
Part Number: 9788062
Cubic Displacement: 326-ci
Usage: 1966 Tempest with 326-ci

Interchange Number: 33
Part Number: 9792266
Cubic Displacement: 400-ci
Usage: 1968-early 1969 Grand Prix, full-size Pontiac and Tempest with 400-ci 2-bbl V-8
Notes: (1) Casting number 14 (2) Intake valves have 30-degree angle.

Interchange Number: 34
Part Number: 9798601
Cubic Displacement: 400-ci
Usage: Late 1969 Grand Prix, full-size Pontiac and Tempest with 400-ci 2-bbl V-8
Notes: Intake valves have 30-degree angle.

Interchange Number: 35
   Part Number: 9799362
   Cubic Displacement: 455-ci
   Usage: 1970 Tempest, Grand Prix, full-size Pontiac with 455-ci 4-bbl V-8

Interchange Number: 36
   Part Number: 9788065
   Cubic Displacement: 421-ci
   Usage: 1965-66 2+2 with 421-ci 338-hp V-8 ; 1965-66 full-size Pontiac with 389-ci 4-bbl V-8; 1967 full-size Pontiac with 400-ci 4-bbl V-8.(without valve guides)
   Notes: Casting numbers 76 for 1965, 092 for 1966 and 143 for 1967

Interchange Number: 37
   Part Number: 9788066
   Cubic Displacement: 428-ci
   Usage: 1967 2+2 with 428-ci 4-bbl V-8 with 360 or 370-hp out put; 1967 Grand Prix 400-ci V-8.

Internal Engine Components

   Great care should be used when buying internal engine parts, they are easily damaged and worn past the point of usability. In fact, some parts like pistons, bearings, and lifters should never be purchased as a used item. These parts are easily worn out, and worn to the specific engine they came out of, and may not fit. However, parts such as connecting rods and crankshafts can be purchased used and rebuilt, or if little wear is present, be reused. Camshafts can be purchased used but you should examine them carefully, this is a part that is better bought new.

CRANKSHAFT
   Crankshafts are made of two different materials. Cast iron, which was used in the majority of standard performance engines, and forged steel which was used in high performance applications. Of the two, the forged steel unit is the better one, as the steel can take more abuse and thus is able to withstand the internal pressures of higher horsepower. A forged crankshaft can take the place of the cast iron unit, in fact it is highly advised if you're increasing the horsepower greatly, but you may have to rebalance the engine. However, the reverse: a cast iron crank in place of a forged steel unit should never be done. You can check for the casting marking to determine the material of a crank but a quicker method is to *lightly* tap one of the crank's counterweights and listen to the sound. If it rings out, then it is a forged unit, if it is duller then it is cast iron.

   First, check the crankshaft for signs of damage. Check the counterweights for cracks and chips which could fail under load conditions. Next check the condition of the ends of the shaft , making sure all mating areas are solid and free from cracks and are not worn out around bolt holes. Next, check crankshaft alignment, this is best done with dial indicator and the crankshaft setting a set of oil V-blocks. But this task is nearly impossible in salvage yards or at a swap meet. Another method is to stand the crankshaft on it's end and place a straight edge along it's side , or to lay it on it's side and note- floor will have to be perfectly flat for this work- and lightly roll the shaft back and forth to see if the shaft lays flat. If it appears that one end wants to stick up this could indicate an out of alignment shaft. Note if the out of alignment is not too bad it can be straighten by several different methods. However, this procedure is best left done by a professional machine shop.

   Next check the conditions of the journals. Be cautious of rusted over journals, rust indicates that the shaft has been weathered and rust can hide flaws . All journals should be absolutely *smooth*. Any roughness, ridging or scoring will require the journals should be reground. Note- a dark line around the journal is normal, it is caused by the oil groove in the insert and is not a concern unless it's more then .0004 inch above the surface of the journal. This line can be removed with *crocus cloth* (an extremely fine abrasive), which is pulled around the journal in a shoe-shine method. If the journals are in good condition, check for out-of-roundness with a dial micrometer. Measure at each end of each journal, but avoid measuring on the fillet radius, the raised portion that graduates into the counterweights. Write down each measurement. Out of roundness is the difference between the two points, and should not exceed .001 inch.

Pontiac V-8 Crankshaft Specifications							
		Main Bearings			Rod Bearings		
Year	Engine	Journal Dia.	Oil Clearance	End Play	Journal Dia.	Oil Clearance	Side Play
1964-67	326-ci	3.00	.0018*	.006	2.250	.0015	.009
1964-66	421-ci	3.250	.0018	.006	2.250	.0015	.009
1968-72	350-ci	3.00	.0017	.0085	2.250	.0025	.011
1967-72	400-ci	3.00	.0017*	.0085	2.250	.0026*	.017
1970-72	455-ci	3.25	.0021	.0085	2.250	..0031	.0017
*- .0028 Main and .0031 rods							

Crankshaft

Firebird/GTO/Grand Prix/LeMans/Tempest/2+2

1964

326-ci	2
389-ci	1
421-ci	3

1965

326-ci	2
389-ci	1
421-ci	3

1966

326-ci	5
389-ci	4
421-ci	
Early	3
Late	6

1967

326-ci	5
400-ci	7
428-ci	6

1968

350-ci	9
400-ci	
Except Ram Air	7
Ram Air	8
428-ci	6

1969

350-ci	9
400-ci	
Except Ram Air	7
Ram Air	8
428-ci	6

1970

350-ci	9
400-ci	
Except Ram Air	7
Ram Air	8
455-ci	10

1971

350-ci	11
400-ci	12
455-ci	10

1972

350-ci	11
400-ci	12
455-ci	10

Interchange Number: 1
Part Number: 9773383
Cubic Displacement: 389-ci
Usage: 1964-1965 GTO, full-size
Pontiac with 389-ci V-8.
Notes: Forging number 9773383

Interchange Number: 2
Part Number: 9773382
Cubic Displacement: 326-ci
Usage: 1964-1965 Tempest with
326-ci V-8.

Interchange Number: 3
Part Number: 9773384
Cubic Displacement: 421-ci
Usage: 1964-early 1966 full-size
Pontiac with 421-ci V-8.
Notes: Forging number 9773384

Interchange Number: 4
Part Number: 9782646
Cubic Displacement: 389-ci
Usage: 1966 GTO, full-size Pontiac
with 389-ci V-8.
Notes: Forging numbers 9782646 or
9783786

Interchange Number: 5
Part Number: 9782770
Cubic Displacement: 389-ci
Usage: 1966-1967 Tempest; 1967
Firebird. With 326-ci V-8

Interchange Number: 6
Part Number: 9782769
Cubic Displacement: 421/428-ci-ci
Usage: Late 1966 full-size Pontiac with
421-ci V-8. 1967-69 full-size Pontiac;
1969 Grand Prix. With 428-ci V-8.

Interchange Number: 7
Part Number: 9795480
Cubic Displacement: 400-ci
Usage: 1967 Tempest, Firebird,;
1969-70 Grand Prix: 1967-70 full-size
Pontiac. With 400-ci V-8 all out puts
1968-1970 Tempest, Firebird with 400-
ci V-8 except Ram Air.

Interchange Number: 8
Part Number: 9794054
Cubic Displacement: 400-ci
Usage: 1968-70 Tempest, Firebird.
With 400-ci V-8 and Ram Air.

Interchange Number: 9
Part Number: 9795479
Cubic Displacement: 350-ci
Usage: 1968-70 Tempest, Firebird.;
1970 full-size Pontiac. With 350-ci V-8

Interchange Number: 10
Part Number: 9799103
Cubic Displacement: 350-ci
Usage: 1970-1972 Tempest, full-size
Pontiac, Grand Prix; 1971-72
Firebird. With 455-ci V-8.

Interchange Number: 11
Part Number: 481379
Cubic Displacement: 350-ci
Usage: 1971-1972 Tempest, full-size
Pontiac, and Firebird. With 350-ci V-8.
Notes: stamped 79 on counterweight
number 1

Interchange Number: 12
Part Number: 481380
Cubic Displacement: 400-ci
Usage: 1971-1972 Tempest, full-size
Pontiac, Grand Prix, and Firebird. With
400-ci V-8.

CONNECTING RODS

Connecting rods are another internal engine component that can be bought used. As with the crankshaft, the first thing you should look for is damage. Hold the rod up and slight down it's side. The sides should be straight and uniform in shape, with no twist or bends, then flip it over. Both bores should line up. Rods can be twisted bend or both. Twisted means that the upper and lower bores are out of alignment in a horizontal plane. A bend is when the bores are out of alignment in a vertical direction. It is possible to remove a slight bend or twist, but it is always better to start with a straight rod.

Caps will have to be replaced and torque to specifications before the bores are checked with a dial gauge for out roundness. Out of roundness should not exceed .001 inch.

There is good news when it comes to interchanging Pontiac connecting rods. Designers made one rod that fit many different V-8 engines, and cubic displacement was not a big factor in the interchange. The one engine to watch for that did use unique rods is the 1964-early 1965 421-ci V-8. However, it is believed the other rods in interchange number 1 will fit this application.

Firebird/GTO/Grand Prix/LeMans/Tempest/2+2

1964	
326-ci	1
389-ci	1
421-ci	2
1965	
326-ci	1
389-ci	1
421-ci	
Before engine number 113742	2
After engine number 113743	3
1966	
326-ci	1
389-ci	1
421-ci	1
1967	
326-ci	1
400-ci	1
428-ci	1
1968-1969	
350-ci	1
400-ci	1
428-ci	1
1970-1972	
350-ci	1
400-ci	1
455-ci	1

Interchange Number: 1
Part Number: 541000
Cubic Displacement: 326/350/400 421-ci/455-ci
Usage: 1964-1967 Tempest with 326-ci; 1967 Firebird with 326-ci; 1968-1972 Tempest, Firebird with 350-ci; 1970-1972 full-size Pontiac with 350-ci V-8; 1967-72 Firebird, Tempest, full-size Pontiac, Grand Prix with 400-ci V-8; 1970-1972 Tempest, full-size Pontiac, Grand Prix with 455-ci V-8; 1971-72 Firebird with 455-ci V-8; 1968-1969 full-size Pontiac, 1969 Grand Prix with 428-ci V-8; Late 1965-1966 full-size Pontiac with 421-ci V-8.

Interchange Number: 2
Part Number: 544956
Cubic Displacement: 421-ci
Usage: 1964-early 65 421-ci V-8
Notes: Before engine number 1113742

VALVE COVERS

Covers came in two styles. Painted, which was used on the majority of power plants, and was painted the same color as the engine block, and chrome, which was used on the high performance applications. Unlike some other GM divisions, Pontiac did not design their valve covers to fit specific models and applications; thus there is a large interchange available. When selecting a used valve cover, check its over all condition. Watch for rust. Lay the cover down on a table or other flat surface and check it's mating surfaces. They should be flat with no gap. Pay extra special attention to the gasket mating lip, make sure that is not damaged, and does not let the cover seat properly.

Firebird/GTO/Grand Prix/LeMans/Tempest/2+2

1964-65	
326-ci	3
389-c	
Painted covers	3
chrome	4

421-ci	4
1966	
326-ci	5
389-c	
Painted covers	5
chrome	6
421-ci	6
1967	
326-ci	1
400 ci	
Painted covers	1
chrome	2
428-ci	2
1968-69	
350 ci	1
400-ci	
Painted covers	1
chrome	2
428-ci	
Painted	1
Chrome	2
1970	
350 ci	1
400-c	
Painted covers	1
chrome	2
455-ci	
Painted	1
Chrome	2
1971-72	
350 ci	1
400 ci	1
455-ci	1

Interchange Number: 1
Part Number: 9786244 right-hand
                          9786245 left-hand
Usage: 1967-1972 Firebird, Full-size Pontiac, Tempest; 1969-1971 Grand Prix. With any V-8 engine except 307-ci or with Ram Air or decorative engine package
Notes: Covers are painted.

Interchange Number: 2
Part Number: 547293- right hand
                         547294-left hand
Usage: 1967-1970 Firebird, Full-size Pontiac, Tempest; 1969-1970 Grand Prix. With any V-8 engine with Ram Air or decorative engine package. Except 307-ci
Notes: Covers are chrome.

Interchange Number: 3
Usage: 1964- 65 Full-size Pontiac, Tempest with V-8 powerplant.
Notes: Covers are painted.

Interchange Number: 4
Usage: 1964-65 GTO; 2+2 with V-8 engine
Notes: Covers are chrome.

Interchange Number: 5
Usage: 1966 Full-size Pontiac, Tempest with V-8 powerplant.
Notes: Covers are painted.

Interchange Number: 6
Usage: 1966 GTO or 2+2 with V-8 powerplant
Notes: Covers are chrome

Interchange Number: 7
Part Number: 6272227 fits either side
Usage: 1971-72 Ventura with 307-ci V-8; 1969-1972 Camaro, Chevelle, Impala with 307-ci V-8.

OIL PANS

Oil pans have more interchange than you may at first think; model and body style have little effect on the interchange as does engine size. Most V-8s, regardless of the model, will cross fit each other. All oil pans were painted to match the cylinder block. Only three different pans were used throughout this book's time span. All 1964 models used part number 9773322 and 1965-1971 models used part number 481030. The 1972 models used part number 485339, which is the hardest to find of the pans, as it was used for this year only, but was used in all Pontiac models. There is one exception to the rule- the 1971-72 Ventura II with a 307-ci V-8 used a different oil pan listed as part number 3974252, it can be found in a variety of Chevrolet models from 1965-1974 with a small block V-8.

When selecting a used oil pan check its overall condition. Watch for rust. Lay the pan down on a table or other flat surface and check it's mating surfaces. They should be flat with no gap.   Pay extra special attention to the gasket mating lip, make sure that is not damaged , and not let the cover seat properly.   Another factor to check is the drain plug. Make sure it is included, and that it seats properly.

Chapter 2

Fuel Systems

Fuel Tanks

Steel encased fuel tanks are very sturdy parts and are readily available as used parts. When inspecting a fuel tank look for signs of damage. A dent can hide a puncture, while holes in the tank can be filled and dents removed, it is best to start with a solid tank.

Before removing the fuel tank, be sure to drain it first by removing the drain plug. If the drain plug is frozen, do not force it as you can damage the fuel tank. If there is no drain plug or the plug is frozen with rust, remove the fuel by using a siphoning tool. But do not use a tool that is electrical, as it may result in an explosion, and do not remove it by sucking on the hose. Place the fuel you remove in an appropriate container and dispose of it in the proper manner, don't just let it pour on to the ground.

Next remove the fuel lines, filler pipe and any external vents. Remove the tank supporting straps and lower the tank. With the tank removed, it is best to remove the sender gauge assembly, then tilt the tank over and drain out any remaining fuel. This rids the tank of any other fuel plus allows you to inspect the interior of the tank. If the interior is rusty reject the tank.

To clean the tank, place a quart and a half of clean gasoline in the tank and cover all openings with a cloth and shake the tank vigorously. Drain. Repeat. Dry the tank out with compressed air and inspect again. If dirt still remains, steam clean the interior of the tank.

Repairing Fuel Tanks

Dents can be straighten to some measure by filling the clean tank completely with water. Stand the tank on its end, and fill with water till it is running out of the filler neck. Plug the vent lines and place a no vented cap on the filler neck. Place compressed air through the pickup tube. Apply short blasts of air, just enough pressure to push the dent outward. Note: this only works with shallow dents that are not damaged to the point that the metal tank itself is stretched and cannot be repaired. ALWAYS MAKE SURE TO FILL THE TANK WITH WATER BEFORE APPLYING AIR. AIR ALONE CAN CAUSE THE TANK TO RUPTURE AND FLY APART CAUSING INJURIES OR DEATH.

Small holes can also repaired by brazing or soldering, BUT ONLY AFTER THE TANK IS CAREFULLY STEAM CLEANED INSIDE, AND THEN COMPLETELY FILLED WITH WATER. After repairs are made, test the area by applying a soapy mixture over the repair and the applying air into the water-filled tank. If your repair is good, bubbles will not form.

After any repairs, drain the water out of the tank. Place a quart and a half of gasoline in the tank, slosh around, and pour out. Blow dry tank. At this point, tank is ready for installation or restoration. The model usually dominates interchange of tanks. However, emission factors can have an affect on the interchange process.

Be sure to check the condition of the fuel gauge and filter openings.

Firebird

1967

All	1

1968

All	1

1969

All	2

1970

Without E.E.C	3
With E.E.C. (California cars)	4

1971

All	5

1972

All	6

Grand Prix

1969

All	7

1970

Without E.E.C.	7
With E.E.C. (California cars)	8

1971

All	9

1972

All	10

GTO/Tempest/LeMans

1964

All	11

1965

All	12

1966

All	13

1967

All	13

1968

All	14

1969

All	7

1970

Without E.E.C.	7
With E.E.C (California cars)	15

1971

All	16

1972

All	16

2+2

1964

All	17

1965

All	18

1966

All	18

1967

All	19

Interchange Number: 1
Part Number: 3912377
Gallons: 18
Usage: 1967-68 Firebird, Camaro

Interchange Number: 2
Part Number: 3953844
Gallons: 21 1/2
Usage: 1969 Firebird, Camaro

Interchange Number: 3
Part Number: 6263025
Gallons: 19 1/2
Usage: 1970 Firebird, Camaro without E.E.C.

Interchange Number: 4
Part Number: 6263026
Gallons: 18 1/2
Usage: 1970 Firebird, Camaro with E.E.C.
Notes: Interchange number 5 will fit but capacity is different.

Interchange Number: 5
Part Number: 3995719
Gallons: 17
Usage: 1971 Firebird, Camaro

Interchange Number: 6
Part Number: 6272127
Gallons: 17
Usage: 1972 Firebird, Camaro

Interchange Number: 7
Part Number: 478116
Gallons: 20
Usage: 1969 Grand Prix, Tempest except station wagon; 1970 Grand Prix, Tempest without E.E.C. except station wagon.

Interchange Number: 8
   Part Number: 485919
   Gallons: 24 1/2
   Usage: 1970 Grand Prix with E.E.C.
   (California cars)

Interchange Number: 9
   Part Number: 484471
   Gallons: 23 1/2
   Usage: 1971 Grand Prix
   Notes: It is reported that Interchange
   number 10 will fit.

Interchange Number: 10
   Part Number: 484471
   Gallons: 26
   Usage: 1972 Grand Prix

Interchange Number: 11
   Part Number: 381458
   Gallons: 21 1/2
   Usage: 1964 Tempest, all lines and
   models except Station wagon.

Interchange Number: 12
   Part Number: 388091
   Gallons: 20
   Usage: 1965 Tempest, all lines and models
   except Station wagon.

Interchange Number: 13
   Part Number: 9787294
   Gallons: 21 ½
   Usage: 1966-67 Tempest, all lines and
   models except Station wagon.

Interchange Number: 14
   Part Number: 9790355
   Gallons: 21 ½
   Usage: 1968 Tempest, all lines and models
   except Station wagon.

Interchange Number: 15
   Part Number: 47819
   Gallons: 20
   Usage: 1970 Tempest, all lines and models
   with E.E.C. California cars except Station
   wagon.

Interchange Number: 16
   Part Number: 485131
   Gallons: 20
   Usage: 1971-72 Tempest, all lines and
   models except Station wagon.

Interchange Number: 17
   Part Number: 9776546
   Gallons: 25
   Usage: 1961-64 full-size Pontiac all models
      and lines except station wagon.

Interchange Number: 18
   Part Number: 9785459
   Gallons: 26 ½
   Usage: 1965-66 full-size Pontiac all models
      and lines except station wagon.
   Notes: Interchange with filler neck.

Interchange Number: 19
   Part Number: 9786636
   Gallons: 26 ½
   Usage: 1967 full-size Pontiac all models
   and lines except station wagon.

Fuel Pump

   Fuel pump condition is hard to determine if it cannot be tested on the car, but it should have resistance when the pump is operated by hand, and pressure felt when your finger is placed over inlet or outlet valves. Fuel pumps are identified by their model numbers, which usually appear on the mounting flange. Fuel pumps are interchanged by engine displacement and model, but options like air conditioning can affect the interchange.

Firebird

1967

326-ci	
without a/c	12
with a/c	13
400-ci	13

1968

350-ci	
2-bbl	
without a/c	6
with a/c	7
4-bbl	7
400-ci	7

1969

350-ci	8
400-ci	8

1970

350-ci	
2-bbl	
Without a/c	15
With a/c	16
4-bbl	17

400-ci		
2-bbl		
Without a/c	15	
With a/c	16	
4-bbl	17	

1971

350-ci	
2-bbl	
Without a/c	15
With a/c	16
4-bbl	17
400-ci	
2-bbl	
Without a/c	15
With a/c	16
4-bbl	17

1972

350-ci	
2-bbl	
Without a/c	18
With a/c	19
4-bbl	19

Grand Prix

1969

All	20

1970

2-bbl	20
4-bbl	
Early	10
Late	11

1971

All	11

1972

All	11

GTO/LeMans/Tempest

1964

326-ci	
2-bbl	1
4-bbl	2

1965

326-ci	3
389-ci	3

1966

326-ci	3
389-ci	3

1967

326-ci	
Early	4
Late	5
400-ci	
Early	4
Late	5

1968

350-ci	
2-bbl	
Without a/c	6
With a/c	7
4-bbl	7
400-ci	
Without a/c	6
With a/c	7
4-bbl	7

1969

350-ci	
without E.E.C.	9
With E.E.C.	8
400-ci	
without E.E.C.	9
With E.E.C.	8

1970

350-ci

2-bbl

without E.E.C.	9
With E.E.C.	8

4-bbl

Early	10
Late	11

400-ci

2-bbl

without E.E.C.	9
With E.E.C.	8

4-bbl

Early	10
Late	11

455-ci

4-bbl

Early	10
Late	11

1971

350-ci

2-bbl	8
4-bbl	11

400-ci

2-bbl	8
4-bbl	11
455-ci	11

1972

350-ci

2-bbl	8
4-bbl	11

400-ci

2-bbl	8
4-bbl	11
455-ci	11

2+2

1964

389-ci	2
421-ci	2

1965

389-ci	2
421-ci	3

1966

389-ci	3
421-ci	3

1967

400-ci

Without a/c	6
Without a/c	13
428-ci	13

Interchange Number: 1
Part Number: 6416531
ID Number: 6550
Usage: 1963-64 full-size Pontiac 389-ci 4-bbl; 1964 Tempest 326-ci 2-bbl.
Notes: Interchange number 2 will fit as heavy-duty unit.

Interchange Number: 2
Part Number: 6416531
ID Number: 40455 or 0455
Usage: 1963-65 full-size Pontiac 389-ci 4-bbl with heavy-duty fuel pump or with 1964 421-ci V-8; 1964-65 Tempest 326-ci 4-bbl.

Interchange Number: 3
Part Number: 6416732
ID Number: 40239 or 0239
Usage: 1965 full-size Pontiac 421-ci V-8; 1965 Tempest 326-ci or 389-ci V-8; 1966 full-size Pontiac all power plants.

Interchange Number: 4
Part Number: 6416911
ID Number: 40521 or 0521
Usage: Early 1967 Tempest 326-ci with V-8 power plant.

Interchange Number: 5
Part Number: 6417175
ID Number: 40610 or 0610
Usage: Late 1967 Tempest 326-ci with V-8 power plant.

Interchange Number: 6
Part Number: 6417211
ID Number: 40601 or 0601
Usage: 1968 Tempest 2-bbl V-8
power plant.; 1968 Firebird 350-ci 2-bbl;
1968 full-size Pontiac with 400-ci V-8.
All models without air conditioning.

Interchange Number: 7
Part Number: 6417212
ID Number: 40607 or 0607
Usage: 1968 Tempest 2-bbl V-8
power plant.; 1968 Firebird 350-ci 2-bbl;
1968 full-size Pontiac with 400-ci V-8.
All models with air conditioning. 1968
Tempest, Firebird 4-bbl V-8; 1968 Pontiac
with 428-ci V-8.

Interchange Number: 8
Part Number: 6417419
ID Number: 40679 or 0679
Usage: 1969 Tempest , Firebird full-size
Pontiac with V-8 power plant and fuel
return.; 1970-72 Tempest with 2-bbl V-8
with fuel return; Early 1970 full-size Pontiac
with V-8 power plant and fuel return.

Interchange Number: 9
Part Number: 6417420
ID Number: 40680 or 0680
Usage: 1969-70 Tempest , Firebird full-size
          Pontiac with V-8 power plant without fuel
return.; 1970-72 Tempest with 2-bbl V-8 without
fuel return; Early 1970 full-size Pontiac with V-8
power plant without fuel return.

Interchange Number: 10
Part Number: 6470222
ID Number: 40710 or 0710
Usage: Early 1970 Tempest, Grand Prix
with 4-bbl V-8; 1970 full-size Pontiac with
455-ci 370-hp V-8 power plant.

Interchange Number: 11
Part Number: 6470513
ID Number: 40863 or 0863
Usage: Late 1970-72 Tempest, Grand Prix
with 4-bbl V-8; Late 1970 full-size Pontiac
with 455-ci 360-hp V-8 power plant.

Interchange Number: 12
Part Number: 6416910
ID Number: 40506 or 0506
Usage: 1967 Firebird with V-8 power plant
without air conditioning

Interchange Number: 13
Part Number: 6417139
ID Number: 40590 or 0590
Usage: 1967 Firebird with V-8 power plant
with air conditioning ; 1967 full-size
Pontiac with 428-ci V-8; 1967 Firebird
with 400-ci V-8.

Interchange Number: 14
Part Number: 6416910
ID Number: 40506 or 0506
Usage: 1967 Firebird with V-8 power plant
without air conditioning

Interchange Number: 15
Part Number: 6470498
ID Number: 40837 or 0837
Usage: 1970-71 Firebird with 2-bbl V-8
power plant without air conditioning; 1971
full-size Pontiac with 2-bbl V- 8 without air
conditioning.

Interchange Number: 16
Part Number: 6470497
ID Number: 40836 or 0836
Usage: 1970-71 Firebird with 2-bbl V-8
power plant with air conditioning; 1971
full-size Pontiac with 2-bbl V-8 with air
conditioning.

Interchange Number: 17
Part Number: 6470499
ID Number: 40838 or 0838
Usage: 1970-71 Firebird with 4-bbl V-8
power plant; 1971-72 full-size Pontiac with
4-bbl V-8 with air conditioning.

Interchange Number: 18
Part Number: 6470668
ID Number: 40929 or 0929
Usage: 1972-74 Firebird, full-size Pontiac
with 2-bbl V-8 power plant; 1973-74
LeMans, Ventura II with 350-ci or
400-ci 2-bbl V-8; 1972 Ventura II with
350-ci V-8. All models without air
conditioning.

Interchange Number: 19
Part Number: 6470670
ID Number: 40931 or 0931
Usage: 1972-74 Firebird, full-size Pontiac
with 2-bbl V-8 power plant; 1973-74
LeMans, Ventura II with 350-ci or
400-ci 2-bbl V-8; 1972 Ventura II with
350-ci V-8. All models without air
conditioning. 1972-74 Firebird with
4-bbl V-8; 1973-1974 Grand Prix; 1973
LeMans with 4-bbl V-8; 1974 LeMans with
455-ci V-8; 1973-1974 Ventura II 350-ci
4-bbl V-8.

Interchange Number: 20
Part Number: 6417418
ID Number: 40678 or 0678
Usage: 1969 Grand Prix all power plants;
1970 Grand Prix with 2-bbl V-8 power plant.

Intake Manifold

The intake manifold is the sturdiest component in the fuel system. It is readily sold as a used part, and a general inspection is all needed. The manifold should be free of any signs of damage. Cracks or chips are sure signs of damage. Take extra time in inspecting the mounting edges, and if the intake has one, the center divider, these areas are more prone to damage.

Intake manifolds were made of two materials: cast iron or forged aluminum. Aluminum intakes are more likely to find a home on high performance applications. And many times an aluminum intake will fit other engines that were originally equipped with a cast iron unit. However, carburetors may have to be swapped also.

Intake manifolds can be easily identified by their casting numbers.

INTAKE MANIFOLD CASTING NUMBERS

Displacement	Model Years	Casting Numbers				Notes
		2-bbl	**4-bbl**	**3x2-bbl**	**Type**	
326/389/421	1964	9770273	9770274	9777508	Iron	
326/389/421	1965	9778817	9778816	9778818	Iron	
326/389/421	1966	9782894	9782896	9782898	Iron	
326/400/428	1967	9784438	9782896	N/A	Iron	
400/428	1967		9786286(1)	N/A		(1) Q-jet
350/400/428	1968	9790418	9790140	N/A	Iron	
350/400/428	1969	9794233	9794234	N/A	Iron	Except Ram Air
400	1969	N/A	9796614	N/A	Aluminum.	Ram Air IV
350/400/455	1970	9799067	9799068	N/A	Iron	Except Ram Air
400	1970	N/A	9799084	N/A	Aluminum	Ram Air IV
350/400/455	1971	481732	481733	N/A	Iron	Except H.O.
455	1971	N/A	483674	N/A	Aluminum	H.O. Only

Firebird

1967

326-ci

2-bbl	1
4-bbl	2
400-ci	3

1968

350-ci

2-bbl	4
4-bbl	5
400-ci	5

1969

350-ci

2-bbl	4
4-bbl	5

400-ci

Without Ram Air IV	5
With Ram Air IV	6

1970

350-ci	
2-bbl	4
4-bbl	5
400-ci	
Without Ram Air IV	5
With Ram Air IV	6

1971

350-ci	7
400-ci	
2-bbl	7
4-bbl	8
455-ci	8

1972

350-ci	9
400-ci	
2-bbl	9
4-bbl	10
455-ci	11

GTO/LeMans/Tempest

1964

326-ci	
2-bbl	12
4-bbl	13
389-ci	
4-bbl	13
3x2-bbl	14

1965

326-ci	
2-bbl	1
4-bbl	2
389-ci	
4-bbl	2

3x2-bbl	15

1966

326-ci	
2-bbl	1
4-bbl	2
389-ci	
4-bbl	2
3x2-bbl	16

1967

326-ci	
2-bbl	1
4-bbl	2
400-ci	
2-bbl	17
4-bbl	3

1968

350-ci	
2-bbl	4
4-bbl	5
400-ci	5

1969

350-ci	
2-bbl	4
4-bbl	5
400-ci	
2-bbl	4
4-bbl	
Without Ram Air IV	5
With Ram Air IV	6

1970

350-ci	
2-bbl	4
4-bbl	5
400-ci	
Without Ram Air IV	5
With Ram Air IV	6

1971

350-ci	7
400-ci	
2-bbl	7
4-bbl	8
455-ci	8

1972

350-ci	9
400-ci	
2-bbl	9
4-bbl	10
455-ci	11

Grand Prix

1969

400-ci	
2-bbl	4
4-bbl	5
428-ci	5

1970

400-ci	
2-bbl	4
4-bbl	5
455-ci	5

1971

400-ci	8
455-ci	8

1972

400-ci	10
455-ci	10

2+2

1964

389-ci	13
421-ci	
4-bbl;	13
3x2-bbl	14

1965

389-ci	2
421-ci	
4-bbl	2
3x2-bbl	15

1966

389-ci	2
421-ci	
4-bbl	2
3x2-bbl	16

1967

400-ci	
2-bbl	17
4-bbl	3
428-ci	3

Interchange Number: 1
    Part Number: 9782893
    Usage: 1966-1967 Tempest; 1967 Firebird.
    All with 326-ci 2-bbl V-8.
Interchange Number: 2
    Part Number: 9782895
    Usage: 1965-1967 Tempest; 1967 Firebird.
    All with 326-ci 4-bbl V-8; 1965-1966 full-
    size Pontiac, GTO with 389-ci 4-bbl; 1967 full-size
    Pontiac with 400-ci 4-bbl.
Interchange Number: 3
    Part Number: 9786285
    Usage: 1967 Tempest; Firebird with 400-ci
    4-bbl V-8; 1967 full-size Pontiac with 428-ci V-8.

Interchange Number: 4
Part Number: 9799067
Usage: 1968-70 Firebird ,Tempest, full-size
Pontiac with 350-ci or 400-ci 2-bbl V-8;
1969-70 Grand Prix 400-ci 2-bbl V-8.

Interchange Number: 5
Part Number: 9799068
Usage: 1968-70 Firebird ,Tempest, full-size
Pontiac with 350-ci, 400-ci or 455-ci 4-bbl
V-8; 1969-70 Grand Prix 400-ci 428-ci or
455-ci 4-bbl V-8.

Interchange Number: 6
Part Number: 9799084
Usage: 1969-70 Firebird ,Tempest with
400-ci with Ram Air IV

Interchange Number: 7
Part Number: 481732
Usage: 1971 Firebird ,Tempest , full-size
Pontiac with 350-ci or 400-ci 2-bbl V-8.

Interchange Number: 8
Part Number: 481733
Usage: 1971 Firebird , Grand Prix,
Tempest, full-size Pontiac with 400-ci or
455-ci 4-bbl V-8. Except High output
335-hp version.

Interchange Number: 9
Part Number: 485911
Usage: 1972 Firebird ,Tempest, full-size
Pontiac, Ventura II with 350-ci or 400-ci
2-bbl V-8.

Interchange Number: 10
Part Number: 485912
Usage: 1972 Firebird ,Grand Prix, Tempest
full-size Pontiac with 400-ci 4-bbl V-8;
1972 Grand Prix, full-size Pontiac with 455-ci 4-bbl.

Interchange Number: 11
Part Number: 488945
Usage: 1972 Firebird ,Tempest with 455-ci 4-bbl V-8.

Interchange Number: 12
Part Number: 9770273
Usage: 1963-64 Tempest with 326-ci 2-bbl
V-8; 1963-64 full-size Pontiac with 389-ci
2-bbl V-8.

Interchange Number: 13
Part Number: 9770274
Usage: 1963-64 Tempest with 326-ci 4-bbl
V-8; 1963-64 full-size Pontiac with 389-ci
4-bbl V-8; 1964 GTO 389-ci 4-bbl V-8.

Interchange Number: 14
Part Number: 9775088
Usage: 1964 GTO with 389-ci 3x2-bbl V-8;
1964 full-size Pontiac with 421-ci 3x2-bbl
V-8.

Interchange Number: 15
Part Number: 9778815
Usage: 1965 GTO with 389-ci 3x2-bbl V-8;
1965 full-size Pontiac with 421-ci 3x2-bbl
V-8.

Interchange Number: 16
Part Number: 9784440
Usage: 1966 GTO with 389-ci 3x2-bbl V-8;
1966 full-size Pontiac with 421-ci 3x2-bbl
V-8.

Interchange Number: 17
Part Number: 9784437
Usage: 1967 GTO, full-size Pontiac with
400-ci 2-bbl V-8; 1966 full-size Pontiac
with 389-ci 2-bbl V-8.

Carburetor

Because of their design with jets and interior components, it is hard to check the condition of a carburetor with any assurance that it is going to work. Carburetors can be rebuilt. This makes them a favorite used parts buy. When inspecting a carburetor, look over the body. Look for cracks and other signs of damage. Flip the throttle linkage back and forth a couple of times; watch for any binding that may occur. Inspect the butterfly flappers, make sure they are not damaged and work properly. And check linkage to make sure it works properly and is all there.

Carburetors were selected by engine size, output, and transmission type. However, options like emissions can effect their usage. And while a carburetor with emission controls can be used somewhat effectively on cars without emissions, [provided you plug the not needed nipples], you cannot effectively use a non-emissions carburetor on a car with emissions, and still have the emissions in operable condition.

Identification of Carter AFB 4-bbl Identification number is found stamped on a metal tag that is attached to the top of the unit. Or is stamped on the base.	**Identification of Rochester 4-MV 4-bbl** Identification number is found stamped on a round shaped metal tag that is attached to the side of the float bowl . Or is stamped into the side, just behind the throttle control linkage..
Identification of Rochester 2GC 2-bbl Identification number is found stamped on a metal tag that is attached to the top of the unit. Or is stamped on the base.	**Identification of Rochester 2 BC 2-bbl or 4BC 4-bbl** Identification number is found stamped on tag that is attached to the top of the float bowl .

Firebird

1967

Without A.I.R.

326-ci

2-bbl

Manual	1
Automatic	2

4-bbl

Manual	3
Automatic	4

400-ci

Without Ram Air

Manual	5
Automatic	6
with Ram Air	7

With A.I.R.

326-ci

2-bbl

Manual	8
Automatic	9

4-bbl

Manual	10
Automatic	10

400-ci

Without Ram Air

Manual	11
Automatic	12

1968

350-ci

2-bbl

Manual	13
Automatic	14

4-bbl

Manual	15
Automatic	16

400-ci

Without Ram Air

Manual	17
Automatic	18

High output 335 hp

Manual	20
Automatic	18

Ram Air

Manual

Early	21
Late	23

Automatic

Early	22
Late	24

1969

350-ci

2-bbl

Manual	13
Automatic	25

4-bbl

Manual	26
Automatic	27

400-ci

Without Ram Air

Manual	26
Automatic	27

With Ram Air

Manual	23
Automatic	24

Ram Air IV

Manual	23
Automatic	24

1970

350-ci

Without E.E.C.

Manual	28
Automatic	29

With E.E.C.

Manual	30
Automatic	31

400-ci

2-bbl

without E.E.C.

Manual	32
Automatic	33

with E.E.C.

Manual	34
Automatic	35

4-bbl

Without Ram Air

Without E.E.C.

Manual	36
Automatic	37

With E.E.C

Manual	38
Automatic	39

With Ram Air

Without E.E.C.

Manual	40
Automatic	41

With E.E.C.

Manual	42
Automatic	43

1971

350-ci

Manual	44
Automatic	45

400-ci

2-bbl

Manual	Not used
Automatic	46

4-bbl

Manual	47
Automatic	48

455-ci

Without High Output or Ram Air

Manual	not used	Automatic	68
Automatic	49	389-ci	
High Output		4-bbl	
Manual	50	Manual	67
Automatic	51	Automatic	4
Ram Air		3x2-bbl	
Manual	52	Front	68
Automatic	53	Center	
1972		Manual	69
350-ci		Automatic	70
Manual	54	Rear	71
Automatic	55	**1965**	
400-ci		326-ci	
2-bbl		2-bbl	
Except California or High Altitude		Manual	72
Automatic	56	Automatic	73
High Altitude	57	4-bbl	
California	58	Manual	3
4-bbl		Automatic	4
Manual	59	389-ci	
Automatic		4-bbl	
Except California	60	Manual	3
High Altitude	61	Automatic	4
California	62	3x2-bbl	
455-ci		Front	68
Manual	63	Center	
Automatic	64	Manual	74
		Automatic	75
GTO/LeMans/Tempest		Rear	
1964		Manual	76
326-ci		Automatic	71
2-bbl			
Manual	65		
Automatic	66		
4-bbl			
Manual	67		

1966

Without A.I.R.

326-ci

2-bbl

Manual	1
Automatic	2

4-bbl

Manual	3
Automatic	4

389-ci

4-bbl

Manual	3
Automatic	4

3x2-bbl

Front	68

Center

Manual	77
Automatic	78

Rear

Manual	76
Automatic	71

With A.I.R.

326-ci

2-bbl

Manual	8
Automatic	9

4-bbl

Manual	10
Automatic	10

389-ci

4-bbl

Manual	11
Automatic	12

3x2-bbl

Front	68

Center

Manual	79
Automatic	80

Rear

Manual	76
Automatic	71

1967

Without A.I.R.

326-ci

2-bbl

Manual	1
Automatic	2

4-bbl

Manual	3
Automatic	4

400-ci

2-bbl	81

Without Ram Air

Manual	5
Automatic	6
with Ram Air	7

With A.I.R.

326-ci

2-bbl

Manual	8
Automatic	9

4-bbl

Manual	10
Automatic	10

400-ci

2-bbl	82

Without Ram Air

Manual	11
Automatic	12

1968

350-ci

2-bbl

Without Ram Air

Manual	90
Automatic	91

With Ram Air

Manual	40
Automatic	41

With E.E.C.

Without Ram Air

Manual	92
Automatic	93

With Ram Air

Manual	42
Automatic	43

1971

350-ci

Manual	44
Automatic	45

400-ci

2-bbl

Manual	Not used
Automatic	46

4-bbl

Manual	47
Automatic	48

455-ci

Without High output or Ram Air

Manual	not used
Automatic	49

High Out Put

Manual	50
Automatic	51

Ram Air

Manual	52
Automatic	53

1972

350-ci

Manual	54
Automatic	55

400-ci

2-bbl

Except California or High Altitude

Automatic	56
High Altitude	57
California	58

4-bbl

Manual	59

Automatic

Except California	60
High Altitude	61
California	62

455-ci

Without Ram Air

Except California	93
High Altitude	94
California	95

With Ram Air

Manual	63
Automatic	64

Grand Prix

1969

400-ci

400-ci

2-bbl	89

4-bbl

Manual	26
Automatic	27

Automatic	75
Rear	
Manual	76
Automatic	71
421-ci	
4-bbl	
Manual	3
Automatic	4
3x2-bbl	
Front	97
Center	
Manual	101
Automatic	102
Rear	
Manual	103
Automatic	100
1966	
Without A.I.R.	
389-ci	
4-bbl	
Manual	3
Automatic	4
3x2-bbl	
Front	68
Center	
Manual	77
Automatic	78
Rear	
Manual	76
Automatic	71
421-ci	
4-bbl	
Manual	3
Automatic	4
3x2-bbl	
Front	97
Center	
Manual	101
Automatic	102
Rear	
Manual	103
Automatic	100
With A.I.R.	
389-ci	
4-bbl	
Manual	11
Automatic	12
1967	
Without A.I.R.	
400-ci	
2-bbl	81
4-bbl	
Manual	5
Automatic	6
428-ci	
Manual	5
Automatic	6
With A.I.R.	
With A.I.R.	
400-ci	
2-bbl	82
4-bbl	
Manual	11
Automatic	12
428-ci	
Manual	11
Automatic	12

Interchange Number: 1
Type: Rochester 2GC
ID Number: 7037071
Usage: 1967 Firebird, Tempest with 326-ci 2-bbl V-8 without A.I.R. With manual transmission.

Interchange Number: 2
Type: Rochester 2GC
ID Number: 7037062
Usage: 1967 Firebird, with 326-ci 2-bbl V-8 without A.I.R; 1966-67 Tempest with 326-ci 2-bbl V-8 without A.I.R. With Automatic transmission.

Interchange Number: 3
Type: Carter AFB
ID Number: 3895
Usage: 1967 Firebird, Tempest with 326-ci 2-bbl V-8 without A.I.R. ; 1964-67 Tempest 326-ci or 389-ci 4-bbl; 1967 full-size Pontiac 400-ci 4-bbl without A.I.R. 1963-1965 full-size Pontiac with 389-ci 4-bbl; 1966 full-size Pontiac with 421-ci 4-bbl V-8. All models have manual transmission

Interchange Number: 4
Type: Carter AFB
ID Number: 3896 or 3898
Usage: 1967 Firebird, Tempest with 326-ci 4-bbl V-8 without A.I.R. ; 1964-67 Tempest 326-ci or 389-ci 4-bbl; 1967 Pontiac 400-ci 4-bbl without A.I.R. 1963-1965 full-size Pontiac with 389-ci 4-bbl; 1966 full-size Pontiac with 421-ci 4-bbl V-8. All models have automatic transmission

Interchange Number: 5
Type: Rochester 4 MV
ID Number: 7027263
Usage: 1967 Firebird, Tempest with 400-ci 4-bbl V-8 without A.I.R. ; 1967 full-size Pontiac with 428-ci 4-bbl without A.I.R.. All models have manual transmission.

Interchange Number: 6
Type: Rochester 4 MV
ID Number: 7027262
Usage: 1967 Firebird, Tempest with 400-ci 4-bbl V-8 without A.I.R. without Ram Air; 1967 full-size Pontiac with 428-ci 4-bbl without A.I.R.. All models have automatic transmission.

Interchange Number: 7
Type: Rochester 4 MV
ID Number:
Usage: 1967 Firebird, Tempest with 400-ci 4-bbl V-8 with Ram Air.; 1967 full-size Pontiac with 428-ci 4-bbl with A.I.R with automatic transmission.

Interchange Number: 8
Type: Rochester 2GC
ID Number: 7036071
Usage: 1967 Firebird, Tempest with 326-ci 2-bbl V-8 with A.I.R. With manual transmission.

Interchange Number: 9
Type: Rochester 2GC
ID Number: 7036072
Usage: 1967 Firebird, Tempest with 326-ci 2-bbl V-8 with A.I.R. With automatic transmission.

Interchange Number: 10
Type: Carter AFB
ID Number: 4041 or 4030
Usage: 1967 Firebird, Tempest 326-ci 4-bbl, 1966 Tempest with 326-ci or 389-ci 4-bbl; 1967 full-size Pontiac with 400-ci 4-bbl V-8. All models have A.I.R.

Interchange Number: 11
Type: Rochester 4 MV
ID Number: 7027272
Usage: 1967 Firebird, Tempest with 400-ci 4-bbl V-8 with A.I.R; 1967 full-size Pontiac with 428-ci with A.I.R. All models equipped with manual transmission.

Interchange Number: 12
Type: Rochester 4 MV
ID Number: 7027273
Usage: 1967 Firebird, Tempest with 400-ci 4-bbl V-8 with A.I.R; 1967 full-size Pontiac with 428-ci with A.I.R. All models equipped with automatic transmission.

Interchange Number: 13
Type: Rochester 2GC
ID Number: 7028061
Usage: 1968-69 Firebird, Tempest with 350-ci 2-bbl V-8. All models equipped with manual transmission.

Interchange Number: 14
Type: Rochester 2GC
ID Number: 7028062
Usage: 1968-69 Firebird, Tempest with 350-ci 2-bbl V-8. All models equipped with automatic transmission.

Interchange Number: 15
Type: Rochester 4MV
ID Number: 7028269
Usage: 1968-69 Firebird, Tempest with 350-ci 2-bbl V-8. All models equipped with manual transmission.

Interchange Number: 16
Type: Rochester 4MV
ID Number: 7028266
Usage: 1968-69 Firebird, Tempest with 350-ci 2-bbl V-8. All models equipped with automatic transmission.

Interchange Number: 17
Type: Rochester 4MV
ID Number: 7028265
Usage: 1968 Firebird 400-ci 4-bbl with High output or Ram Air. Manual transmission

Interchange Number: 18
Type: Rochester 4MV
ID Number: 7028264
Usage: 1968 Firebird 400-ci 4-bbl with or without High output without Ram Air. Automatic transmission

Interchange Number: 19
Type: Rochester 4MV
ID Number: 7028168
Usage: 1968 Firebird 400-ci 4-bbl without High output or Ram Air. Manual transmission

Interchange Number: 20
Type: Rochester 4MV
ID Number: 7028265
Usage: 1968 Firebird 400-ci 4-bbl with High output. Manual transmission

Interchange Number: 21
Type: Rochester 4MV
ID Number: 7028277
Usage: Early 1968 Firebird 400-ci 4-bbl with Ram Air. Manual transmission

Interchange Number: 22
Type: Rochester 4MV
ID Number: 7028276
Usage: 1968 Firebird 400-ci 4-bbl with Ram Air. Automatic transmission

Interchange Number: 23
Type: Rochester 4MV
ID Number: 7029273
Usage: Late 1968-1969 Firebird 400-ci 4-bbl with Ram Air. Manual transmission

Interchange Number: 24
Type: Rochester 4MV
ID Number: 7029270
Usage: Late 1968-1969 Firebird 400-ci 4-bbl with Ram Air. Automatic transmission.

Interchange Number: 25
Type: Rochester 2CG
ID Number: 7029072
Usage: 1969 Firebird, Tempest 350-ci 2-bbl with Ram Air. Automatic transmission

Interchange Number: 26
Type: Rochester 4MV
ID Number: 7029263
Usage: 1969 Firebird Tempest with 350-ci or 400-ci 4-bbl V-8 without Ram Air; 1969 Grand Prix, full-size Pontiac with 428-ci 4-bbl V-8. Manual Transmission

Interchange Number: 27
Type: Rochester 4MV
ID Number: 7029268
Usage: 1969 Firebird Tempest with 350-ci or 400-ci 4-bbl V-8 without Ram Air; 1969 Grand Prix, full-size Pontiac with 428-ci 4-bbl V-8. Automatic transmission

Interchange Number: 28
Type: Rochester 2CG
ID Number: 7040071
Usage: 1970 Firebird , Tempest full-size Pontiac with 350-ci 2-bbl V-8 without E.E.C.. Manual transmission.

Interchange Number: 29
Type: Rochester 2CG
ID Number: 7040062
Usage: 1970 Firebird , Tempest full-size Pontiac with 350-ci 2-bbl V-8 Without E.E.C.. Automatic transmission.

Interchange Number: 30
Type: Rochester 2CG
ID Number: 7040471
Usage: 1970 Firebird , Tempest full-size Pontiac with 350-ci 2-bbl V-8 With E.E.C. Manual transmission.

Interchange Number: 31
Type: Rochester 2CG
ID Number: 7040462 or 704063
Usage: 1970 Firebird , Tempest full-size Pontiac with 350-ci 2-bbl V-8 with E.E.C.. Automatic transmission.

Interchange Number: 32
Type: Rochester 2BC
ID Number: 7040066
Usage: 1970 Firebird full-size Pontiac with 400 2-bbl V-8 without E.E.C.. Manual transmission.

Interchange Number: 33
Type: Rochester 2BC
ID Number: 7040060 or 7040064
Usage: 1970 Firebird , Grand Prix, Tempest ,full-size Pontiac with 400 2-bbl V-8 without E.E.C. Automatic transmission.

Interchange Number: 34
Type: Rochester 2BC
ID Number: 7040462 or 7040463
Usage: 1970 Firebird full-size Pontiac with
400 2-bbl V-8 with E.E.C.. Manual
transmission.

Interchange Number: 35
Type: Rochester 2BC
ID Number: 7040460 or 7040461
Usage: 1970 Firebird , Grand Prix,
Tempest ,full-size Pontiac with 400 2-bbl
V-8 with E.E.C. Automatic transmission.

Interchange Number: 36
Type: Rochester 4BC
ID Number: 7040263
Usage: 1970 Firebird, Tempest, Grand Prix
with 400-ci 4-bbl V-8 without E.E.C
without Ram Air. Manual transmission

Interchange Number: 37
Type: Rochester 4BC
ID Number: 7040264
Usage: 1970 Firebird, Tempest, Grand Prix
with 400-ci 4-bbl V-8 without E.E.C
without Ram Air. Automatic transmission

Interchange Number: 38
Type: Rochester 4BC
ID Number: 7040563
Usage: 1970 Firebird, Grand Prix, Tempest
with 400-ci 4-bbl V-8 with E.E.C without
Ram Air. Manual transmission

Interchange Number: 39
Type: Rochester 4BC
ID Number: 7040564
Usage: 1970 Firebird, Grand Prix, Tempest
with 400-ci 4-bbl V-8 with E.E.C without
Ram Air. Automatic transmission

Interchange Number: 40
Type: Rochester 4MV
ID Number: 7040273
Usage: 1970 Firebird, Tempest with 400-ci
4-bbl V-8 without E.E.C with Ram Air.
Manual transmission

Interchange Number: 41
Type: Rochester 4MV
ID Number: 7040270
Usage: 1970 Firebird, Tempest with 400-ci
4-bbl V-8 without E.E.C with Ram Air.
Automatic transmission

Interchange Number: 42
Type: Rochester 4MV
ID Number: 7040573
Usage: 1970 Firebird, Tempest with 400-ci
4-bbl V-8 with E.E.C with Ram Air.
Manual transmission

Interchange Number: 43
Type: Rochester 4MV
ID Number: 7040570
Usage: 1970 Firebird, Tempest with 400-ci
4-bbl V-8 with E.E.C with Ram Air.
Automatic transmission

Interchange Number: 44
Type: Rochester 2BC
ID Number: 7041171
Usage: 1971 Firebird, Tempest, full-size
Pontiac with 350-ci 2-bbl V-8. Manual
transmission

Interchange Number: 45
Type: Rochester 2BC
ID Number: 7041162 or 7041163
Usage: 1971 Firebird, Tempest, full-size
Pontiac with 350-ci 2-bbl V-8. Automatic
transmission

Interchange Number: 46
Type: Rochester 2BC
ID Number: 7041060 or 7041061
Usage: 1971 Firebird, Tempest, full-size
Pontiac with 400-ci 2-bbl V-8. Automatic
transmission

Interchange Number: 47
Type: Rochester 4MV
ID Number: 7041263
Usage: 1971 Firebird, Grand Prix,
Tempest, full-size Pontiac with 400-ci
4-bbl V-8. Manual transmission

Interchange Number: 48
Type: Rochester 4MV
ID Number: 7041264
Usage: 1971 Firebird, Grand Prix,
Tempest, full-size Pontiac with 400-ci
4-bbl V-8. Automatic transmission

Interchange Number: 49
Type: Rochester 4MV
ID Number: 70
Usage: 1971 Firebird, Grand Prix,
Tempest, full-size Pontiac with 455-ci
4-bbl V-8 without Ram Air or High output.
Automatic transmission

Interchange Number: 50
Type: Rochester 4MV
ID Number: 7041267
Usage: 1971 Firebird, Tempest, with 455-ci
4-bbl V-8 High Output (335-hp). Manual
transmission

Interchange Number: 51
Type: Rochester 4MV
ID Number: 7041268
Usage: 1971 Firebird, Tempest, with 455-ci
4-bbl V-8 High Output (335-hp).Automatic
transmission

Interchange Number: 52
Type: Rochester 4MV
ID Number: 7041273
Usage: 1971 Firebird, Tempest, with 455-ci
4-bbl V-8 Ram Air (335-hp). Manual
transmission

Interchange Number: 53
Type: Rochester 4MV
ID Number: 7041270
Usage: 1971 Firebird, Tempest, with 455-ci
4-bbl V-8 Ram Air (335-hp). Manual
transmission

Interchange Number: 54
Type: Rochester 2BC
ID Number: 7042071
Usage: 1972 Firebird, Tempest, with 350-ci
2-bbl V-8 . Manual transmission.

Interchange Number: 55
Type: Rochester 2BC
ID Number: 7042062
Usage: 1972 Firebird, Tempest, Ventura II
with 350-ci 2-bbl V-8 . Automatic
transmission.

Interchange Number: 56
Type: Rochester 2BC
ID Number: 7024062
Usage: 1972 Firebird, Tempest, full-size
Pontiac with 400-ci 2-bbl V-8 except
California or high altitude.
Automatic transmission.

Interchange Number: 57
Type: Rochester 2BC
ID Number: 7042078
Usage: 1972 Firebird, Tempest, full-size
Pontiac with 400-ci 2-bbl V-8 high altitude
except California . Automatic
transmission.

Interchange Number: 58
Type: Rochester 2BC
ID Number: 7042067
Usage: 1972 Firebird, Tempest, full-size
Pontiac with 400-ci 2-bbl V-8 California .
Automatic transmission.

Interchange Number: 59
Type: Rochester 4MV
ID Number: 7042263
Usage: 1972 Firebird, Tempest, with 400-ci
4-bbl V-8. Manual transmission.

Interchange Number: 60
Type: Rochester 4MV
ID Number: 7042274
Usage: 1972 Firebird, Tempest, Grand
Prix, full-size Pontiac with 400-ci 4-bbl V-8
except California or high altitude.
Automatic transmission.

Interchange Number: 61
Type: Rochester 4MV
ID Number: 7042278
Usage: 1972 Firebird, Tempest, Grand
Prix, full-size Pontiac with 400-ci 4-bbl V-8
high altitude. Automatic transmission.

Interchange Number: 62
Type: Rochester 4MV
ID Number: 7042264
Usage: 1972 Firebird, Tempest, Grand
Prix, full-size Pontiac with 400-ci 4-bbl V-8
California. Automatic transmission

Interchange Number: 63
Type: Rochester 4MV
ID Number: 7042263
Usage: 1972 Firebird, Tempest, with 455-ci
4-bbl V-8. Manual transmission.

Interchange Number: 64
Type: Rochester 4MV
ID Number: 7042264
Usage: 1972 Firebird, Tempest, with 455-ci
4-bbl V-8. Automatic transmission.

Interchange Number: 65
Type: Rochester 2GC
ID Number: 7023071
Usage: 1964 Tempest 326-ci 2-bbl V-8.
Manual transmission

Interchange Number: 66
Type: Rochester 2GC
ID Number: 7023062
Usage: 1964 Tempest 326-ci 2-bbl V-8.
Automatic transmission

Interchange Number: 67
Type: Carter AFB
ID Number: 3477 or 3479 or 3647 or 3650
Usage: 1964 Tempest 326-ci 4-bbl V-8;
1964 GTO 389-ci 4-bbl; 1963-64 full- size
Pontiac with 389-ci 4-bbl V-8; 1964 full-
size Pontiac with 421-ci 4-bbl V-8.
Manual transmission

Interchange Number: 68
Type: Rochester 2G
ID Number: 7024178
Usage: 1964-66 GTO 389-ci 3x2-bbl V-8;
1964-66 full- size Pontiac with 42i-ci
3x2-bbl V- 8.

Interchange Number: 69
Type: Rochester 2G
ID Number: 70313067 or 7015068 or
7019064 or 7020064 or 7023075 or
7024175
Usage: 1964 GTO 389-ci 3x2-bbl V-8;
1959-64 full- size Pontiac with 3x2-bbl
V- 8. Center Carburetor with
manual transmission.
Notes: Bold is 1964 part number

Interchange Number: 70
Type: Rochester 2G
ID Number: 7015066 or 7015076 or
7019067 or 7019069 or 7020067 or
7020069 or 7023073 or 7023077 or
7024173
Usage: 1964 GTO 389-ci 3x2-bbl V-8;
1959-64 full- size Pontiac with 3x2-bbl
V- 8. Center Carburetor with automatic
transmission.
Notes: Bold is 1964 part number

Interchange Number: 71
Type: Rochester 2G
ID Number: 7024179
Usage: 1964-66 GTO 389-ci 3x2-bbl V-8;
1964-66 full- size Pontiac with 3x2-bbl
V- 8. Automatic only for 1965-66

Interchange Number: 72
Type: Rochester 2GC
ID Number: 7025071
Usage: 1965 Tempest with 326-ci 2-bbl
V-8. Manual transmission.

Interchange Number: 73
Type: Rochester 2GC
ID Number: 7025062
Usage: 1965 Tempest with 326-ci 2-bbl
V-8. Automatic transmission.

Interchange Number: 74
Type: Rochester 2G
ID Number: 7025175
Usage: 1965 GTO with 389-ci 3x2-bbl V-8.
Manual transmission.

Interchange Number: 75
Type: Rochester 2G
ID Number: 7025173
Usage: 1965 GTO with 389-ci 3x2-bbl V-8.
Automatic transmission.

Interchange Number: 76
Type: Rochester 2G
ID Number: 7025179
Usage: 1965-66 GTO with 389-ci 3x2-bbl
V-8. Manual transmission.

Interchange Number: 77
Type: Rochester 2G
ID Number: 7026075
Usage: 1966 GTO, full-size Pontiac with
389-ci 3x2-bbl V-8. Manual transmission.

Interchange Number: 78
Type: Rochester 2G
ID Number: 7026074
Usage: 1966 GTO, full-size Pontiac with
389-ci 3x2-bbl V-8. Automatic
transmission.

Interchange Number: 79
Type: Rochester 2G
ID Number: 7036175
Usage: 1966 GTO, with 389-ci 3x2-bbl V-8
with A.I.R.. Manual transmission.

Interchange Number: 80
Type: Rochester 2G
ID Number: 7026074
Usage: 1966 GTO, with 389-ci 3x2-bbl V-8
with A.I.R.. Automatic transmission.

Interchange Number: 81
Type: Rochester 2BC
ID Number: 7027060 or 7027061
Usage: 1967 GTO, full-size Pontiac with
400-ci 2-bbl V-8 without A.I.R. Automatic
transmission.

Interchange Number: 82
Type: Rochester 2BC
ID Number: 7037162
Usage: 1967 GTO, full-size Pontiac with
400-ci 2-bbl V-8 with A.I.R... Automatic
transmission.

Interchange Number: 83
Type: Rochester 2BC
ID Number: 7028060
Usage: 1968 GTO, full-size Pontiac with
400-ci 2-bbl V-8 . Automatic
transmission.

Interchange Number: 84
Type: Rochester 4MV
ID Number: 7028263
Usage: 1968 GTO, full-size Pontiac with
400-ci 4-bbl V-8. Manual transmission.

Interchange Number: 85
Type: Rochester 4MV
ID Number: 7028268
Usage: 1968 GTO, with 400-ci 4-bbl V-8;
1968 full-size Pontiac with 428-ci 4-bbl
V-8. Automatic transmission.

Interchange Number: 86
Type: Rochester 4MV
ID Number: 7028267
Usage: 1968 GTO, with 400-ci 4-bbl
360-hp V-8 without Ram Air; 1968 full-size
Pontiac with 428-ci 4-bbl V-8. Manual
transmission.

Interchange Number: 87
Type: Rochester 4MV
ID Number: 7028275
Usage: Early 1968 GTO, with 400-ci 4-bbl
V-8 with Ram Air. Manual transmission

Interchange Number: 88
Type: Rochester 4MV
ID Number: 7028274
Usage: Early 1968 GTO, with 400-ci 4-bbl
V-8 with Ram Air. Automatic transmission

Interchange Number: 89
Type: Rochester 2BC
ID Number: 7029060 or 7029070
Usage: 1969 GTO, Grand Prix, full-size
Pontiac with 400-ci 2-bbl V-8. Automatic
transmission

Interchange Number: 90
Type: Rochester 4MV
ID Number: 7040267
Usage: 1970 GTO, Grand Prix, full-size
Pontiac with 455-ci 4-bbl V-8 without
E.E.C. or Ram Air. Manual transmission

Interchange Number: 91
Type: Rochester 4MV
ID Number: 7040268
Usage: 1970 GTO, Grand Prix, full-size
Pontiac with 455-ci 4-bbl V-8 without
E.E.C. or Ram Air. Automatic transmission

Interchange Number: 92
Type: Rochester 4MV
ID Number: 7040567
Usage: 1970 GTO, Grand Prix, full-size
Pontiac with 455-ci 4-bbl V-8 with E.E.C.
with out Ram Air. Manual transmission

Interchange Number: 93
Type: Rochester 4MV
ID Number: 7040568
Usage: 1970 GTO, Grand Prix, full-size
Pontiac with 455-ci 4-bbl V-8 with E.E.C
without Ram Air. Automatic transmission

Interchange Number: 94
Type: Rochester 4MV
ID Number: 7042272
Usage: 1972 GTO, Grand Prix, full-size
Pontiac with 455-ci 4-bbl V-8 except
California or high altitude.

Interchange Number: 95
Type: Rochester 4MV
ID Number: 7042276
Usage: 1972 GTO, Grand Prix, full-size
Pontiac with 455-ci 4-bbl V-8 high
altitude.

Interchange Number: 96
Type: Rochester 4MV
ID Number: 7042262
Usage: 1972 GTO, Grand Prix, full-size
Pontiac with 455-ci 4-bbl V-8 California.

Interchange Number: 97
Type: Rochester 2G
ID Number: 7024078 or 7025078
Usage: 1964-66 full-size Pontiac with
421-ci 3x2-bbl V-8.

Interchange Number: 98
Type: Rochester 2G
ID Number: 7023161
Usage: 1963-64 full-size Pontiac with
421-ci 3x2-bbl V-8. Manual transmission

Interchange Number: 99
Type: Rochester 2G
ID Number: 7024074
Usage: 1964 full-size Pontiac with 421-ci
3x2-bbl V-8. Automatic transmission.

Interchange Number: 100
Type: Rochester 2G
ID Number: 7024079 or 7025079
Usage: 1964-66 full-size Pontiac with
421-ci 3x2-bbl V-8. Automatic only
1965-66

Interchange Number: 101
Type: Rochester 2G
ID Number: 7025075
Usage: 1965 full-size Pontiac with 421-ci
3x2-bbl V-8. Manual transmission

Interchange Number: 102
Type: Rochester 2G
ID Number: 7025074
Usage: 1965 full-size Pontiac with 421-ci
3x2-bbl V-8. Automatic transmission

Interchange Number: 103
Type: Rochester 2G
ID Number: 7025079
Usage: 1965-66 full-size Pontiac with 421-ci 3x2-bbl.
Manual transmission

Original air cleaners can be identified by using this decal repaired

Minor damage like this can be easily

Typical salvage yard find. This air cleaner assembly is in good shape and can be repainted

Air Cleaner Assembly

When buying a used air cleaner assembly, first make sure the unit is complete. Small items like vacuum diaphragms can be hard to locate by themselves, especially in classic cars.. Next look at the base and be sure it is undamaged, many individuals modified air cleaner assemblies to make it fit a different carburetor or a home made ram air system. Play attention to the snorkels and the lid lip, these areas are more prone to damage. And be sure that lid and base match up properly. Also be sure it has the right provisions for your model, for example: cars with an automatic transmission require special vacuum provisions, and clearance for the kick down rod so an air cleaner from a car with a manual transmission make not necessarily interchange.

Air Cleaner Interchange

Firebird

1967

326-ci

2-bbl

Without A.I.R. or Closed PCV

Manual Transmission

Standard Air Cleaner	1
Heavy-duty	2

Automatic

Standard Air Cleaner	3
Heavy-duty	4

Manual

Standard Air Cleaner	5
Heavy-duty	6

Automatic

Standard Air Cleaner	7
Heavy-duty	8

With A.I.R.

Manual

Standard Air Cleaner	9
Heavy-duty	10

Automatic

Standard Air Cleaner	11
Heavy-duty	12

4-bbl

Without A.I.R. or Closed P.C.V.

Standard Air Cleaner	42
Heavy-duty	43

With A.I.R.

Standard	36
Heavy-duty	46

With Closed P.C.V.

Standard	44
Heavy-duty	45

400-ci

Without Ram Air

Without A.I.R. or Closed P.C.V.	47
With A.I.R	48
With Closed P.C.V.	48
With Ram Air	49

1968

350-ci

2-bbl	29
4-bbl	56

400-ci

4-bbl	57

1969

350-ci

2-bbl

All	29

350-ci

2-bbl	29
4-bbl	56

400-ci

4-bbl	57

1970

350-ci

2-bbl	30

400-ci

2-bbl	30
4-bbl	
Except Trans Am or	
Formula 400	60
Formula with Ram Air	61
Trans Am	
Ram Air III	63
Ram Air IV	62

1971

350-ci	
2-bbl	
All	30
400-ci	
2-bbl	30
4-bbl	
Except High output Ram Air	
or Trans Am	60
Ram Air III	67
Trans Am	
Ram Air II	68
Ram Air III	72
High Output	69

1972

350-ci	
2-bbl	
All	30
400-ci	
2-bbl	30
4-bbl	
Except High output Ram Air	
or Trans Am	60
Ram Air III	67
Trans Am	
Ram Air II	68
Ram Air III	72
High Output	69

GTO/LeMans/Tempest

1964

326-ci	
2-bbl	
Standard Air Cleaner	13
Heavy-duty	14
4-bbl	
Without Closed PCV	32
With Closed PCV	33
389-ci	
Without Closed PCV	34
With Closed PCV	35

1965

326-ci	
2-bbl	
Standard	15
Heavy-duty	16
4-bbl	
Without Closed P.C.V.	36
With Closed P.C.V.	37
389-ci	
Without Closed P.C.V.	39
With Closed P.C.V	38

1966

2-bbl	
Without A.I.R. or closed PCV	17
With A.I.R.	19
With Closed PCV	18

1967

326-ci	
2-bbl	
Without A.I.R. or Closed PCV	
Manual Transmission	20
Automatic	25
WITH A.I.R.	
Manual	

Standard	23	**1969**		
Heavy-duty	24	350-ci		
Automatic	28	2-bbl		
With Closed PCV		All	29	
Manual		4-bbl	56	
Standard	21	400-ci		
Heavy-duty	22	2-bbl	29	
Automatic		4-bbl		
Standard	26	Standard Air Cleaner	58	
Heavy-duty	27	Heavy-duty	59	
4-bbl		**1970**		
Without A.I.R.		350-ci		
Standard Air Cleaner	36	2-bbl	31	
Heavy-duty	50	400-ci		
With A..I..R.		4-bbl		
Standard Air Cleaner	36	Except GTO	64	
Heavy-duty	46	GTO	65	
400-ci		455-ci	65	
2-bbl		**1971**		
Without A.I.R. or Closed PCV		350-ci		
Manual Transmission	20	2-bbl	31	
Automatic	25	4-bbl	70	
Without Ram Air, A.I.R		400-ci		
or Closed P.C.V.	47	Except Ram Air.		
With Ram Air or High Output		4-bbl	70	
Without A.I.R.	49	Ram Air	61	
With A.I.R.		455-ci	70	
Standard Air cleaner	51	**1972**		
Heavy-duty	52	350-ci		
1968		2-bbl	31	
350-ci		4-bbl	70	
2-bbl	29	400-ci		
4-bbl	56	Except Ram Air.		
400-ci		4-bbl	70	
2-bbl	29	Ram Air	61	
4-bbl	57	455-ci	70	

Grand Prix

1969

400-ci	56
428-ci	57

1970

400-ci	
2-bbl	
4-bbl	64
455-ci	66

1971

400-ci	
2-bbl	
4-bbl	71
455-ci	70

1971

400-ci	
2-bbl	
4-bbl	71
455-ci	70

2+2

1964

389-ci	
Without Closed P.C.V	
4-bbl	40
With Closed P.C.V.	
4-bbl	41
421-ci	
Without Closed P.C.V	
4-bbl	40
With Closed P.C.V.	
4-bbl	41

1965

Without Closed P.C.V	
4-bbl	38
With Closed P.C.V.	
4-bbl	39
421-ci	
Without Closed P.C.V	
4-bbl	38
With Closed P.C.V.	
4-bbl	39

1966

Without Closed P.C.V	
4-bbl	38
With Closed P.C.V.	
4-bbl	39
421-ci	
Without Closed P.C.V	
4-bbl	38
With Closed P.C.V.	
4-bbl	39

1967

400-ci	
Without A.I.R. or Closed P.C.V.	
Standard	53
Heavy-duty	54
With A.I.R.	
Standard	36
Heavy-duty	46
With Closed P.C.V.	
Standard	36
Heavy-duty	55
428-ci	
Without A.I.R. or High Output	47
With A.I.R.	48
High Output	49

Interchange Number: 1
Part Number: 6424882
Usage: 1967 Firebird with 326-ci 2-bbl, manual transmission without A.I.R. or heavy-duty air cleaner.

Interchange Number: 2
Part Number: 6424885
Usage: 1967 Firebird with 326-ci 2-bbl, manual transmission with heavy-duty air cleaner. Without A.I.R.

Interchange Number: 3
Part Number: 6424793
Usage: 1967 Firebird with 326-ci 2-bbl, automatic transmission without A.I.R. or heavy-duty air cleaner.

Interchange Number: 4
Part Number: 6424796
Usage: 1967 Firebird with 326-ci 2-bbl, automatic transmission with heavy-duty air cleaner. Without A.I.R.

Interchange Number: 5
Part Number: 6424883
Usage: 1967 Firebird with 326-ci 2-bbl, manual transmission without heavy-duty air cleaner. With closed PCV.

Interchange Number: 6
Part Number: 6424886
Usage: 1967 Firebird with 326-ci 2-bbl, manual transmission with heavy-duty air cleaner. With closed PCV.

Interchange Number: 7
Part Number: 6424794
Usage: 1967 Firebird with 326-ci 2-bbl, automatic transmission without heavy duty air cleaner. With closed PCV.

Interchange Number: 8
Part Number: 6424797
Usage: 1967 Firebird with 326-ci 2-bbl, automatic transmission heavy-duty air cleaner. With closed PCV.

Interchange Number: 9
Part Number: 6424884
Usage: 1967 Firebird with 326-ci 2-bbl, manual transmission with A.I.R. without heavy-duty air cleaner.

Interchange Number: 10
Part Number: 6424887
Usage: 1967 Firebird with 326-ci 2-bbl, manual transmission with A.I.R. with heavy-duty air cleaner.

Interchange Number: 11
Part Number: 6424795
Usage: 1967 Firebird with 326-ci 2-bbl, automatic transmission with A.I.R. without heavy-duty air cleaner.

Interchange Number: 12
Part Number: 6424798
Usage: 1967 Firebird with 326-ci 2-bbl, manual transmission with A.I.R. with heavy-duty air cleaner.

Interchange Number: 13
Part Number: 5554159
Usage: 1964 Tempest 326-ci 2-bbl without heavy-duty air cleaner. All transmission types.

Interchange Number: 14
Part Number: 5646357
Usage: 1964 Tempest with 326-ci 2-bbl, with heavy-duty air cleaner. All transmission types.

Interchange Number: 15
Part Number: 6420969
Usage: 1964 Tempest with 326-ci 2-bbl, without heavy-duty air cleaner. All transmission types.

Interchange Number: 16
Part Number: 6420967
Usage: 1964 Tempest with 326-ci 2-bbl, with heavy-duty air cleaner. All transmission types.

Interchange Number: 17
Part Number: 6422846
Usage: 1966 Tempest with 326-ci 2-bbl, without A.I.R or closed PCV. All transmission types.

Interchange Number: 18
Part Number: 6420971
Usage: 1966 Tempest with 326-ci 2-bbl, with closed PCV. All transmission types.

Interchange Number: 19
Part Number: 6422252
Usage: 1966 Tempest with 326-ci 2-bbl, with A.I.R. All transmission types.

Interchange Number: 20
Part Number: 6422846
Usage: 1967 Tempest, full-size Pontiac with 326-ci or 400-ci 2-bbl, manual transmission without A.I.R or heavy-duty air cleaner.

Interchange Number: 21
Part Number: 6423196
Usage: 1967 Tempest, full-size Pontiac with 326-ci or 400-ci 2-bbl, manual transmission without A.I.R or heavy-duty air cleaner. With Closed PCV.

Interchange Number: 22
Part Number: 6423199
Usage: 1967 Tempest with 326-ci 2-bbl, manual transmission without A.I.R with heavy-duty air cleaner and closed PCV.

Interchange Number: 23
Part Number: 6423197
Usage: 1967 Tempest with 326-ci 2-bbl, manual transmission with A.I.R withoutr heavy-duty air cleaner.

Interchange Number: 24
Part Number: 6423200
Usage: 1967 Tempest with 326-ci 2-bbl, manual transmission with A.I.R with heavy-duty air cleaner.

Interchange Number: 25
Part Number: 6484482
Usage: 1967 Tempest with 326-ci 2-bbl, automatic transmission without A.I.R or heavy-duty air cleaner.

Interchange Number: 26
Part Number: 6424572
Usage: 1967 Tempest with 326-ci 2-bbl, automatic transmission without A.I.R without heavy-duty air cleaner. With Closed PCV

Interchange Number: 27
Part Number: 6424575
Usage: 1967 Tempest with 326-ci 2-bbl, automatic transmission without A.I.R with heavy-duty air cleaner. With closed PCV.

Interchange Number: 28
Part Number: 6424576
Usage: 1967 Tempest with 326-ci 2-bbl, automatic transmission with A.I.R.

Interchange Number: 29
Part Number: 6424820
Usage: 1968-69 Firebird, Tempest with 350-ci, 400-ci 2-bbl; 1968-69, full-size Pontiac, Tempest with 400--ci 2-bbl,; 1969 Grand Prix with 400-ci 2-bbl. All transmissions.

Interchange Number: 30
Part Number: 6485785
Usage: 1970-71 Firebird, with 350-ci 2-bbl. All transmissions.

Interchange Number: 31
Part Number: 6486107
Usage: 1970-72 Tempest, Grand Prix, full-size Pontiac with 350-ci or 400-ci 2-bbl V-8. All transmissions.

Interchange Number: 32
Part Number: 6484456
Usage: 1964 Tempest with 326-ci 4-bbl V-8. Without closed PCV.

Interchange Number: 33
Part Number: 6419724
Usage: 1964 Tempest with 326-ci 4-bbl V-8. With closed PCV.

Interchange Number: 34
Part Number: 6420754
Usage: 1964 GTO without closed PCV.
Notes: Chrome

Interchange Number: 35
Part Number: 6420765
Usage: 1964 GTO with closed PCV.
Notes: Chrome

Interchange Number: 36
Part Number: 6484472
Usage: 1965-67 Tempest with 326-ci 4-bbl V-8 without closed PCV; 1967 Firebird with 326-ci 4-bbl with A.I.R. without heavy-duty air cleaner; 1967 full-size Pontiac with 400-ci 4-bbl V-8 with and without A.I.R. with closed P.C.V. without heavy-duty air cleaner.

Interchange Number: 37
Part Number: 6420968
Usage: 1965-66 Tempest with 326-ci 4-bbl V-8 with closed PCV.

Interchange Number: 38
Part Number: 6420984
Usage: 1965-66 GTO, 2+2 with 389-ci or 421-ci 4-bbl V-8 with closed PCV.

Interchange Number: 39
Part Number: 6421289
Usage: 1965-66 GTO, 2+2 with 389-ci or 421-ci 4-bbl V-8 without closed PCV.

Interchange Number: 40
Part Number: 6418019
Usage: 1964 Catalina, Bonneville with 389-ci 4-bbl or 421-ci 4-bbl V-8. Without closed PCV.

Interchange Number: 41
Part Number: 6419802
Usage: 1964 Catalina, Bonneville with 389-ci 4-bbl or 421-ci 4-bbl V-8. Without closed PCV.

Interchange Number: 42
Part Number: 6424789
Usage: 1967 Firebird with 326-ci 4-bbl. Without A.I.R. without closed P.C.V or heavy-duty air cleaner.

Interchange Number: 43
Part Number: 6424791
Usage: 1967 Firebird with 326-ci 4-bbl. Without A.I.R. without closed P.C.V with heavy-duty air cleaner.

Interchange Number: 44
Part Number: 6424790
Usage: 1967 Firebird with 326-ci 4-bbl. Without A.I.R. with closed P.C.V without heavy-duty air cleaner.

Interchange Number: 45

Part Number: 6424792

Usage: 1967 Firebird with 326-ci 4-bbl. Without A.I.R. without closed P.C.V or heavy-duty air cleaner.

Interchange Number: 46

Part Number: 6424505

Usage: 1967 Firebird, Tempest with 326-ci 4-bbl. With A.I.R. with heavy-duty air cleaner; 1967 full-size Pontiac with 400-ci 4-bbl V-8 with A.I.R.

Interchange Number: 47

Part Number: 6422168

Usage: 1967 Firebird, Tempest with 400-ci 4-bbl. Without Ram Air, A.I.R. or closed P.C.V. Or High output package; 1967 2+2 with 428-ci V-8 without A.I.R.

Interchange Number: 48

Part Number: 6484473

Usage: 1967 Firebird, Tempest with 400-ci 4-bbl. With closed P.C.V; 1967 full-size Pontiac with 428-ci with A.I.R.

Interchange Number: 49

Part Number: 6424590

Usage: 1967 Firebird, Tempest with 400-ci 4-bbl. With Ram Air, without A.I.R; 1967 full-size Pontiac with 428-ci High Output.

Interchange Number: 50

Part Number: 6423202

Usage: 1967 Tempest with 326-ci 4-bbl with heavy-duty air cleaner without A.I.R.

Interchange Number: 51

Part Number: 6423211

Usage: 1967 Firebird, Tempest with 400-ci 4-bbl. With Ram Air, with A.I.R. Without Heavy-duty air cleaner.

Interchange Number: 52

Part Number: 6423209

Usage: 1967 Firebird, Tempest with 400-ci 4-bbl. With Ram Air, with A.I.R. With Heavy-duty air cleaner.

Interchange Number: 53

Part Number: 6420972

Usage: 1967 full-size Pontiac with 400-ci 4-bbl V-8. Without A.I.R. or Closed P.C.V. or heavy-duty air cleaner.

Interchange Number: 54

Part Number: 6422849

Usage: 1967 full-size Pontiac with 400-ci 4-bbl V-8. Without A.I.R. or Closed P.C.V. with heavy-duty air cleaner.

Interchange Number: 55

Part Number: 6423213

Usage: 1967 full-size Pontiac with 400-ci 4-bbl V-8. Without A.I.R. with Closed P.C.V. with heavy-duty air cleaner.

Interchange Number: 56

Part Number: 6485501

Usage: 1968 Firebird, Tempest with 350-ci 4-bbl; 1968-69 full-size Pontiac with 400-ci 4-bbl; 1969 Grand Prix with 400-ci 4-bbl V-8.

Interchange Number: 57

Part Number: 6424827

Usage: 1968-69 Firebird, 1968 Tempest with 400-ci 4-bbl V-8; 1968-69 full-size Pontiac, Grand Prix with 428-ci V-8.

Interchange Number: 58

Part Number: 684994

Usage: 1969 Tempest with 400-ci 4-bbl V-8.

Interchange Number: 59

Part Number: 6421746

Usage: 1969 Tempest with 400-ci 4-bbl V-8. With heavy-duty air cleaner.

Interchange Number: 60

Part Number: 66486117

Usage: 1970-71 Firebird with 400-ci 4-bbl V-8. Except Trans Am or Formula 400.

Interchange Number: 61

Part Number: 6486474

Usage: 1970-72 Firebird Formula; 1971-72 GTO with 400 with Ram Air.

Interchange Number: 62

Part Number: 6486669

Usage: 1970 Trans Am with Ram Air IV.

Interchange Number: 63

Part Number: 6486668

Usage: 1970 Trans Am with Ram Air III

Interchange Number: 64

Part Number: 6486138

Usage: 1970-72 Tempest with 400-ci or 455-ci 4-bbl V-8 except GTO; 1970 Grand Prix with 455-ci V-8.

Interchange Number: 65

Part Number: 6485778

Usage: 1970 GTO with 400-ci 4-bbl V-8. Notes: Chrome cover.

Interchange Number: 66

Part Number: 6485800

Usage: 1970 Grand Prix with 400-ci; 1970 full-size Pontiac with 400-ci or 455-ci 4-bbl V-8.

Interchange Number: 67

Part Number: 6486684

Usage: 1971-72 Firebird with Ram Air III.

Interchange Number: 68

Part Number: 6486686

Usage: 1971-72 Firebird Trans Am

Interchange Number: 69

Part Number: 6486812

Usage: 1971-72 Firebird with 400-ci or 350-ci High output.

Interchange Number: 70
Part Number: 6466182
Usage: 1971-72 Tempest 350-ci, 400-ci or 455- ci 4-bbl V-8; 1971-72 Grand Prix with 455-ci V-8.

Interchange Number: 71
Part Number: 6486680
Usage: 1971-72 Grand Prix with 400-ci 4-bbl V-8; 1971-72 full-size Pontiac with 400-ci or 455-ci 4-bbl V-8 except police car.

Interchange Number: 72
Part Number:
Usage: 1971-72 Firebird Trans Am with Ram Air III.

Ram Air

Various components made up the Ram Air System, and to list all interchangeable parts would be a book in it's self. Also some Ram Air parts can be found in other interchanges, such as exhaust manifolds. This section focuses the 1967-70 Air cleaner assemblies. You may have noticed them missing from the above interchange. This was done because more components can be grouped here.

Ram Air/ Air Cleaner Interchange

Firebird

1967

Shroud	1
Cover	22
Seal	
Baffle to shroud	10
Baffle to Hood	24

1968

Shroud	3
Baffle	17
Cover	22
Seal	
Baffle to shroud	12
Baffle to Hood	24

1969

Shroud	
Ram Air III or H.O.	4
Ram Air IV	5
Baffle	
Ram Air III	19
Ram Air IV	
Except Trans Am	18
Trans Am	20
Seal	
Baffle to shroud	
Except Trans Am	13
Trans Am	14
Baffle to Hood	
Except Trans Am	26
Trans Am	27

GTO

1967

Shroud	2
Cover	22
Seal	
Hood to Shroud	11

1968

Shroud	3
Baffle	16
Cover	22
Seal	
Baffle to shroud	12
Baffle to Hood	25

1969

Shroud	
Ram Air III or H.O.	7
Ram Air IV	6
Baffle	21
Cover	23

Seal

Baffle to shroud	15
Baffle to Hood	28

1970

Shroud

455-ci or Ram Air III	9
Ram Air IV	8
Baffle	21
Cover	23

Seal

Baffle to shroud	15
Baffle to Hood	28

Interchange Number: 1
Part Number: 9789884
Part: Bottom Pan (shroud)
Usage: 1967 Firebird with Ram Air.

Interchange Number: 2
Part Number: 9788921
Part: Bottom Pan (shroud)
Usage: 1967 Tempest with H.O. and Ram Air.

Interchange Number: 3
Part Number: 9792987
Part: Bottom Pan (shroud)
Usage: 1968 Firebird, GTO with Ram Air.

Interchange Number: 4
Part Number: 97981121
Part: Bottom Pan (shroud)
Usage: 1969 Firebird with 400-ci H.O.

Interchange Number: 5
Part Number: 9798113
Part: Bottom Pan (shroud)
Usage: 1969 Firebird with Ram Air IV..

Interchange Number: 6
Part Number: 9794639
Part: Bottom Pan (shroud)
Usage: 1969 GTO with Ram Air IV.

Interchange Number: 7
Part Number: 9794638
Part: Bottom Pan (shroud)
Usage: 1969 GTO with Ram AIr III or H.O.

Interchange Number: 8
Part Number: 478135
Part: Bottom Pan (shroud)
Usage: 1970 GTO with Ram Air IV.

Interchange Number: 9
Part Number: 478136
Part: Bottom Pan (shroud)
Usage: 1970 GTO with Ram Air III.

Interchange Number: 10
Part Number: 9789885
Part: seal baffle to shroud
Usage: 1967 Firebird With Ram Air

Interchange Number: 11
Part Number: 9788922
Part: seal shroud to hood
Usage: 1967 GTO with Ram Air.

Interchange Number: 12
Part Number: 9793163
Part: seal baffle to shroud
Usage: 1968 Firebird, GTO with Ram air

Interchange Number: 13
Part Number: 9798061
Part: Seal baffle to shroud
Usage: 1969 Firebird with Ram Air, except Trans Am.

Interchange Number: 14
Part Number: 546282
Part: Seal baffle to shroud
Usage: 1969 Firebird Trans Am

Interchange Number: 15
Part Number: 9797429
Part: Seal baffle to shroud
Usage: 1969-70 GTO with Ram air

Interchange Number: 16
Part Number: 9792984
Part: Baffle
Usage: 1968 GTO with Ram air

Interchange Number: 17
Part Number: 9793161
Part: Baffle
Usage: 1968 Firebird with Ram air

Interchange Number: 18
Part Number: 9797838
Part: Baffle
Usage: 1969 Firebird with Ram air IV or H.O., except Trans Am.

Interchange Number: 19
Part Number: 9797839
Part: Baffle
Usage: 1969 Firebird with Ram air III

Interchange Number: 20
Part Number: 546284
Part: Baffle
Usage: 1969 Firebird Trans Am.

Interchange Number: 21
Part Number: 979436
Part: Baffle
Usage: 1969-70 GTO with Ram air

Interchange Number: 22
> Part Number: 6424398
> Part: Cover
> Usage: 1967 Firebird, GTO with Ram air

Interchange Number: 23
> Part Number: 6485198
> Part: Cover
> Usage: 1969-70 GTO with Ram air

Interchange Number: 24
> Part Number: 9789883
> Part: Seal Baffle to Hood
> Usage: 1967-68 Firebird with Ram air

Interchange Number: 25
> Part Number: 9792986
> Part: Seal Baffle to Hood
> Usage: 1968 GTO with Ram air

Interchange Number: 26
> Part Number: 9798061
> Part: Seal Baffle to Hood
> Usage: 1969 Firebird with Ram air, except
> Trans Am.

Interchange Number: 27
> Part Number: 546282
> Part: Seal Baffle to Hood
> Usage: 1969 Firebird Trans Am.

Interchange Number: 28
> Part Number: 9797423
> Part: Seal Baffle to Hood
> Usage: 1969-70 GTO with Ram Air

Chapter 3

Exhaust Systems

Exhaust Manifolds

Cast iron exhaust manifolds were designed to be maintenance free. But due to the high temperatures that they receive from engine exhaust fumes, and water vapors, this makes them susceptible to corrosion, resulting in frozen parts. Penetrating oil and heat may be required to remove a manifold. Though the manifolds are tough items, care should still be used in examining the parts. Look for cracks and broken areas, especially around the mounting areas. Also look for signs of repair, like weld marks. Cast iron does not repair well, so be suspicious for these. Another factor to test is the heat valve, check to see if it is free and moves correctly. In many old exhaust manifolds the heat valves are stuck, and this is common.

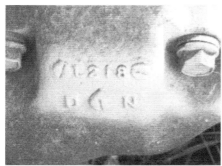

Date code. Letter is month A-January-L December, and day of the month and the last digit of the casting year. The arrow straight up indicates the third shift.

Casting number on manifold.

Firebird

1967

326-ci

Drivers	1
Passengers	2

400-ci

Without Ram Air

Drivers	1
Passengers	2

With Ram Air

Drivers	3
Passengers	4

1968

350-ci

Drivers	1
Passengers	2

400-ci

Without Ram Air

Drivers	1
Passengers	2

With Ram Air Except 360-hp

Drivers	3
Passengers	5

360-hp

Drivers	6
Passengers	7

1969

350-ci

Drivers	8
Passengers	9

400-ci

Without Ram Air

Drivers	8
Passengers	9

With Ram Air III

Drivers	3
Passengers	10

Ram Air IV

Drivers	6
Passengers	11

1970

350-ci

Drivers	12
Passengers	9

400-ci

Without Ram Air

Drivers	12
Passengers	9

With Ram Air

Drivers	13
Passengers	14

1971

350-ci

Drivers	12
Passengers	9

400-ci

Drivers	12
Passengers	9

455-ci

325-hp

Drivers	12
Passengers	9

335-hp

Drivers	15
Passengers	16

1972

350-ci

Drivers	12
Passengers	9

400-ci

Drivers	12
Passengers	9

455-ci

Drivers	15
Passengers	16

Grand Prix

1969

400-ci

Drivers	8
Passengers	9

428-ci

370-hp

Drivers	8
Passengers	9

390-hp

Drivers	3
Passengers	10

1970

Drivers	8
Passengers	9

1971

Drivers	12
Passengers	9

1972

Drivers	12
Passengers	9

GTO/Tempest/LeMans

1964

326-ci, 389-ci

Drivers	12
Passengers	17

1965

326-ci, 389-ci

Drivers	12
Passengers	2

1966

326-ci, 389-ci

Drivers	12
Passengers	2

1967

326-ci

Drivers	12
Passengers	2

400-ci

Except Ram Air

Drivers	12
Passengers	2

With Ram Air

Drivers	18
Passengers	2

1968

350-ci

Drivers	12
Passengers	2

400-ci

Except Ram Air

Drivers	12
Passengers	2

With Ram Air 360-hp

Drivers

engine codes XP and XS	20
engine codes WY and XW	15

Passengers

engine codes XP and XS	19
engine codes WY and XW	21

1969

350-ci

Drivers	8
Passengers	9

400-ci

Without Ram Air

Drivers	8
Passengers	9

Ram Air III or H.O.

Drivers	20
Passengers	14

Ram Air IV

Drivers	15
Passengers	22

1970

350-ci

Drivers	8
Passengers	9

400-ci

Without Ram Air

Drivers	8
Passengers	9

Ram Air III

Drivers	20
Passengers	13

Ram Air IV

Drivers	15
Passengers	16

1971

350-ci 400-ci

Drivers	8
Passengers	9

455-ci 325-hp

Drivers	8
Passengers	9

455-ci 335-hp

Drivers	15
Passengers	16

1972

350-ci 400-ci

Drivers	8
Passengers	9

455-ci 220-hp

Drivers	8
Passengers	9

455-ci 300-hp

Drivers	15
Passengers	16

2+2

1964

Except 421-ci H.O.

Drivers	23
Passengers	17

421-ci H.O.

Drivers	24
Passengers	25

1965

Except 421-ci H.O.

Drivers	18
Passengers	2

421-ci H.O.

Drivers	3
Passengers	4

1966

Except 421-ci H.O.

Drivers	18
Passengers	2

421-ci H.O.

Drivers	3
Passengers	4

1967

428-ci Except H.O.

Drivers	18
Passengers	2

428-ci H.O.

Drivers	3
Passengers	4

Interchange Number: 1
    Part Number: 9777755
    Side: Drivers
    Usage: 1967-68 Firebird 350-ci or 400-ci without Ram Air.

Interchange Number: 2
    Part Number: 9779325
    Side: Passengers
    Usage: 1967 Firebird 350-ci or 400-ci without Ram Air; 1965-66 full size Pontiac, except 421-ci H.O.   1967 full-size Pontiac except 428-ci H.O.; 1965-67 Tempest except H.O. or Ram Air.
    Notes: Casting Number 9779325

Interchange Number: 3
    Part Number: 9779495
    Side: Drivers
    Usage: 1967-69 Firebird 400-ci with Ram Air or H.O, except Ram Air IV; 1965-66 full size Pontiac with 421-ci H.O. 1967 full-size Pontiac with 428-ci H.O.; 1968-69 full size Pontiac, Grand Prix 428-ci 390-hp.

Interchange Number: 4
    Part Number: 9779493
    Side: Passengers
    Usage: 1967 Firebird 400-ci with Ram Air; 1965-66 full size Pontiac ,with 421-ci H.O. 1967 full-size Pontiac with 428-ci H.O.

Interchange Number: 5
    Part Number: 9791607
    Side: Passengers
    Usage: 1968 Firebird 400-ci with Ram Air III; 1968 full-size Pontiac with 428-ci 390-hp.

Interchange Number: 6
Part Number: 9794038
Side: Drivers
Usage: 1968-69 Firebird 400-ci with Ram
Air IV, 360-hp in 1968.

Interchange Number: 7
Part Number: 9794036
Side: Passengers
Usage: 1968 Firebird 400-ci with 360-hp
Ram Air

Interchange Number: 8
Part Number: 490144
Side: Drivers
Usage: 1969 Firebird, Tempest 350-ci ,
400-ci except with Ram Air; 1969-70 full
size Pontiac , except 390-hp 428-ci
1969-1970 Grand Prix except 390-hp 428-
ci.

Interchange Number: 9
Part Number: 490142
Side: Drivers
Usage: 1969-72 Firebird, Tempest 350-ci ,
400-ci except with Ram Air; 1971 Firebird
455-ci 325-hp ; 1969-72 full size Pontiac
except 390-hp 428-ci; 1969-1972 Grand
Prix except 390-hp 428-ci.

Interchange Number: 10
Part Number: 9797073
Side: Passengers
Usage: 1969 Firebird 400-ci with Ram
Air III or H.O.; 1969 Grand Prix, full-size
Pontiac with 390-h 428-ci.

Interchange Number: 11
Part Number: 9797074
Side: Passengers
Usage: 1969 Firebird 400-ci with Ram Air
IV

Interchange Number: 12
Part Number: 490143
Side: Drivers
Usage: 1970 Firebird 350-ci, 400-ci
without Ram Air; 1971-72 Firebird 455-ci
250-hp; 1971-72 full-size Pontiac;
1971-72 Grand Prix; 1964-72 GTO without
Ram Air; 1964-66 Tempest 326-ci; 1968-
1972 Tempest with 350-ci V-8.

Interchange Number: 13
Part Number: 478140
Side: Drivers
Usage: 1970 Firebird, GTO with 400-ci
with Ram Air III;

Interchange Number: 14
Part Number: 9799720
Side: Passengers
Usage: 1970 Firebird with 400-ci with
Ram Air III; 1969-70 Tempest 400-ci with
Ram Air III

Interchange Number: 15
Part Number: 478141
Side: Drivers
Usage: 1971 Firebird with 455-ci with
455-ci 335-hp; 1972 Firebird 455-ci;
1968-70 GTO with Ram Air IV;
1971-72 Tempest with 455-ci 335 or
300-hp
Notes: Ram Air III in 1968 engine codes
WY or XW

Interchange Number: 16
Part Number: 9799721
Side: Passengers
Usage: 1971 Firebird with 455-ci with
455-ci 335-hp; 1972 Firebird 455-ci;
1970-72 Tempest with 455-ci 335
or 300-hp or with Ram Air IV.

Interchange Number: 17
Part Number: 9779325
Side: Passengers
Usage: 1963-64 Tempest with 326-ci or
389-ci; 1963-64 full-size Pontiac except
421-ci H.O.

Interchange Number: 18
Part Number: 9779033
Side: Drivers
Usage: 1967 Tempest with 400-ci H.O.;
1965-66 full-size Pontiac 421-ci H.O.;
1967-68 full size Pontiac 428-ci
H.O.

Interchange Number: 19
Part Number: 9777641
Side: Passengers
Usage: 1968 Tempest with 400-ci H.O or
Ram Air engine codes XP and XS

Interchange Number: 20
Part Number: 9791637
Side: Drivers
Usage: 1968-69 Tempest with 400-ci H.O
or Ram Air III, engine codes XP and XS in
1968.

Interchange Number: 21
Part Number: 9794033
Side: Drivers
Usage: 1968 Tempest with 400-ci H.O or
Ram Air III, engine codes WY and XW

Interchange Number: 22
Part Number: 9797075
Side: Passengers
Usage: 1969 Tempest with 400-ci Ram Air
IV.

Interchange Number: 23
Part Number: 545470
Side: Drivers
Usage: 1963-64 Full-size Pontiac except
421-ci H.O.

Interchange Number: 24
Part Number: 537455
Side: Drivers
Usage: 1963-64 full-size Pontiac 421-ci H.O.

Interchange Number: 25
Part Number: 545106
Side: Passengers
Usage: 1963-64 full-size Pontiac 421-ci H.O.

Tail Pipe Extensions

Firebird

1967	4
1968	4
1969	4
1970	
2-bbl	8
4-bbl	9
1971	
2-bbl	8
Formula or Trans Am	9
1972	
2-bbl	8
Formula or Trans Am	9

GTO/LeMans/Tempest

1964	2
1965	2
1966	3
1967	3, 5
1968	3, 5
1969	6
1970	
GT-37	7
GTO	7
1971	
GT-37	7
GTO	7

1972	
GTO	7

2+2

1964	1
1965	1
1966	1
1967	1

Interchange Number: 1
Part Number: 536690
Side: Either Side
Usage: 1959-1969 full-size Pontiac station wagon; 1963-64 full-size Pontiac 421-ci H.O.

Interchange Number: 2
Part Number: 9776486 Right and 9776487 Left
Usage: 1964-65 Tempest except station wagon or six cylinder.

Interchange Number: 3
Part Number: 9785205
Side: Either Side
Usage: 1966-68 Tempest.

Interchange Number: 4
Part Number: 9789850 right 9789851 left
Usage: 1967-68 Firebird

Interchange Number: 5
Part Number: 9789224
Side: Either Side
Usage: 1967-68 Tempest with 4-bbl and manual transmission.

Interchange Number: 6
Part Number: 979245
Side: Either Side
Usage: 1969 GTO with manual transmission.

Interchange Number: 7
Part Number: 478022
Side: Either Side
Usage: 1970-71 GT-37, GTO

Interchange Number: 8
Part Number: 481526
Usage: 1970-1971 Firebird 2-bbl

Interchange Number: 9
Part Number: 481525
Usage: 1970-1971 Firebird Formula or Trans Am. All four-barrel versions in 1970.

Chapter 4 Cooling Systems

Radiator

Buying a used radiator core can be a risky venture, as the core can hide flaws. However, with careful inspection you can improve your chances in selecting a quality unit. First off, give the core a general inspection: check the cooling fins. The fins should be straight and not bent or missing. The core it's self should be in one solid piece. Take care in checking the condition of the neck and the hose nipples. These areas are easily damaged, and a bent hose nipple can cause problems in mounting the inlet or outlet hoses.

Never buy a used radiator core that is laying on the ground. Weeds can grow into the core, blocking the fins, also degeneration of the core can also occur. It is also a wise idea not to buy a core that is sitting in a car, especially if there is water in the core. During freezing temperatures the core can be damaged, this is also true if you live in a warm climate or if there is anti-freeze in the core. Anti-freeze or even plain water in a core for long periods of time can cause scale deposits, blocking the effective usage of the unit. The best way to store a core, and the way you should purchase one, is to drain it and store it inside.

As for being able to interchange the core: The below interchange is for an original replacement, it does not mention of improved cooling choices. However, improved cooling can usually be had if you select an upgraded core. An example of an upgrade in core is using a core that was used with air conditioning when your car did not come with air conditioning. The cores are usually larger, wider, and or have better cooling fins. Note you can use a core from an automatic car in a car with manual transmission, by blocking off the transmission cooling ports, but it is not wise to use a core form a manual car in a car with automatic transmission because there is no transmission-cooling tank. Some cores allow you to swap the bottom tanks.

When upgrading, it is best to stick to the same general model group. For example: your 1968 Firebird came without air conditioning, so a core from a 1968 Firebird with air conditioning will most likely fit and give you better cooling.

Firebird

1967

326-ci

Without Air Conditioning

Manual transmission	1
Automatic	2

With Air Conditioning

Manual transmission	3
Automatic transmission	4

400-ci

Manual transmission	3
Automatic transmission	4

1968

350-ci

Without Air Conditioning	5
With Air Conditioning	4

400-ci

Without Air Conditioning

Manual	4

Automatic

without Ram Air	5
With Ram Air	4
With Air Conditioning	4

1969

350-ci

Without Air Conditioning	2
With Air Conditioning	4

With Heavy-duty Cooling

Manual	1
Automatic	4

1970

350-ci

Without Air Conditioning	6
With Air Conditioning	7

400-ci 2-bbl

Without Air Conditioning	7
With Air Conditioning	8

400-ci 4-bbl

Without Air Conditioning	7
With Air Conditioning	
Manual	7
Automatic	8

1971

350-ci

Without Air Conditioning	
Manual	9
Automatic	6
With Air Conditioning	
Manual	8
Automatic	7

400-ci 2-bbl

Without Air Conditioning	6
With Air Conditioning	7

400-ci 4-bbl

Without Air Conditioning	
Manual	7
Automatic	10
With Air Conditioning	8

455-ci 325-hp

Without Air Conditioning	7
With Air Conditioning	8

455-ci 335-hp

Without Air Conditioning	
Manual	10
Automatic	7
With Air Conditioning	8

1972

350-ci or 400-ci

Without Air Conditioning	11
With Air Conditioning	12

455-ci

Without Air Conditioning	
Manual	11
Automatic	12
With Air Conditioning	12

Grand Prix

1969

400-ci

Without Air Conditioning	14
With Air Conditioning	13

428-ci

Without Air Conditioning	
Manual	14
Automatic	15
With Air Conditioning	
Manual	13
Automatic	16

1970

400-ci 2-bbl

Without Air Conditioning	17
With Air Conditioning	14

4-bbl

Without Air Conditioning	
Manual	18
Automatic	17
With Air Conditioning	
Manual	13
Automatic	14
Heavy-duty Cooling	14

455-ci

Without Air Conditioning	14

With Air Conditioning	
Manual	13
Automatic	16
Heavy-duty Cooling	
Manual	13
Automatic	14

1971

400-ci

Without Air Conditioning	
Manual	16
Automatic	13
with Air Conditioning	
Manual	14
Automatic	19

455-ci

Without Air Conditioning	14
With Air Conditioning	13

1972

400-ci

Without Air Conditioning	21
With Air Conditioning	20

455-ci

Without Air Conditioning	22
With Air Conditioning	20

GTO/Tempest/LeMans

1964

326-ci 2-bbl

Without Air Conditioning	23
With Air Conditioning	25

326-ci 4-bbl

Without Air Conditioning	24
With Air Conditioning	25

389-ci

Without Air Conditioning	26
With Air Conditioning	27

1965

326-ci

Without Air Conditioning	30
With Air Conditioning	29
Heavy-duty Cooling	28

389-ci 4-bbl

Without Air Conditioning

Manual	31
Automatic	28
With Air Conditioning	29
389-ci 3x2-bbl	28

1966

326-ci 2-bbl

Without Air Conditioning

Manual	32
Automatic	
With Air Conditioning	

4-bbl

Without Air Conditioning	32
Automatic	33
With Air Conditioning	4

389-ci 4-bbl

Without Air Conditioning	32
With Air Conditioning	34
389-ci 3x2-bbl	35

1967

326-ci, 400-ci 2-bbl

Without Air Conditioning	36
With Air Conditioning	37
With Heavy-duty Cooling	38

400-ci 4-bbl Without Ram Air

Without Air Conditioning	38
With Air Conditioning	37
With Ram Air	37

1968

350-ci

Without Air Conditioning	14
With Air Conditioning	
Manual	13
Automatic	
Without Trailer tow (2-bbl only)	14
With Trailer tow (2-bbl Only)	13
4-bbl	13
400-ci	
Without Air Conditioning	
Manual	13
Automatic	
Except Ram Air or H.O.	14
Ram Air or H.O.	13
With Air Conditioning	13
Heavy-duty Cooling	
2-bbl	14
4-bbl	13

1969

350-ci	
Without air Conditioning	14
With Air Conditioning	
Manual	13
Automatic	
Without Trailer tow (2-bbl only)	14
With Trailer Tow (2-bbl only)	13
4-bbl	13
400-ci	
Without Air Conditioning	14
With Air Conditioning	13
With Ram Air IV	13
Heavy-duty Cooling	
2-bbl	14
4-bbl	13

1970

350-ci	
Without Air Conditioning	
Manual	18
Automatic	17
With Air Conditioning	
Manual	13
Automatic	14
Heavy-duty Cooling	14
400-ci	
Without Ram Air	
or Air Conditioning	17
With Air Conditioning	14
With Ram Air III	
Without Air Conditioning	14
With Air Conditioning	
Manual	13
Automatic	39
Ram Air IV	
Manual	13
Automatic	16
455-ci	
Without Air Conditioning	14
With Air Conditioning	
Manual	13
Automatic	16

1971

350-ci	
Without Air Conditioning	17
With Air Conditioning	
Manual	16
Automatic	14
Heavy-duty Cooling	14
400-ci 2-bbl	
Without Air Conditioning	17
With Air Conditioning	14

400-ci 4-bbl

Without Air Conditioning	14
With Air Conditioning	
Manual	40
Automatic	13
Heavy-duty Cooling	
Manual	16
Automatic	13

455-ci 325-hp

Without Air Conditioning	19
With Air Conditioning	40
With Heavy-duty Cooling	
Manual	16
Automatic	13

455-ci 335-hp

Without Air Conditioning	14
With Air Conditioning	
Manual	16
Automatic	40
Heavy-duty Cooling	
Manual	16
Automatic	13

1972

350-ci

Without Air Conditioning	41
With Air Conditioning	
Manual	20
Automatic	22
Heavy-duty Cooling	22

400-ci 2-bbl

Without Air Conditioning	41
With Air Conditioning	22

400-ci 4-bbl or 455-ci

Without Air Conditioning	22
With Air Conditioning	20

2+2

1964

Without Air Conditioning

Manual	42
Automatic	43
With Air Conditioning	44

1965

Without Air Conditioning

Three-speed

389-ci 4-bbl	46
389-ci 3x2-bbl	47
421-ci 4-bbl	48
421-ci 3x2-bbl	
Except H.O.	48
H.O.	49

Four-speed

389-ci	48
421-ci 4-bbl	48
421-ci 3x2-bbl	
Except H.O.	48
H.O.	49

Automatic

389-ci	47
421-ci	50

With Air Conditioning

3-speed

389-ci 2-bbl or 4-bbl	50
389-ci 3x2-bbl	51
421-ci	51
4-speed	51

Automatic

389 2-bbl or 4-bbl	50
3x2-bbl	52
421-ci	51

1966

Without Air Conditioning

389-ci or 421-ci	53

With Air Conditioning

389-ci Manual transmission	54

Automatic

without A.I.R.	53
With A.I.R.	55

421-ci

Manual	56
Automatic	57

1967

428-ci

Without air conditioning

Manual	58
Automatic	59
With Air Conditioning	55

Interchange Number: 1
Part Number: 3010183
Usage: 1967 Firebird 326-ci Manual transmission without air conditioning; 1969 Firebird 350-ci manual transmission with heavy-duty cooling; 1969 Firebird 400-ci manual transmission without heavy-duty cooling, air conditioning or Ram Air.

Interchange Number: 2
Part Number: 3014096
Usage: 1967 Firebird 326-ci automatic transmission without air conditioning; 1969 Firebird 350-ci without heavy-duty cooling or air conditioning; 1969 Firebird 400-ci automatic transmission without heavy-duty cooling, air conditioning or Ram Air.

Interchange Number: 3
Part Number: 3014091
Usage: 1967 Firebird 326-ci Manual transmission with air conditioning; 1967 Firebird 400-ci manual transmission without air conditioning.

Interchange Number: 4
Part Number: 3014090
Usage: 1967 Firebird 326-ci automatic transmission with air conditioning; 1967 Firebird 400-ci automatic; 1968 Firebird 400-ci manual transmission 350-ci without heavy-duty cooling or air conditioning; 1968 Firebird 400-ci automatic with Ram Air without air conditioning and heavy-duty cooling; 1968-69 Firebird 350-ci automatic transmission with air conditioning or 400-ci automatic with air conditioning and heavy-duty cooling; 1969 Firebird 350-ci automatic with heavy-duty cooling, or 400-ci Ram Air without air conditioning and heavy-duty cooling.

Interchange Number: 5
Part Number: 3010181
Usage: 1968 Firebird 350-ci without air conditioning or 400-ci automatic without Ram Air, heavy-duty cooling and air conditioning; Late 1968 Camaro 327-ci 4-bbl or 350-ci with automatic transmission and air conditioning or heavy-duty cooling

Interchange Number: 6
Part Number: 3021527
Usage: 1970 Firebird 350-ci without air conditioning or heavy-duty cooling; 1971 Firebird 350-ci automatic without air conditioning or heavy-duty cooling or 400-ci 2-bbl without air conditioning or heavy-duty cooling.

Interchange Number: 7
Part Number: 3021528
Usage: 1970 Firebird 350-ci with air conditioning or heavy-duty cooling or 400-ci 2-bbl without air conditioning; 1970 Firebird 400-ci 4-bbl with or without Ram Air III without air conditioning or heavy-duty cooling; 1970 Firebird 400-ci manual transmission Ram Air IV; 1971 Firebird 350-ci or 400-ci 2-bbl automatic with air conditioning or heavy-duty cooling; 1971 Firebird 400-ci 4-bbl manual transmission without air conditioning or heavy-duty cooling; 1971 Firebird 455-ci without air conditioning or heavy-duty cooling.

Interchange Number: 8
Part Number: 3021532
Usage: 1970 Firebird 400-ci 2-bbl with air conditioning, or 400-ci 4-bbl automatic with Ram Air III and air conditioning or heavy-duty cooling; 1970 Firebird 400-ci 4-bbl automatic with Ram Air IV; 1970 Firebird 400-ci 4-bbl automatic with air conditioning except Ram Air; 1971 Firebird 350-ci manual transmission with air conditioning or heavy duty cooling or 400-ci 4-bbl or 455-ci both with air conditioning;

Interchange Number: 9
Part Number: 3025371
Usage: 1971 Firebird 350-ci manual without air conditioning or heavy-duty cooling.

Interchange Number: 10
Part Number: 3023920
Usage: 1971 Firebird 400-ci automatic without air conditioning or heavy-duty cooling; 1971 Firebird 455-ci 335-hp manual transmission without air conditioning or heavy-duty cooling.

Interchange Number: 11
Part Number: 3025915
Usage: 1972 Firebird 350-ci or 400-ci automatic without air conditioning or heavy-duty cooling; 1972 Firebird 455-ci manual transmission without air conditioning or heavy-duty cooling.

Interchange Number: 12
Part Number: 3025900
Usage: 1972 Firebird 350-ci or 400-ci or 455-ci with air conditioning or heavy-duty cooling; 1972 Firebird 455-ci automatic transmission without air conditioning or heavy-duty cooling.

Interchange Number: 13
Part Number: 3025764
Usage: 1969 Grand Prix 400-ci with air conditioning or heavy-duty cooling, or 428-ci manual with air conditioning or heavy-duty cooling; 1970 Grand Prix 400-ci 4-bbl or 455-ci manual transmissions with air conditioning or heavy-duty cooling; 1971 Grand Prix 400-ci automatic or 455-ci both with air conditioning or heavy-duty cooling; 1968 Tempest 400-ci manual without air conditioning or heavy-duty cooling; 1968 GTO 400-ci 360-hp automatic, without air conditioning or heavy-duty cooling; 1968-69 Tempest 350-ci with air conditioning or heavy-duty cooling; 1968-70 Tempest 350-ci manual with air conditioning or heavy-duty cooling; 1969 Tempest 400-ci with Ram Air IV without air conditioning or heavy-duty cooling; 1970 GTO with Ram Air II manual with air conditioning or heavy duty cooling; 1970 GTO 400-ci with Ram Air IV manual transmission; 1970 Tempest 455-ci manual with air conditioning or heavy duty cooling; 1971 Tempest 400-ci 4-bbl automatic with air conditioning or heavy duty cooling; 1971 Tempest 455-ci with heavy-duty cooling.

Interchange Number: 14
Part Number: 3019205
Usage: 1969 Grand prix 400-ci without air conditioning or 428-ci manual transmission without air conditioning; 1970 Grand Prix 400-ci 4-bbl automatic with air conditioning or heavy-duty cooling or 2-bbl with air conditioning; 1970-71 Grand Prix 455-ci without air conditioning or heavy-duty cooling; 1970 Grand Prix 455-ci automatic with heavy-duty cooling; 1971 Grand Prix 400-ci manual transmission with air conditioning or heavy-duty cooling; 1968-69 Tempest 350-ci or 400-ci 2-bbl without air conditioning or heavy-duty cooling; 1968 Tempest 400-ci 350-hp automatic without air conditioning or heavy-duty cooling; 1968-69 Tempest 350-ci 2-bbl automatic with air conditioning or heavy-duty cooling, except trailer tow package; 1969 Tempest 400-ci without air conditioning or heavy-duty cooling or Ram Air IV, or with 350-ci manual transmission with heavy duty cooling; 1970-71 Tempest 350-ci with heavy-duty cooling; 1970 Tempest 400-ci Ram Air III without air conditioning or heavy-duty cooling; 1970 Tempest 400-ci with air conditioning or heavy duty cooling except Ram Air; 1970 Tempest 455-ci without air conditioning or heavy-duty cooling; 1971 Tempest 400-ci 2-bbl with air conditioning or heavy-duty cooling; 1971 Tempest 400-ci 4-bbl or 455-ci 335-hp without air conditioning or heavy duty cooling; 1969 full-size Pontiac 400-ci automatic with air conditioning or heavy-duty cooling, or 428-ci 360-hp without air conditioning or heavy-duty cooling; 1970-71 full-size Pontiac 350-ci or 400-ci or 455-ci 2-bbl with air conditioning or heavy-duty cooling.

Interchange Number: 15
Part Number: 3017240
Usage: 1969 Grand Prix 428-ci automatic without air conditioning; 1969 Tempest 350-ci automatic with air conditioning or heavy-duty cooling; 1969 full-size Pontiac 428-ci 390-hp automatic without air conditioning or heavy-duty cooling

Interchange Number: 16
Part Number: 3017248
Usage: 1969 Grand Prix 428-ci automatic with air conditioning or heavy-duty cooling; 1970 Grand Prix 455-ci automatic with air conditioning, or 400-ci manual transmission without air conditioning or heavy-duty cooling; 1970 GTO 400-ci automatic Ram Air IV, or 455-ci automatic with air conditioning or heavy-duty cooling; 1971 Tempest 350-ci or 400-ci 4-bbl or 455-ci 335-hp all with manual and air conditioning; 1970-71 full-size Pontiac 350-ci or 400-ci automatic with extra heavy-duty cooling usually used with trailer package.

Interchange Number: 17
Part Number: 3014754
Usage: 1970 Grand Prix 400-ci 2-bbl without air conditioning or 400-ci 4-bbl automatic without air conditioning; 1970 Tempest 350-ci or 400-ci automatic without air conditioning or heavy-duty cooling or Ram Air; 1971 Tempest 400-ci 2-bbl without air conditioning without air conditioning or heavy-duty cooling.

Interchange Number: 18
Part Number: 3016908
Usage: 1970 Grand Prix 400-ci 4-bbl manual with air conditioning; 1970 Tempest 350-ci manual transmission without air conditioning or heavy-duty cooling.

Interchange Number: 19
Part Number: 3023917
Usage: 1971 Grand Prix 400-ci automatic with air conditioning; 1971 Tempest 455-ci 325-hp without air conditioning; 1971 full-size Pontiac 455-ci without air conditioning without air conditioning or heavy-duty cooling.

Interchange Number: 20
Part Number: 3025911
Usage: 1972 Grand Prix 400-ci or 455-ci with air conditioning ; 1972 Tempest 350-ci , 400-ci 4-bbl or 455-ci with air conditioning or heavy-duty cooling; 1972 full-size Pontiac 400-ci or 455-ci with air conditioning without air conditioning or heavy-duty cooling.

Interchange Number: 21
Part Number: 3025169
Usage: 1972 Grand Prix 400-ci without air conditioning ; 1972 full-size Pontiac 400-ci or 455-ci without air conditioning or heavy-duty cooling.

Interchange Number: 22
Part Number: 3025159
Usage: 1972 Grand Prix 455-ci without air conditioning ; 1972 Tempest automatic 350-ci or 400-ci 2-bbl with air conditioning or heavy-duty cooling; 1972 Tempest 400-ci 4-bbl or 455-ci without air conditioning without air conditioning or heavy-duty cooling; 1972 full-size Pontiac 400-ci 2-bbl or 455-ci 2-bbl with air conditioning.

Interchange Number: 23
Part Number: 3158853 and 3158855
Usage: 1964 Tempest 326-ci 2-bbl without air conditioning.
Notes: To swap between automatic and manual transmissions bottom tanks must be switched.

Interchange Number: 24
Part Number: 3158956
Usage: 1964 Tempest 326-ci 4-bbl without air conditioning.
Notes: To swap between automatic and manual transmissions bottom tanks must be switched.

Interchange Number: 25
Part Number: 3158854
Usage: 1964 Tempest 326-ci 2 and 4-bbl with air conditioning.
Notes: To swap between automatic and manual transmissions bottom tanks must be switched.

Interchange Number: 26
Part Number: 3002157
Usage: 1964 Tempest 389-ci without air conditioning.
Notes: To swap between automatic and manual transmissions bottom tanks must be switched.

Interchange Number: 27
Part Number: 3002158
Usage: 1964 Tempest 389-ci with air conditioning.
Notes: To swap between automatic and manual transmissions bottom tanks must be switched.

Interchange Number: 28
Part Number: 3003154
Usage: 1965 Tempest 326-ci with heavy duty cooling; 1965 GTO 389-ci Manual 3x2-bbl without air conditioning; 1965 GTO 389-ci automatic without air conditioning.
Notes: To swap between automatic and manual transmissions bottom tanks must be switched.

Interchange Number: 29
Part Number: 3003158
Usage: 1965 Tempest 326-ci or 389-ci with air conditioning.
Notes: To swap between automatic and manual transmissions bottom tanks must be switched.

Interchange Number: 30
Part Number: 3003153
Usage: 1965 Tempest 326-ci without air conditioning.
Notes: To swap between automatic and manual transmissions bottom tanks must be switched.

Interchange Number: 31
Part Number: 3003154
Usage: 1965 GTO 389-ci 4-bbl without air conditioning.
Notes: To swap between automatic and manual transmissions bottom tanks must be switched.

Interchange Number: 32
Part Number: 3008356
Usage: 1966 Tempest 326-ci 2-bbl manual without air conditioning; 1965 Tempest 326-ci 4-bbl or 389-ci 4-bbl without air conditioning.
Notes: Stamped 3005850,30058856 and 3009950. Cores from automatic will fit manual, but cores form a car with manual transmission will *not* fit cars with an automatic.

Interchange Number: 33
Part Number: 3005853
Usage: 1966 Tempest 326-ci 2-bbl automatic without air conditioning.
Notes: Stamped same as part number.

Interchange Number: 34
Part Number: 3009875
Usage: 1966 Tempest 326-ci or 389-ci with air conditioning.
Notes: Stamped 3005858, 3005859 or 3009955

Interchange Number: 35
Part Number: 3008354
Usage: 1966 GTO 389-ci 3x2-bbl.
Notes: Stamped 3005854 or 3009059

Interchange Number: 36
Part Number: 3010456
Usage: 1967 Tempest 326-ci or 400-ci 2-bbl without air conditioning or heavy-duty cooling.

Interchange Number: 37
Part Number: 3158851
Usage: 1967 Tempest 326-ci with air conditioning or heavy-duty cooling; 1967 GTO 400-ci Ram Air without air conditioning or heavy-duty cooling.

Interchange Number: 38
Part Number: 3010454
Usage: 1967 Tempest 326-ci or 400-ci with heavy duty cooling. 1967 GTO 400-ci without Ram Air or air conditioning.

Interchange Number: 39
Part Number: 3021744
Usage: 1970 GTO 400-ci Ram Air II automatic with air conditioning or heavy-duty cooling.

Interchange Number: 40
Part Number: 3022040
Usage: 1971 Tempest 400-ci 4-bbl manual transmission with air conditioning or 455-ci with air conditioning; 1970-71 Chevelle 307-ci or 350-ci 1968-71 Nova 307-ci or 350-ci.

Interchange Number: 41
Part Number: 3025166
Usage: 1972 Tempest 350-ci or 400-ci 2-bbl without air conditioning or heavy-duty cooling; 1972 full-size Chevrolet, Chevelle, Monte Carlo 402-ci or 454-ci without air conditioning.

Interchange Number: 42
Part Number: 3158954
Usage: 1963-64 full-size Pontiac manual without air conditioning.
Notes: To swap between automatic and manual transmissions bottom tanks must be switched.

Interchange Number: 43
Part Number: 3151053
Usage: 1963-64 full-size Pontiac automatic without air conditioning.
Notes: To swap between automatic and manual transmissions bottom tanks must be switched.

Interchange Number: 44
Part Number: 3155350
Usage: 1963-64 full-size Pontiac automatic with air conditioning.
Notes: To swap between automatic and manual transmissions bottom tanks must be switched.

Interchange Number: 45
Part Number: 3004656
Usage: 1965 full-size Pontiac with 389-ci or 421-ci 3x2-bbl except H.O.; 1965 full-size Pontiac 389-ci or 421-ci 4-speed manual without air conditioning.
Notes: To swap between automatic and manual transmissions bottom tanks must be switched.

Interchange Number: 46
Part Number: 3002559
Usage: 1965 full-size Pontiac with 389-ci 3-speed manual, without air conditioning..
Notes: To swap between automatic and manual transmissions bottom tanks must be switched.

Interchange Number: 47
Part Number: 3002554 or 3003955
Usage: 1965 full-size Pontiac with 389-ci 3x2-bbl 3-speed manual, without air conditioning; 1965 full-size Pontiac with 389-ci and T.H. 400 automatic Without air conditioning or heavy-duty cooling.
Notes: To swap between automatic and manual transmissions bottom tanks must be switched.

Interchange Number: 48
Part Number: 3004656
Usage: 1965 full-size Pontiac 421-ci 4-bbl or 3x2-bbl with 3-speed manual, without air conditioning. Except H.O.; 1964 full-size Pontiac 389-ci or 421-ci 4-speed except H.O.
Notes: To swap between automatic and manual transmissions bottom tanks must be switched.

Interchange Number: 49
Part Number: 3005151
Usage: 1965 full-size Pontiac 421-ci H.O.or 389-ci 3x2-bbl automatic with air conditioning.
Notes: To swap between automatic and manual transmissions bottom tanks must be switched.

Interchange Number: 50
Part Number: 3004957
Usage: 1965 full-size Pontiac 421-ci automatic;
Notes: Stamped 3005053, 3002556, 3002557,3003250
Notes: To swap between automatic and manual transmissions bottom tanks must be switched.

Interchange Number: 51
Part Number: 3005250
Usage: 1965 full-size Pontiac 389-ci 3x2-bbl 3-speed air conditioning, or 421-ci with air conditioning or 4-speed manual transmission.
Notes: Stamped 3005150, 3003254 or 3003255
Notes: To swap between automatic and manual transmissions bottom tanks must be switched.

Interchange Number: 52
Part Number: 3005252
Usage: 1965 full-size Pontiac 389-ci or 421-ci 3x2-bbl with air conditioning
Notes: Stamped 3005151, 3003752
Notes: To swap between automatic and manual transmissions bottom tanks must be switched.

Interchange Number: 53
Part Number: 3006254
Usage: 1966 full-size Pontiac 389-ci or 421-ci without air conditioning
Notes: Automatic cores will fit manual transmissions. But Manual transmission will *not* fit automatic. Stamped 3006254, 3006156, 3006251, 3006255,3006256 or 3006257

Interchange Number: 54
Part Number: 3009855
Usage: 1966 full-size Pontiac 389-ci or 421-ci manual with air conditioning; 1967 full-size Pontiac 400-ci with air conditioning.
Notes: Automatic cores will fit manual transmissions. But Manual transmission will not fit automatic.

Interchange Number: 55
Part Number: 3009053
Usage: 1966 full-size Pontiac 389-ci automatic with air conditioning and A.I.R. emissions

Interchange Number: 56
Part Number: 3006258
Usage: 1966 full-size Pontiac 421-ci manual with air conditioning and A.I.R. emissions

Interchange Number: 57
Part Number: 3006257
Usage: 1966 full-size Pontiac 421-ci automatic with air conditioning and A.I.R. emissions

Interchange Number: 58
Part Number: 3013352
Usage: 1967 full-size Pontiac 400-ci with air conditioning or 428-ci manual without air conditioning.

Interchange Number: 58
Part Number: 3013355
Usage: 1967 full-size Pontiac 400-ci manual or 428-ci automatic without air conditioning

Interchange Number: 58
Part Number: 3013352
Usage: 1967 full-size Pontiac 400-ci with air conditioning or 428-ci without air conditioning

Water Pump

It is best to inspect the water pump off the car, at least the belts should be disconnected, if taking the water pump off the car is not possible. A general inspection: looking for cracks in the body and bent rotor shafts. A common place for damage is around the mounting bolt perimeter. Next grasp the hub and attempt to move the rotor shaft up and down, it should have little or no play. Spin the shaft noting any signs of bearing roughness. Also shake the water pump, listening for sounds that could indicate damage. Rattling could indicate a broken propeller.

Water pumps can be identified by their casting numbers

Firebird		GTO/LeMans/Tempest	
1967		**1964**	
326-ci	1	326-ci	1
400-ci	1	389-ci	1
1968		**1965**	
350-ci	1	326-ci	1
400-ci	1	389-ci	1
1969		**1966**	
350-ci	2	326-ci	1
400-ci	2	389-ci	1
1970		**1967**	
350-ci	3	326-ci	1
400-ci	3	400-ci	1
1971		**1968**	
350-ci	3	350-ci	1
400-ci	3	400-ci	1
455-ci	3	**1969**	
1972		350-ci	2
350-ci	3	400-ci	2
400-ci	3	**1970**	
455-ci	3	350-ci	3
Grand Prix		400-ci	3
1969		455-ci	3
400-ci	3	**1971**	
428-ci	3	350-ci	3
1970		400-ci	3
400-ci	3	455-ci	3
455-ci	3	**1972**	
1971		350-ci	3
400-ci	3	400-ci	3
455-ci	3	455-ci	3
1972			
400-ci	3		
455-ci	3		

2+2

1964

389-ci	1
421-ci	1

1965

389-ci	1
421-ci	1

1966

389-ci	1
421-ci	1

1967

400-ci	1
428-ci	1

Interchange Number: 1
Part Number: 9793130
Usage: 1967-68 Firebird 326-ci 350-ci or   400-ci V-8;
1964-1967 Tempest, full-size Pontiac 326-ci, 350-ci
389-ci 400-ci ,421-ci V-8 or 428-ci V-8.

Interchange Number: 2
Part Number: 9797581
Usage: 1969 Firebird 326-ci or 400-ci V-8

Interchange Number: 3
Part Number: 488377
Usage: 1970-72 Firebird 350-ci, 400-ci or 455-ci V-8,
1969-1972 Grand Prix, Tempest, full-size Pontiac
350-ci, 400-ci or 455-ci V-8.

Fan Blade

Fan blades should be stripped of their clutch and spacers before being checked. Blades are usually identified by their diameter and number of blades, but also may be classified by the diameter of the center hole, indicating what type of drive was used. A fan design for use with a fan clutch will not necessarily fit a model that was design to use a fan spacer. Even though they have the same diameter and number of blades.

The fan assembly should be check for warpage, by laying it down on a solid flat surface, like a cement floor. The assembly should lay flush or parallel to the floor, one side should not be higher than the other. Next check each individual blades, make sure they are straight and free of damage. This is especially true of flex fans, which contain flexible aluminum tips on the blades that are easily bent.

Firebird

1967

Without Air Conditioning

4-blade	1
5-blade	2
7-blade	3
With Air Conditioning	4

1968

Except Air Conditioning

4-blade	1
5-blade	5
7-blade	3
With Air Conditioning	4

1969

4-blade	1
5-blade	5
7-blade	6
With Air Conditioning	4
14-Blade	1
5-Blade	5
7-Blade	7
With Air Conditioning	4

1970-1972

Except Air Conditioning

4-blade	1
5-Blade	8
7-Blade	7

With Air Conditioning

350-ci	9
Except 350-ci	10

Grand Prix

1969

5-blade	5
7-blade	6
With Air Conditioning	4

1970

5-Blade	5
7-Blade	7
With Air Conditioning	4

1971-1972

Except Air Conditioning

5-Blade	8
7-Blade	7
With Air Conditioning	10

GTO/LeMans/Tempest

1964

326-ci

Except Air Conditioning	1
With Air Conditioning	12
With Heavy-duty	11
389-ci	12

1965-1966

326-ci

Four Blade	1
Five Blade	13

Seven Blade

Except Heavy-duty	14
Heavy-duty	11
389-ci	14

1967

Without Air Conditioning

4-blade	1
5-blade	2
7-blade	3
With Air Conditioning	4

1968

Except Air Conditioning

4-blade	1
5-blade	5
7-blade	3
With Air Conditioning	4

1969

4-blade	1
5-blade	5
7-blade	6
With Air Conditioning	4

1970

4-Blade

350-ci or 400-ci

Except Ram Air	15
Ram Air	1
455-ci	1
5-Blade	5
7-Blade	7
With Air Conditioning	4

1971-1972

Except Air Conditioning

4-blade	1
5-Blade	8
7-Blade	7

With Air Conditioning

350-ci	9
Except 350-ci	10

2+2

1964

4-Blade	1
5-Blade	16
Seven Blade	12

1965-1966

Four Blade	1
Five Blade	17
Seven Blade	
389-ci	14
421-ci	11

1967

Without Air Conditioning

4-blade	1
5-blade	2
7-blade	3
With Air Conditioning	4

Interchange Number: 1
Part Number: 9798940
Number of Blades: 4 Diameter: 19 Pitch: 2- 5/16
Usage: 1967-72 Firebird 326-ci 350-ci or 400-ci V-8 or 455-ci; 1964-1965 Tempest 326-ci; 1968-1969 Tempest; 1970 Tempest, full-size Pontiac except 350-ci or 400-ci; 1971-1972 Tempest all V-8s; 1972 Grand Prix; 1971-1972 full-size Pontiac all V-8s. All models listed above are without air conditioning.

Interchange Number: 2
Part Number: 9779005
Number of Blades: 5 Diameter: 19- Pitch: 2-1/4
Usage: 1967 Firebird V-8 without air conditioning; 1965-1967 full-size Pontiac without air conditioning; Early 1968 Tempest without air conditioning. All above models are with heavy-duty fan.

Interchange Number: 3
Part Number: 9777012
Number of Blades: 7 Diameter: 19 ½ -Pitch 1-7/8
Usage: 1964-1966 full-size Pontiac all V-8s except air conditioning; 1967 Firebird , Tempest, full-size Pontiac 400-ci except air conditioning or Ram Air; 1966 Tempest V-8 without air conditioning; 1968 Firebird, Tempest, full-size Pontiac all V-8's without air conditioning; 1867 full-size Pontiac 400-ci with air conditioning

Interchange Number: 4
Part Number: 9784546
Number of Blades: 7 Diameter: 19 ½ Pitch: 2-1/4
Usage: 1967-68 Firebird, Tempest, full-size Pontiac V-8 with air conditioning .

Interchange Number: 5
Part Number: 9791346
Number of Blades: 5 Diameter: 19 ½ Pitch: 2 ¾
Usage: 1968-70 Firebird ,Tempest, full-size Pontiac with heavy-duty fan except air conditioning.

Interchange Number: 6
Part Number: 9796135
Number of Blades: 7 Diameter: 19 Pitch: 2 ¾
Usage: 1969 Firebird, Grand Prix, Tempest, full-size Pontiac except air conditioning; 1971-74 full-size Pontiac except air conditioning; 1971 Tempest except air conditioning.

Interchange Number: 7
Part Number: 480035
Number of Blades: 7 Diameter: 18 ¾ Pitch: 2 ¼
Usage: 1970-72 Firebird with air conditioning

Interchange Number: 8
Part Number: 480033
Number of Blades: 5 Diameter 18 13/16
Pitch: 2 5/16
Usage: 1971-72 Firebird, Grand Prix, Tempest, full-size Pontiac, except air conditioning.

Interchange Number: 9
Part Number: 3947772
Number of Blades: 7 Diameter: 18 Pitch: 2.00
Usage: 1971 Firebird 350-ci with air conditioning; 1970-1971 Tempest 250-ci six cylinder with air conditioning; 1969-70 Camaro, Nova, Chevelle, full-size Chevrolet with fan clutch; 1969 Buick, Oldsmobile six cylinder with air conditioning. Notes: Stamped with part number.

Interchange Number: 10
Part Number: 9796134
Number of Blades: 7 Diameter: 19 ½ Pitch: 2 ¼
Usage: 1971-72 Firebird ,Tempest, full-size Pontiac with air conditioning, except 1971 Firebird 350-ci.

Interchange Number: 11
Part Number: 9777014
Number of Blades: 7 Diameter: 18
Usage: 1964-67 Tempest heavy-duty cooling except GTO; 1967 GTO 400-ci 2-bbl; 1964 Tempest with dealer installed air conditioning.

Interchange Number: 12
Part Number: 9777013
Number of Blades: 7 Diameter: 19 ½
Usage: 1964 Tempest, full-size Pontiac with air conditioning; 1964 GTO 389-ci; 1964 2+2 421-ci and air conditioning.

Interchange Number: 13
Part Number: 9777139
Number of Blades: 5 Diameter: 18 Pitch: 2-¼
Usage: 1965-67 Tempest Heavy-duty cooling except GTO or air conditioning.

Interchange Number: 14

Part Number: 9779004

Number of Blades: 7   Diameter: 19 ½

Usage: 1965 Tempest with air conditioning; 1965 GTO; 1965 full-size Pontiac 421-ci H.O. except Grand Prix.

Interchange Number: 15

Part Number: 9798938

Number of Blades: 4 Diameter: 19   Pitch: 2.00

Usage: 1970 Tempest, full-size Pontiac 350-ci or 400-ci except Ram Air or Air conditioning; 1969 Bonneville 400-ci except air conditioning.

Interchange Number: 16

Part Number: 530912

Number of Blades: 5

Usage: 1962-1964 full-size Pontiac with heavy-duty fan.

Interchange Number: 17

Part Number: 9779005

Number of Blades: 5   Diameter: 19   Pitch: 2-1/4

Usage: 1965 full-size Pontiac except air conditioning or H.O.

Chapter 5 Transmissions

Manual

IDENTIFICATION

There are two types of manual transmissions, three-speed and four-speed. Four different manufacturers supplied transmissions to the Pontiac line. They were Warner, Saginaw and Muncie; in 1965 the Ford-built Dearborn unit was added. Each has their specific usage and will not necessarily interchange. An identification code was painted in yellow on the right-hand side of all manual transmissions. To view these codes may require you to clean the transmission case. A date stamp can be found on the right-hand side of the case near the rear. For further identification look for the VIN which was stamped on a small pad on the right-hand side of the transmission case, except the Dearborn three-speed manual unit, which was stamped on the left-hand side of the case.

General Manual Transmission Identification

Type	Manufacture	General Identification
3-spd.	Saginaw	7 bolt side cover. Three holes top row, 2 bolt holes bottom row.
3-spd.	Muncie	7 bolt side cover 2 bolt hole top row, 3 bolt holes bottom row.
3-spd	Warner	9-bolt side cover
3-spd.	Dearborn	Top side cover
4-spd.	Saginaw	Cast iron case and extension housing. 7-bolt cover has 3 shift levers. Input shaft has 19 teeth
4-spd.	Muncie wide ratio	Aluminum case and extension housing.. 7-bolt side cover has 2 shift levers. Reverse gear and reverse shift lever are located at extension housing. 24 teeth on input shaft.
4-spd.	Muncie close ratio	Aluminum case and extension housing.. 7-bolt side cover has 2 shift levers. Reverse gear and reverse shift lever are located at extension housing. 26 teeth on input shaft.

INSPECTION

Over all inspection to the transmission unit should be the condition of the transmission case. Damage to the case, such as a crack, could indicate that there is more damage inside, and any damaged transmission case should be passed on.

Remove the cover, turn the input shaft while shifting through the gears. The shaft should turn freely with no catching. Note: if there is no oil in the case, pour oil, of the correct viscosity, over the gears before doing this operation.

Unfortunately, the best method of checking the condition of a manual transmission is to open it up, with some units removing the inspection cover can do this. However, to accurately check the gears you will have to flush the insides of the transmission out, since this requires the removal of the internal lubricate, some sellers may object to this. So ask first.

To flush the unit: Drain the oil from the transmission. Then pour a pint of cleaning solvent into the case. Shake and roll the case to disperse to solvent. Drain. Repeat. This will allow you to remove the grease, and make a visual inspection of the gears. With the cover removed, turn the gears over slowly while you inspect the teeth for wear chips or damage, such as a missing tooth. Rock the gears on the shaft while you check for excessive play and wear. Check for endplay in the reverse idler gear, input and output, and the cluster gear. Visually inspect the synchronizer for excessive wear and looseness. While this inspection will not guarantee you a workable transmission, it can give you an indication of the part or parts that may need to be replaced.

MANUAL TRANSMISSION IDENTIFICATION CODES

Code	Type	Manufacture	Models	Code	Type	Manufacture	Models
THREE-SPEED MANUAL				**FOUR-SPEED MANUAL**			
5	3-spd	Muncie	1966-67 GTO Col. Shift	8	4-spd	Muncie	1966-67 GTO (C.R.)
DB	3-spd	Muncie	1968-69 GTO	DL	4-spd	Muncie	1970 Tempest (C.R.)
DG	3-spd	Muncie	1970 GTO H.D.	DP	4-spd	Muncie	1970 Grand Prix, Tempest (C.R.)
FA	3-spd	Saginaw	1968-69 Tempest	FM	4-spd	Muncie	1968 Pontiac (W.R.)
FB	3-spd	Saginaw	1968-69 Tempest	FO	4-spd	Muncie	1968-69 GTO (W.R.)
FC	3-spd	Saginaw	1968-69 Tempest	FS	4-spd	Saginaw	1968 Tempest
R4	3-spd	Muncie	1970, 1972 Firebird 1972 Tempest	FT	4-spd	Muncie	1968-69 GTO (C.R.)
S	3-spd	Dearborn	1965-67 GTO	W	4-spd	Muncie	1964-67 GTO (W.R.)
X	3-spd	Muncie	1964-65 GTO	WC	4-spd	Muncie	1972 Firebird
DE	3-spd.	Saginaw	1970 Tempest Col. Shift.	WD	4-spd	Muncie	1972 Firebird
DG	3-spd.	Muncie	1970, Firebird, Tempest	WJ	4-spd	Muncie	1972 Firebird
FK	3-spd.	Saginaw	1968-69 Firebird	WL	4-spd	Muncie	1971 Firebird (W.R.)
FY	3-spd.	Saginaw	1968-69 Firebird Col. Shift.	9	4-spd.	Muncie	1964-65 GTO (C.R.)
R3	3-spd.	-Muncie	1970-72 Firebird	DJ	4-spd.	Muncie	1970 Grand Prix, Tempest (W.R.)
RA	3-spd.	Muncie	1971 Firebird, Tempest	FF	4-spd.	Muncie	1968-69 Firebird (W.R.)
RJ	3-spd.	Saginaw	1968-69 Firebird	FH	4-spd.	Saginaw	1968-69 Firebird
				FN	4-spd.	Muncie	1968 Pontiac (C.R.)
				FO	4-spd.	Muncie	1968-69 Tempest, 1969 Grand Priix
				FT	4-spd.	Muncie	1968-69 Tempest, 1969 Grand Prix. (C.R.)
				FX	4-spd.	Muncie	1968-69 Firebird (C.R.)
				WO	4-spd.	Muncie	1971 Firebird (C.R.)

Abbreviations: (C.R.) Close Ratio

(W.R.) Wide Ratio

Col. Shift- Column Shift

H.D. Heavy-duty

Firebird

1967

326-ci, 400-ci

Three-Speed Manual

Warner Heavy-duty	1
Saginaw	2

4-speed

Saginaw	3

Muncie

Wide Ratio	5
Close Ratio	4

1968

Three-Speed Manual

Saginaw

Column	7
Floor	6
Dearborn	8

Four-Speed Manual

Saginaw	9

Muncie

Wide Ratio	5
Close Ratio	4

1969

Three-Speed-Manual

Column	7
Floor	8

Four-Speed Manual

Saginaw	9

Muncie

Wide Ratio	10
Close Ratio	11

1970

Three-Speed Manual

Column	12
Floor	13

Four-Speed Manual

Wide Ratio	15
Close Ratio	14

1971-1972

Three-Speed Manual

Standard	16
Heavy-duty	17

Four-Speed Manual

Wide Ratio	19
Close Ratio	18

Grand Prix

1969

Three-Speed Manual	8

Four-Speed

Wide Ratio	20
Close Ratio	21

1970

Three-speed	13

Four-Speed Manual

Wide Ratio	22
Close Ratio	23

1971

Four-Speed Manual

Wide Ratio	19
Close Ratio	18

1972

Manual Transmission Not available

GTO/LeMans/Tempest

1964

Three-Speed Manual

Column

Except Inter Lock	24
With Inter-Lock	25
Floor	24

Four-Speed

Wide Ratio	26
Close Ratio	27

1965

Three-Speed Manual

Column	24
Floor Heavy-duty	8

Four-Speed

Wide Ratio	26
Close Ratio	27

1966-1967

Three-Speed Manual

Column	29
Floor	8

Four-Speed

Wide Ratio	26
Close Ratio	30

1968

Three-Speed Manual

Column	31
Floor	8

Four-Speed

Wide Ratio	26
Close Ratio	32

1969

Three-Speed Manual

Column	31
Floor	8

Four-Speed

Wide Ratio	20
Close Ratio	21

1970

Three-speed	13

Four-Speed Manual

Wide Ratio	22
Close Ratio	23

1971-1972

Four-Speed Manual

Wide Ratio	19
Close Ratio	18

2+2

1964

Three-Speed Manual

Standard	33

Heavy-duty

Early	34
Late	35

Four-speed Manual

421-ci	38

421 H.O.

Except 3.91 axle.	36
With 3.91 Axle	37

1965-1967

Three-speed Manual	35

Four-speed Manual

Wide Ratio	40
Close Ratio	39

Interchange Number: 1
Part Number: 3890533
Usage: 1967 Firebird, 326-ci or 400-ci; 1967-1968 Camaro; 1966-68 Chevelle; 1968 Nova; 1965-68 f full-size Chevrolet.
Notes: Has 9-bolt side cover.

Interchange Number: 2
Part Number: 9789553
Usage: 1967 Firebird 326-ci or 400-ci
Notes: Interchange number 6 will fit.

Interchange Number: 3
Part Number: 9777732
Usage: 1967 Firebird 326-ci or 400-ci
Notes: It is believed that 9 will fit but has different ratio.

Interchange Number: 4
Part Number: 545769 or 545869
Usage: 1967-68 Firebird 326-ci, 350-ci or 400-ci.
Notes Close ratio Interchange Number 11 will fit.

Interchange Number: 5
Part Number: 9792530
Usage: 1967-68 Firebird 326-ci, 350-ci or 400-ci
Notes Wide ratio   Interchange Number 10
will fit.

Interchange Number: 6
Part Number: 9793093
Usage: 1968-69 Firebird 350-ci, or 400-ci with floor shift.
Notes: Interchange 7 will fit if levers are switched and balances in extension drilled out to accommodate lever.

Interchange Number: 7
Part Number: 9793095
Usage: 1968-69 Firebird 350-ci, or 400-ci with column shift

Interchange Number: 8
Part Number: 9793425
Usage: 1968-69 Firebird 350-ci, or 400-ci; 1965-1969 GTO; 1969 Grand Prix; 1965-69 Skylark; Late 1965-69 Cutlass; 1966 Wildcat.
Notes: Top cover

Interchange Number: 9
Part Number: 9791992
Usage: 1968-69 Firebird 350-ci, or 400-ci with floor shift.
Notes Ratio 2.85

Interchange Number: 10
Part Number: 9798974
Usage: 1969 Firebird 350-ci, or 400-ci with floor shift
Notes: Wide Ratio

Interchange Number: 11
Part Number: 9798975
Usage: 1969 Firebird 350-ci, or 400-ci with floor shift
Notes Close Ratio

Interchange Number: 12
Part Number: 3974485
Usage: 1970 Firebird, Tempest, Cutlass with column shift.

Interchange Number: 13
Part Number: 477781
Usage: 1970 Firebird, Tempest, Grand Prix Cutlass; with floor shift.
Notes: 2.42 first gear.

Interchange Number: 14
Part Number: 3968011
Usage: 1970 Firebird 4-speed
Notes: Close Ratio.

Interchange Number: 15
Part Number: 3952659
Usage: 1970 Firebird 4-speed
Notes: Wide Ratio.

Interchange Number: 16
Part Number: 3974484
Usage: 1971-72 Firebird, Tempest 3-speed
Notes: Wide Ratio.

Interchange Number: 17
Part Number: 3952657
Usage: 1971-72 Firebird, Tempest 3-speed
Notes: Close Ratio. Heavy-duty

Interchange Number: 18
Part Number: 3978766
Usage: 1971-72 Firebird, Tempest; 1971 Grand Prix 4-speed
Notes: Close Ratio.

Interchange Number: 19
Part Number: 3981709
Usage: 1971-72 Firebird, Tempest; 1971 Grand Prix. 4-speed
Notes: Wide Ratio.

Interchange Number: 20
Part Number: 9798972
Usage: 1969 Grand Prix, Tempest 4-speed.
Notes: Wide Ratio

Interchange Number: 21
Part Number: 9798973
Usage: 1969 Grand Prix, Tempest 4-speed.
Notes: Close Ratio

Interchange Number: 22
Part Number: 478173
Usage: 1970 Grand Prix, Tempest 4-speed.
Notes: Wide Ratio

Interchange Number: 23
Part Number: 478174
Usage: 1970 Grand Prix, Tempest 4-speed.
Notes: Close Ratio

Interchange Number: 24
Part Number: 9778723
Usage: 1964 Tempest with column shift without interlock; or with floor shift

Interchange Number: 25
Part Number: 9776543
Usage: 1964 Tempest with column shift with interlock shift.

Interchange Number: 26
Part Number: 545770
Usage: 1964-68 Tempest with 4-speed.
Notes: Wide Ratio

Interchange Number: 27
Part Number: 545767
Usage: 1964-65 Tempest with 4-speed.
Notes: Close Ratio

Interchange Number: 28
Part Number: 9785187
Usage: 1966-67 Tempest with 3-speed. Column shift.

Interchange Number: 29
Part Number: 9785187
Usage: 1966-67 Tempest with 3-speed. Column shift.

Interchange Number: 30
Part Number: 545767
Usage: 1966-67 Tempest with 4-speed. Floor shift.
Notes: Close Ratio

Interchange Number: 31
Part Number: 9793094
Usage: 1968-69 Tempest with 3-speed. Column shift.

Interchange Number: 32
Part Number: 9793330
Usage: 1968 GTO with 4-speed. Floor Shift.
Notes: Close Ratio

Interchange Number: 33
Part Number: 9774626
Usage: 1964 full-size Pontiac Catalina. 3- speed except Heavy-duty.

Interchange Number: 34
Part Number: 9770586
Usage: 1963 Early 1964 full-size Pontiac Catalina. 3-speed Heavy-duty.
Notes: Side cover

Interchange Number: 35
Part Number: 9793426
Usage: Late 1964-1970 full-size Pontiac. 3- speed Heavy-duty; 1969-71 full-size Buick, Oldsmobile.
Notes: Top cover

Interchange Number: 36
Part Number: 9771280
Usage: 1963- 1964 full-size Pontiac 421-ci H.O. except 3.91 axle; 1964 full-size Pontiac 389-ci 3x2-bbl with 3.91 or 4.11 axle; 1961-62 full-size Pontiac 389-ci Super Duty.

Interchange Number: 37
Part Number: 9771281
Usage: 1963- 1964 full-size Pontiac 421-ci H.O. with 3.91 axle; 1962-1963 full-size Pontiac 421-ci Super Duty.

Interchange Number: 38
Part Number: 9771710
Usage: 1963- 1964 full-size Pontiac 421-ci

Interchange Number: 39
Part Number: 545768
Usage: 1965-68 full-size Pontiac. Four-speed
Notes: Close Ratio

Interchange Number: 40
Part Number: 545771
Usage: 1965-68 full-size Pontiac. Four-speed
Notes: Wide Ratio

Automatic

IDENTIFICATION

There are two types of automatic transmissions, the Pontiac division 2-speed, and the three-speed Turbo-Hydra-Matic. There are two different versions of the Turbo-Hydra-Matic. For the big power plants (389-ci, 400-ci, 428-ci and 455-ci) there was the Turbo-Hydra-Matic 400. It became available in the 1964 Pontiac, and the `1965 Tempest. The other Turbo-Hydra-Matic is the 350 version, which was used with the smaller 350-ci power plant; it was phased into production in the 1969 models. Automatic transmissions can be identified by a code that is stamped on the unit or a tag that is attached to the unit. On the Pontiac division two-speed it can be found on a metal tag that is attached to the passengers side of the case for 1964 and early 1965 models. After this date the code is found stamped on the low servo cover.

Example of Two-speed code. Top number are model year. Bottom line ID code followed by the day of the calendar of manufacture. The code 026 means the 26 th day of the year.

The Turbo-Hydra-Matic 350 can be identified by it's pan which is square in shape. It's identification numbers are found stamped on the servo cover on the passengers side of the case. While the 400 version has an uniformed shaped pan, its identification numbers are stamped on tag on the passenger's side, or on the left-hand side of the converter housing.

Transmission usage is based on many applications. These include engine size, out put, and some case options such as emission controls or air conditioning can affect the usage. Many transmissions have a cross-fit, meaning they fit more than the application listed. These cross fits are listed in the notes section of those particular interchanges. If no cross-fit is noted, then that interchange has no other usage.

INSPECTION

An automatic transmission is very hard to inspect once it is off the car. Since their internal system is made up of bands and valves that require fluid to be operating through their system, the best way to check out an automatic transmission is through a drive test. You should note how the transmission shifts in DRIVE there should be not sluggish or sharp shifts (unless a shift kit is installed, then shifts can be sharp) and each gear, including reverse, should function.

In most cases, vehicle testing of an automatic transmission will not be possible, thus you should inspect the case. Look for cracks and other signs of damage.   Be wary of oil pans that are heavily dented. The valve body assembly is very close to the inner pan surfaces, and a dent may have damaged internal components. Another thing to check is the fluid. Check the level and then perform a "sniff test", if the oil has a burned smell, it can indicate burned bands. However, be suspicious of clean new red fluid in a used transmission, this could be a way of hiding the burnt bands.

If possible, if the seller doesn't object, pull the pan off the unit, this will first require you to drain the transmission oil. With the pan off, visually inspect the bands and valves. Look for wear and a sludge build up. With the pan off, you should turn the transmission over and around, listening for rattling, or watch for pieces falling out of the unit, which can indicate broken bands or other broken parts. Many times transmissions will be found just lying in the yard. If your transmission choice is found this way there should be some standards to follow. First, never buy a transmission that has no protection, for example: a cup placed over the end to keep the water out. A transmission sitting on its end with the driveshaft end open allowing rain to enter, is best left alone. Also the end that is resting on the ground can deteriorate, and become a mouse or snake haven so be careful when lifting the transmission. The best method to store a transmission in inside a building.

Firebird

1967

326-ci

2-bbl

Except Air Conditioning	6
Air Conditioning	8

4-bbl

Except Air Conditioning	7
Air Conditioning	8

400-ci

2-bbl	15

4-bbl

Except Ram Air

Early	16
Late	17

Ram Air	14

1968

350-ci

2-bbl

Except Air Conditioning	9
Air Conditioning	11

4-bbl

Except Air Conditioning	10
Air Conditioning	11

400-ci

2-bbl	15

4-bbl

Except Ram Air	17
Ram Air	14

1969

2-bbl

Except Air Conditioning	12
Air Conditioning	13
T.H. 350	21

400-ci

2-bbl	18

4-bbl

Except Ram Air IV	19
Ram Air IV	20

1970-1972

350-ci 2-bbl	22
350-ci 4-bbl	xxx

400-ci

2-bbl	26
Except Ram Air	23
With Ram Air	24
455-ci	25

Grand Prix

1969

400-ci

2-bbl	18
4-bbl	19
455-ci	27

1970-1972

400-ci 2-bbl	26
400-ci 4-bbl	23
455-ci	25

GTO/LeMans/Tempest

1964-1965

326-ci

2-bbl

Except Air Conditioning	1
Air Conditioning	5

4-bbl

Except Air Conditioning	2
Air Conditioning	5

389-ci

Except Air Conditioning	3
Air Conditioning	4

1966

326-ci

2-bbl

Except Air Conditioning	3
Air Conditioning	4

4-bbl

Except Air Conditioning	2
Air Conditioning	5

389-ci

Except Air Conditioning	3
Air Conditioning	4

1967

326-ci

2-bbl

Except Air Conditioning	6
Air Conditioning	8

4-bbl

Except Air Conditioning	7
Air Conditioning	8

400-ci

2-bbl	15

4-bbl

Except Ram Air

Early	16
Late	17
Ram Air	14

1968

350-ci

2-bbl

Except Air Conditioning	9
Air Conditioning	11

4-bbl

Except Air Conditioning	10
Air Conditioning	11

400-ci

2-bbl	15

4-bbl

Except Ram Air	17
Ram Air	14

1969

2-bbl

Except Air Conditioning	12
Air Conditioning	13
T.H. 350	21

400-ci

2-bbl	18

4-bbl

Except Ram Air IV	19
Ram Air IV	20

1970-1972

350-ci	22
400-ci	
2-bbl	26
Except Ram Air	23
With Ram Air	24
455-ci	25

2+2

1964

3-speed model 10	28
4-speed model 315	29

1965

389-ci except H.O.	33
389-ci H.O. 4-bbl	30
389-ci H.D. Trans.	34
389-ci 3x2-bbl	31
421-ci H.O.	
Without trailer package	32
With trailer package	30
421-ci 3x2-bbl	31

1966

389-ci	
Except H.D.	14
H.D. Transmission	37,38
421-ci 4-bbl	36
421-ci 3x2-bbl	35

1967

400-ci	
Except H.D. Transmission	14
H.D. Transmission	41

428-ci

Except H.O.	40
H.O.	39

Interchange Number: 1
Part Number: 17373419   ID Code: MA
Type: 2-speed
Usage: 1964-66 Tempest 326-ci 2-bbl. except air conditioning.
Notes: Interchange Numbers 2 and 5 will fit

Interchange Number: 2
Part Number: 1373420   ID Code: MB
Type: 2-speed
Usage: 1964-66 Tempest 326-ci 4-bbl. except air conditioning
Notes: Interchange Number 5 will fit

Interchange Number: 3
Part Number: 1373422   ID Code: NA
Type: 2-speed
Usage: 1964-66 GTO 389-ci 4-bbl. except air conditioning; 1966 GTO 389-ci 4-bbl with air conditioning..
Notes: Interchange Number 4 will fit

Interchange Number: 4
Part Number: 1372418   ID Code: NB
Type: 2-speed
Usage: 1964-65 GTO 389-ci 4-bbl. With air conditioning

Interchange Number: 5
Part Number: 1372419   ID Code: MC
Type: 2-speed
Usage: 1964-65 Tempest 326-ci 2 or 4-bbl. With air conditioning

Interchange Number: 6
Part Number: 13777113   ID Code: MA
Type: 2-speed
Usage: 1967 Firebird, Tempest 326-ci 2-bbl. Except air conditioning

Interchange Number: 7
Part Number: 1377114   ID Code: MB
Type: 2-speed
Usage: 1967 Firebird, Tempest 326-ci 4-bbl. except air conditioning.

Interchange Number: 8
Part Number: 1377115   ID Code: MC
Type: 2-speed
Usage: 1967 Firebird, Tempest 326-ci 2 or 4-bbl. With air conditioning.

Interchange Number: 9
Part Number: 1383317   ID Code: MA
Type: 2-speed
Usage: 1968 Firebird, Tempest 350-ci 2-bbl. except air conditioning.
Notes: Interchange 10 and 11 will fit

Interchange Number: 10
Part Number: 1383316   ID Code: MB
Type: 2-speed
Usage: 1968 Firebird, Tempest 350-ci 4-bbl. except air conditioning.
Notes: Interchange Number 11 will fit.

Interchange Number: 11
Part Number: 1383315   ID Code: MC
Type: 2-speed
Usage: 1968 Firebird, Tempest 350-ci 2 or 4-bbl. With air conditioning.

Interchange Number: 12
Part Number: 1386508   ID Code: MA
Type: 2-speed
Usage: 1969 Firebird, Tempest 350-ci 2-bbl. except air conditioning.

Interchange Number: 13
Part Number: 1386510   ID Code: M
Type: 2-speed
Usage: 1969 Firebird, Tempest 350-ci 2 -bbl. With air conditioning.

Interchange Number: 14
Part Number: 9789928   ID Code: PQ
Type: 3-speed
Usage: 1967-68 Tempest 400-ci Ram Air ; 1966-67 full-size Pontiac with 389-ci, 400-ci or 421-ci V-8
Notes: After ID number PQ 67 1143 the direct clutch drive wave plate is eliminated. Five clutch driven plates were added.

Interchange Number: 15
Part Number: 8626155   ID Code: PT
Type: 3-speed
Usage: 1967-68 Tempest 400-ci 2-bbl

Interchange Number: 16
Part Number: 9777928   ID Code: PS
Type: 3-speed
Usage: 1967 Tempest 400-ci 4-bbl and H.O.

Interchange Number: 17
Part Number: 9791682   ID Code: PX
Type: 3-speed
Usage: Late 1967-68 Tempest 400-ci 4-bbl and H.O.

Interchange Number: 18
Part Number: 8626515   ID Code: PT
Type: 3-speed
Usage: 1969 Grand Prix, Tempest 400-ci 2-bbl.

Interchange Number: 19
Part Number: 8626517   ID Code: PX
Type: 3-speed
Usage: 1969 Firebird, Tempest 400-ci 4-bbl except Ram Air IV.

Interchange Number: 20
Part Number: 8626516   ID Code: PQ
Type: 3-speed
Usage: 1969 Firebird, Tempest 400-ci 4-bbl Ram Air IV.

Interchange Number: 21
Part Number: 6260003   ID Code: JF
Type: 3-speed T.H. 350
Usage: 1969 Firebird, Tempest 350-ci 2-bbl.

Interchange Number: 22
Part Number: 626018   ID Code: JF
Type: 3-speed T.H. 350
Usage: 1970 Firebird, Tempest 350-ci 2-bbl.

Interchange Number: 23
Part Number: 8626797   ID Code: PY
Type: 3-speed T.H. 400
Usage: 1970 Tempest 400-ci except Ram Air.

Interchange Number: 24
Part Number: 8626796   ID Code: PD
Type: 3-speed T.H. 400
Usage: 1970 Tempest 400-ci Ram Air.

Interchange Number: 25
Part Number: 8626687   ID Code: PR
Type: 3-speed T.H. 400
Usage: 1970 Tempest, Grand Prix with 455-ci

Interchange Number: 26
Part Number: 8626689   ID Code: PT
Type: 3-speed T.H. 400
Usage: 1970 Tempest Grand Prix 400-ci 2-bbl

Interchange Number: 27
Part Number: 8626519   ID Code: PR
Type: 3-speed T.H. 400
Usage: 1969 Grand Prix 455-ci

Interchange Number: 28
Part Number: varies   ID Code: varies
Type: 3-speed Hydra
Usage: 1964 full-size Pontiac.

Interchange Number: 29
Part Number: varies   ID Code: varies
Type: 4-speed Dyno
Usage: 1961-64 full-size Pontiac.

Interchange Number: 30
Part Number: 9777495   ID Code: PB
Type: 3-speed T.H.400
Usage: 1965 full-size Pontiac 389-ci or 421-ci 4-bbl

Interchange Number: 31
Part Number: 9777494   ID Code: PA
Type: 3-speed T.H.400
Usage: 1965 full-size Pontiac 389-ci or 421-ci with 3x2-bbl or 421-ci with trailer package.

Interchange Number: 32
Part Number: 9777496   ID Code: PC
Type: 3-speed T.H.400
Usage: 1965 full-size Pontiac 421-ci 4-bbl H.O. without trailer package

Interchange Number: 33
Part Number: 9777497   ID Code: PE
Type: 3-speed T.H.400
Usage: 1965 full-size Pontiac 389-ci except high compression.

Interchange Number: 34

Part Number: 9777498   ID Code: PH
Type: 3-speed T.H.400
Usage: 1965 full-size Pontiac 389-ci with heavy duty transmission

Interchange Number: 35

Part Number: 9784613   ID Code: PA
Type: 3-speed T.H.400
Usage: 1965 full-size Pontiac 421-ci with 3x2-bbl, or 421-ci with trailer package.

Interchange Number: 36

Part Number: 9784615   ID Code: PC
Type: 3-speed T.H.400
Usage: 1966 full-size Pontiac 2+2 421-ci 4-bbl

Interchange Number: 37

Part Number: 9784616   ID Code: PD
Type: 3-speed T.H.400
Usage: 1966 full-size Pontiac 389-ci H.D. transmission.

Interchange Number: 38

Part Number: 9784618   ID Code: PH
Type: 3-speed T.H.400
Usage: 1966 full-size Pontiac 389-ci H.D. transmission

Interchange Number: 39

Part Number: N/A   ID Code: PA
Type: 3-speed T.H.400
Usage: 1967 full-size Pontiac 428-c H.O.

Interchange Number: 40

Part Number: N/A   ID Code: PC
Type: 3-speed T.H.400
Usage: 1967 full-size Pontiac 2+2 428-ci 4-bbl except H.O.

Interchange Number: 41

Part Number: N/A   ID Code: PD
Type: 3-speed T.H.400
Usage: 1967 full-size Pontiac 400-ci H.D. transmission.

Shift Levers

Inspect the overall condition of the lever. Check the finish. Most levers were chrome plated, yet with wear and weather conditions in a salvage yard the finish may bubble up and rust will settle in. Make sure the lever is straight, it is true that some levers may have a radius to them making it easier to grab when going through the gears but be the radius is smooth and not altered. Make sure all levers and bars operate smoothly, this includes the tee bar handle, reverse lock out in manuals, or the grip release knob in automatics.

Firebird

1967

Three-speed manual	
Column	9
Floor	11
Four-Speed Manual	12
Automatic	
Column Except Tilt	13
Column With Tilt	14
Floor	49

1968

Three-speed manual	
Column	9
Floor	15
Four-Speed Manual	15
Automatic	
Column Except Tilt	13
Column With Tilt	17
Floor	16

1969

Three-speed manual	
Column	18
Floor	15
Four-Speed Manual	15
Automatic	
Column Except Tilt	19
Column With Tilt	20
Floor	21

1970

Three-speed manual (floor std.)	22
Three-speed manual (floor H.D.)	23
Four-Speed Manual	23
Automatic	

Column

Except tilt	24
With Tilt	26
Floor	25

1971

Three-speed manual (floor std.)	22
Three-speed manual (floor H.D.)	23
Four-Speed Manual	23

Automatic

Column

Except Tilt	24
With Tilt	26

Floor

Except Trans Am or Formula	27
Trans Am or Formula	25

1972

Three-speed manual (floor std.)	22
Three-speed manual (floor H.D.)	23
Four-Speed Manual	23

Automatic

Column

Except Tilt	24
With Tilt	26
Floor	27

Grand Prix

1969

Three-speed manual	28
Four-speed manual	28

Automatic

Column

Except Tilt	29
With Tilt	54
Floor	31

1970

Three-speed manual	28
Four-speed manual	28

Automatic

Column

Except Tilt	29
With Tilt	30
Floor	32

1971-1972

Automatic, Column

Except Tilt	33
With Tilt	30
Automatic, Floor	32

GTO/LeMans/Tempest

1964

Three-speed manual

Column	2
Floor	34

Four-speed manual

Bench seats	36
Bucket Seats	35

Automatic

Column

Except Tilt	37
With Tilt	38
Floor	39

1965

Three-speed manual

Column	4

Floor

Std.	34

H.D.

Bench Seats	5
Bucket Seats	7

Four-speed manual

Automatic

Column

Except Tilt	29
With Tilt	30
Floor	56

1971-1972

Three-speed manual

Column	55
Floor	28

Four-speed manual	28

Automatic

Column

Except Tilt	33
With Tilt	26

Floor

Except GTO	32
GTO	56

2+2

1964

Three-speed manual

Column	3
Four-speed Manual	57

Automatic

Column

Except Tilt	58
With Tilt	59
Floor	60

1965-1966

Three-speed manual

Column	6
Floor	61
Four-speed Manual	62

Automatic

Column

Except Tilt	63
With Tilt	64
Floor	65

1967

Three-speed manual

Column	44
Floor	66
Four-speed Manual	67

Automatic

Column

Except Tilt	47
With Tilt	48
Floor	65

Interchange Number: 1
Part Number: 9789697
Item: Shifter   Shift Location: Floor
Usage: 1969-70 GTO 3-speed

Interchange Number: 2
Part Number: 9774316
Item: Shifter   Shift Location: column
Usage: 1964 Tempest 3-speed

Interchange Number: 3
Part Number: 9774317
Item: Shifter   Shift Location: Column
Usage: 1964 full-size Pontiac 3-speed

Interchange Number: 4
Part Number: 9779399
Item: Shifter   Shift Location: Column
Usage: 1965-66 Tempest 3-speed

Interchange Number: 5
Part Number: 9775834
Item: Shifter   Shift Location: Floor
Usage: 1965 Tempest 3-speed H.D. Bench seat

Interchange Number: 6
Part Number: 9780811
Item: Shifter   Shift Location: Column
Usage: 1965-66 Full-size Pontiac 3-speed

Interchange Number: 7
Part Number: 9781448
Item: Shifter   Shift Location: Floor
Usage: 1965 Tempest 3-speed Bucket seats

Interchange Number: 8
Part Number: 978105
Item: Shifter   Shift Location: Floor
Usage: 1965 full-size Pontiac 3-speed

Interchange Number: 9
Part Number: 9790723
Item: Shifter   Shift Location: Column
Usage: 1967-68 Firebird; 1967-68 Camaro 3-speed

Interchange Number: 10
Part Number: 97779399
Item: Shifter   Shift Location: Column
Usage: 1965-66 Tempest 3-speed

Interchange Number: 11
Part Number:
Item: Shifter   Shift Location: Floor
Usage: 1967 Firebird 3-speed

Interchange Number: 12
Part Number:
Item: Shifter   Shift Location: Floor
Usage: 1967 Firebird 4-speed

Interchange Number: 13
Part Number: 9790724
Item: Shifter   Shift Location: Column
Usage: 1967 Firebird Automatic. Except Tilt steering column.

Interchange Number: 14
Part Number: 3895210
Item: Shifter   Shift Location: Column
Usage: 1967 Firebird Automatic with Tilt steering column.

Interchange Number: 15
Part Number: 9792435
Item: Shifter   Shift Location: Floor
Usage: 1968-69 Firebird 3-speed or 4-speed: 1969 Camaro 3-speed or 4-speed
Notes: Hurst Shifter.

Interchange Number: 16
Part Number: 9791314
Item: Shifter   Shift Location: Floor
Usage: 1968 Firebird automatic with console; 1968 LeMans with 2-speed automatic and console.

Interchange Number: 17
Part Number: 9790725
Item: Shifter   Shift Location: Column
Usage: 1968 Firebird Automatic with Tilt steering column.

Interchange Number: 18
Part Number: 9796421
Item: Shifter   Shift Location: Column
Usage: 1969 Firebird, Tempest, full-size Pontiac. 3-speed

Interchange Number: 19
Part Number: 9795118
Item: Shifter   Shift Location: Column
Usage: 1969 Firebird Automatic except Tilt steering column.

Interchange Number: 20
Part Number: 9795890
Item: Shifter   Shift Location: Column
Usage: 1969 Firebird Automatic with Tilt steering column.

Interchange Number: 21
Part Number: 9796736
Item: Shifter   Shift Location: Floor
Usage: 1969 Firebird Automatic with console.

Interchange Number: 22
Part Number: 478175
Item: Shifter   Shift Location: Floor
Usage: 1970-72 Firebird standard 3-speed

Interchange Number: 23
Part Number: 479048
Item: Shifter   Shift Location: Floor
Usage: 1970-72 Firebird Heavy-duty 3-speed or 4-speed

Interchange Number: 24
Part Number: 480677
Item: Shifter   Shift Location: Column
Usage: 1970-72 Firebird with automatic except tilt steering column.

Interchange Number: 25
Part Number: 478842
Item: Shifter   Shift Location: Floor
Usage: 1970 Firebird automatic with console; 1971 Firebird Trans Am or Formula models only.

Interchange Number: 26
Part Number: 546354
Item: Shifter   Shift Location: Column
Usage: 1970-72 Firebird, Tempest automatic with tilt steering column.

Interchange Number: 27
Part Number: 498974
Item: Shifter   Shift Location: Floor
Usage: 1971 Firebird except Trans Am or Formula; 1972-75 Firebird, all models

Interchange Number: 28
Part Number: 9784385
Item: Shifter   Shift Location: Floor
Usage: 1969-71 Grand Prix 3-speed or 4-speed manual; 1970-72 Tempest 3-speed or 4-speed manual.

Interchange Number: 29
Part Number: 546355
Item: Shifter   Shift Location: Column
Usage: 1969-70 Grand Prix, Tempest automatic except tilt steering column.

Interchange Number: 30
Part Number: 546354
Item: Shifter   Shift Location: Column
Usage: 1970-72 Grand Prix, Tempest, full-size Pontiac automatic with tilt steering column.

Interchange Number: 31
Part Number: 9782398
Item: Shifter   Shift Location: Floor
Usage: 1969 Grand Prix, Tempest automatic with console.

Interchange Number: 32
Part Number: 480654
Item: Shifter   Shift Location: Floor
Usage: 1970-72 Grand Prix; 1971-72 Tempest, except GTO. Automatic with console.

Interchange Number: 33
Part Number: 482505
Item: Shifter   Shift Location: Column
Usage: 1971-72 Grand Prix, Tempest; full-size Pontiac automatic except tilt steering column.

Interchange Number: 34
Part Number: 9781447
Item: Shifter   Shift Location: Floor
Usage: 1964-65 Tempest Standard 3-speed manual.

Interchange Number: 35
Part Number: 9781846
Item: Shifter   Shift Location: Floor
Usage: 1964-66 Tempest 4-speed manual.   Bucket seats.

Interchange Number: 36
Part Number: 9775875
Item: Shifter   Shift Location: Floor
Usage: 1964-66 Tempest 4-speed manual.   Bench seats.

Interchange Number: 37
Part Number: 9776101
Item: Shifter   Shift Location: Column
Usage: 1964 Tempest automatic except tilt steering column.

Interchange Number: 38
Part Number: 9776102
Item: Shifter   Shift Location: Column
Usage: 1964-66 Tempest automatic with tilt steering column.

Interchange Number: 39
Part Number: 9779868
Item: Shifter   Shift Location: Floor
Usage: 1964-65 Tempest automatic with console.

Interchange Number: 40
Part Number: 9780215
Item: Shifter   Shift Location: Column
Usage: 1965-66 Tempest automatic except tilt steering column.

Interchange Number: 41
Part Number: 9785199
Item: Shifter   Shift Location: Floor
Usage: 1966 Tempest 3-speed manual. Bench seats.

Interchange Number: 42
Part Number: 9785094
Item: Shifter   Shift Location: Floor
Usage: 1966 Tempest 3-speed manual. Bucket seats.

Interchange Number: 43
Part Number: 9779349
Item: Shifter   Shift Location: Floor
Usage: 1966-67 Tempest automatic with console.

Interchange Number: 44
Part Number: 9792624
Item: Shifter   Shift Location: Column
Usage: 1967 Tempest, full-size Pontiac 3-speed manual.

Interchange Number: 45
Part Number: 9789783
Item: Shifter   Shift Location: Floor
Usage: 1967 Tempest 3-speed or 4-speed manual. Bucket seats.

Interchange Number: 46
Part Number: 9787944
Item: Shifter   Shift Location: Floor
Usage: 1967-69 Tempest 3-speed or 4-speed manual. Bench seats.

Interchange Number: 47
Part Number: 9787108
Item: Shifter   Shift Location: Column
Usage: 1967 Tempest, full-size Pontiac automatic transmission, except tilt steering column.

Interchange Number: 48
Part Number: 9787089
Item: Shifter   Shift Location: Column
Usage: 1967-68 Tempest, 1967 full-size Pontiac automatic transmission, with tilt steering column.

Interchange Number: 49
Part Number: 9794098
Item: Shifter   Shift Location: Floor
Usage: 1967 Firebird automatic transmission, with console.

Interchange Number: 50
Part Number: 9792434
Item: Shifter   Shift Location: Floor
Usage: 1968-69 Tempest 3-speed or 4-speed manual. Bucket seats.

Interchange Number: 51
Part Number: 9792626
Item: Shifter   Shift Location: Column
Usage: 1968 Tempest automatic except tilt steering column.

Interchange Number: 52
Part Number: 9777924
Item: Shifter   Shift Location: Floor
Usage: 1967 GTO automatic with console.

Interchange Number: 53
Part Number: 9791438
Item: Shifter   Shift Location: Floor
Usage: 1968 Tempest automatic with console, except LeMans with two speed automatic.

Interchange Number: 54
Part Number: 9798737
Item: Shifter   Shift Location: Column
Usage: 1969 Grand Prix, Tempest automatic with tilt steering column.

Interchange Number: 55
Part Number: 546356
Item: Shifter   Shift Location: Column
Usage: 1970-72 Tempest, full-size Pontiac 3-speed
manual.

Interchange Number: 56
Part Number: 481176
Item: Shifter   Shift Location: Floor
Usage: 1970 Tempest, automatic with console;
1971-72 GTO automatic with console

Interchange Number: 57
Part Number: 9771786
Item: Shifter   Shift Location: Floor
Usage: 1963-64 full-size Pontiac 4-speed except
Super Duty.

Interchange Number: 58
Part Number: 9776098
Item: Shifter   Shift Location: Column
Usage: 1964 full-size Pontiac automatic except tilt
steering column.

Interchange Number: 59
Part Number: 9776099
Item: Shifter   Shift Location: Column
Usage: 1964 full-size Pontiac automatic with
steering column.

Interchange Number: 60
Part Number: 9770018
Item: Shifter   Shift Location: Floor
Usage: 1964 2+2 Pontiac automatic with console;
1963 full-size Pontiac automatic with console.

Interchange Number: 61
Part Number: 9781015
Item: Shifter   Shift Location: Floor
Usage: 1965-66 full-size Pontiac 3-speed manual.

Interchange Number: 62
Part Number: 9779485
Item: Shifter   Shift Location: Floor
Usage: 1965-66 full-size Pontiac 4-speed   manual.

Interchange Number: 63
Part Number: 9778821
Item: Shifter   Shift Location: Column
Usage: 1965-66 full-size Pontiac automatic, except
tilt steering column.

Interchange Number: 64
Part Number: 9778822
Item: Shifter   Shift Location: Column
Usage: 1965-66 full-size Pontiac automatic, with tilt
steering column.

Interchange Number: 65
Part Number: 9779349
Item: Shifter   Shift Location: Floor
Usage: 1965-68 full-size Pontiac   automatic, with
console.

Interchange Number: 66
Part Number: 9788891
Item: Shifter   Shift Location: Floor
Usage: 1967 full-size Pontiac 3-speed manual.

Interchange Number: 67
Part Number: 9787946
Item: Shifter   Shift Location: Floor
Usage: 1967-68 full-size Pontiac 4-speed manual.

Chapter 6 Suspension Systems

Front Suspension

The front suspension is made up of several different components, many of which can be bought as used parts. However, some parts should never be purchased used. These include: ball-joints, tie rod ends, shock absorbers and bushings. Other parts like control arms and sway bars are excellent used part buys.

Before you begin purchasing suspension parts, know what type of suspension your car has. Most muscle cars like the GTO and Firebird 400 came standard with a heavy duty Rally type suspension. This suspension utilizes special springs and other components that are stiffer or bigger then the standard duty items that are found on lesser-powered versions. However, there were options like the Soft-ride in 1968, which used lower rated springs and other components. It is vital that you don't mix suspension parts for the suspension to work properly. In other words don't used Rally springs and a standard sway bar.

Control Arms

These extreme duty components are easily obtainable as used parts, and have good interchange range. You should inspect the parts for damage. Check the outer lip, as this area is thinner and more prone to damage. Check the unit for warpage or any signs of welding or repair, which could indicate an accident. Arms that have been repaired should be avoided. Control arms consist of a pair of upper units, and a pair of lower units. They are tailored for a specific side of the automobile and will not swap sides.

Firebird

1967-1968

Upper Arms	1
Lower Arms	9

1969

Upper Arms	2
Lower Arms	9

1970-72

Upper Arms	3
Lower Arms	10

Grand Prix

1969

Upper Arms	4
Lower Arms	
L.H.	11

1970-1972

Upper Arms	5
Lower Arms	
L.H..	11

GTO/LeMans/Tempest

1964-1972

Upper Arms	5
Lower Arms	
L.H.	11
R.H.	
1964-1967	13
1968-1972	12

2+2

1964

Upper Arms	6
Lower Arms	14

1965-1966

Upper Arms	
Except Air Conditioning	8
With Air Conditioning	7
Lower Arms	15

1967

Upper Arms	8
Lower Arms	15

Interchange Number: 1
Part Number: 3963843-L.H. 3963844- R.H.
Part: Upper Arm
Usage: 1967-68 Firebird, Camaro; 1968 Nova

Interchange Number: 2
Part Number: 9796891-L.H. 9796890-R.H.
Part: Upper Arm
Usage: 1969 Firebird
Notes: Will fit interchange number 1

Interchange Number: 3
Part Number: 3964827-L.H. 3964828- R.H.
Part: Upper Arm
Usage: 1970-72 Firebird, Camaro; 1971-72 full-size Pontiac, Chevrolet, Oldsmobile.

Interchange Number: 4
Part Number: 402935-L.H. 402934- R.H.
Part: Upper Arm
Usage: 1969 Grand Prix

Interchange Number: 5
Part Number: 402933-L.H. 402932- R.H.
Part: Upper Arm
Usage: 1970-72 Grand Prix; 1964-72 Tempest, Skylark, Cutlass

Interchange Number: 6
Part Number: 9772890- L.H. 9772889-R.H.
Part: Upper Arm
Usage: 1964 full-size Pontiac

Interchange Number: 7
Part Number: 9778367- L.H. 9778366-R.H.
Part: Upper Arm
Usage: 1965-66 full-size Pontiac with air conditioning

Interchange Number: 8
Part Number: 9796923- L.H. 9796922-R.H.
Part: Upper Arm
Usage: 1965-66 full-size Pontiac except air conditioning; 1967-1970 full-size Pontiac with or without air conditioning.

Interchange Number: 9
Part Number: 6258451-L.H. 6258452-R.H.
Part: Lower Arm
Usage: 1967-69 Firebird, Camaro;1968-72 Nova; 1971-72 Ventura II; 1973-74 Apollo, Omega.

Interchange Number: 10
Part Number: 3964833-L.H. 3964834-R.H.
Part: Lower Arm
Usage: 1970-74 Firebird, Camaro; 1973-74 Chevelle, Monte Carlo; 1973 Grand Prix, Tempest, Regal

Interchange Number: 11
Part Number: 402965-L.H.
Usage: 1964-72 Tempest; 1969-72 Grand Prix, Cutlass.
Notes: Left-hand side only.

Interchange Number: 12
Part Number: 402964-R.H.
Usage: 1968-72 Tempest; 1969-72 Grand Prix, Cutlass.
Notes: Right-hand side only.

Interchange Number: 13
Part Number: 9784869-R.H.
Usage: 1964-67 Tempest..
Notes: Right-hand side only.
Salvage yard owners say interchange number 12 fits.

Interchange Number: 14
Part Number: 542465-L.H. 542464-R.H.
Usage: 1962-64 full-size Pontiac

Interchange Number: 15
Part Number: 9777389-L.H. 9777388-R.H.
Usage: 1965-68 full-size Pontiac

Springs

All Pontiac models covered in this guide used front coil springs. The parts can be bought as used parts. However, you must always inspect the part for damage such as broken coils, and signs of repair. Never buy a spring that has been repaired. Also you must *always replace the springs in pairs* from the same donor car. This is due to the way springs settle over time, and to the fact that many different rates were available. To make your suspension function properly you must use springs that are from a similarly equipped model. For example: if you're looking for springs for your 1968 GTO with a Ram Air, you should try to find a similarly equipped car. Ram Air Cars are hard to find, but the same springs can be found on other Tempest models with a 350-ci V-8 and air conditioning. The purpose of this section is two-fold: to give you a guide line on what springs will fit, plus what models the springs were used in. Pontiac used two methods of identification for the springs. Some have the part number stamped into the coil, while other used color identification. Be careful of identifying springs by color codes, these are easily changed. Use the following charts to cross-reference the spring you need. First look up your model and body style, then the option your car has. Then find the part number. Next scan the other charts looking for the same part number.

The second part of this section is a standard interchange. Due to their design, other GM models may fit your Pontiac; these are not the same part, but will physically fit. When swapping springs from different models remember that there are various tensions available and you should get similar style springs. For example: if you're looking for springs for your 67 GTO, you might find them on a 1967 Chevelle, but use only those from a Super Sport 396 model and not a standard Malibu.

1967 Firebird Front Spring Identification

Option	Body Style	
	Hardtop	Convertible
		Spring ID Part Numbers
Standard 326-ci V-8	397910	397910
326-ci with Air Conditioning	397907	388281
326-ci with Firm Ride (1)	397922	397910
326-ci with Firm Ride (2)	397910	397912
326-ci with Firm Ride (3)	397910	398883
326-ci with Firm Ride (4)	397910	397912
400-ci Standard	397922	397910
400-ci with Air Conditioning	397910	398883

(1)- Without Air Conditioning   (2)- Without Air Conditioning 2-speed automatic (3)- With Air Conditioning T.H. auto

1968 Firebird Front Spring Identification

Option	Body Style	
	Hardtop	Convertible
		Spring ID Part Numbers
Standard 350-ci V-8	397910	397910
350-ci with Air Conditioning	397907	388281
350-ci with Firm Ride (1)	397922	397910
350-ci with Firm Ride (2)	397910	397912
400-ci Standard	397910	397910
400-ci with Air Conditioning	397910	388281
400-ci with Firm Ride (1)	397922	397910
400-ci with Firm Ride (2)	397910	398883
400-ci with Firm Ride (3)	397922	397910
400-ci with Firm Ride (4)	397910	397912

(1)- Without Air Conditioning (2)- With Air Conditioning automatic (3)- Without Air Conditioning manual trans.

(4) With Air Conditioning manual trans.

1969 Firebird Front Spring Identification

Option	Body Style	
	Hardtop	Convertible
		Spring ID Part Numbers
Standard 350-ci 2-bbl or 4-bbl V-8	397910	397910
350-ci 2-bbl with Air Conditioning	388281	388283
350-ci 4-bbl with Air Conditioning	397912	398883
350-ci with Firm Ride (1)	397910	397912
350-ci with Firm Ride (2)	397912	398883
400-ci Standard	388281	388281
400-ci Ram Air IV or H.O.	397910	397912
400-ci with Air Conditioning	388284	388284
400-ci Ram Air or H.O. with air conditioning	397912	397912
400-ci with Firm Ride (1)	397910	397912
400-ci with Firm Ride (2)	397912	397912

(1)- Without Air Conditioning (2)- With Air Conditioning

1970-72 Firebird Front Spring Identification

Options	Model		
	Firebird	Formula 400	Trans Am
Standard*	3996365	344537	344537
T.H.350 automatic or with a/c	344537	not used	not used
400-ci 2-bbl	344537	not used	not used
400-ci 2-bbl with air conditioning	3988104	not used	not used
400-ci Ram Air III with a/c	not used	3988100	3988100
400-ci Ram Air III auto. Transmission without a/c	not used	3988104	3988104

*- Manual transmission or 2-speed automatic and no air conditioning

1964-65 Tempest Front Spring Identification

Option	Body Style		
	Hardtop/Coupe/Sedan	Convertible	Wagon
		Spring ID Part Numbers	
Standard 326-ci	381940	381946	381946
326 with a/c (1)	381940	381946	381946
326-ci with a/c (2)	381946	381946	381946
326-ci Firm Ride	384543	384543	384543
389-ci all applications	384543	384543	384543

(1)- With man. trans. (2)- with automatic

1966 Tempest Front Spring Identification

Option	Body Style	
	Hardtop/Coupe	Convertible
		Spring ID Part Numbers
Standard 326-ci	381940	381946
326 with a/c (1)	381940	381946
326-ci with a/c (2)	381946	381946
326-ci Firm Ride	384543	384543
389-ci except soft-ride or a/c	384543	384543
389-ci with a/c	388283	388283
389-ci Soft Ride (3)	381940	381946
389-ci Soft Ride (4)	381946	381946

(1)- With man. trans. (2)- with automatic (3) without a/c (4) with a/c

1967 Tempest Front Spring Identification

Option	Body Style	
	Hardtop/Coupe	Convertible
		Spring ID Part Numbers
Standard 326-ci	381940	381940
326 with a/c	381940	381946
326-ci Firm Ride (1)	388281	388281
326-ci Firm ride (2)	388283	384752
400-ci no a/c no A.I.R. (3)	388283	384752
400-ci no a/c no A.I.R.	384752	388284
400-ci a/c no A.I.R. (3)	386288	388284
400-ci a/c no A.I.R (4).	388284	388284
400-ci no a/c with A.I.R (3).	386283	384752
400-ci no a/c with A.I.R (4).	384752	386288
400-ci a/c with A.I.R (3).	386288	388284
400-ci a/c with A.I.R (4).	388284	388284

(1)- Without a/c . (2)- with a/cc (3) man. trans. a/c (4) automatic

1968 Tempest Front Spring Identification

Option	Body Style	
	Hardtop/Coupe	Convertible
		Spring ID Part Numbers
350-ci Standard	400874	400874
350-ci with a/c (1)	400883	400980
350-ci with a/c (2)	400881	400883
350-ci H.D. Springs (3)	400975	400980
350-ci H.D. Springs (4)	401174	401174
350-ci Firm Ride (3)	400881	400883
350-ci Firm Ride (4)	400980	401174
400-ci Standard	400880	400881
400-ci with a/c	400980	400980

(1)- Manual trans. (2) Automatic Trans. (3) without a/c (4)- with a/c

400-ci a/c with A.I.R (4).	388284	388284

(1)- Without a/c . (2)- with a/cc (3) man. trans. a/c (4) automatic

1969 Tempest/Grand Prix Front Spring Identification

	Hardtop/Coupe				Convertible			
Body Style								
	Right		Left		Right		Left	
Spring ID Part Numbers								
Position	Right		Left		Right		Left	
Option	Code	Part Number	Code	Part Number	Code	Part Number	Code	Part Number
MANUAL TRANSMISSION								
350-ci 2-bbl	LS	400871	LT	400874	LS	400871	LU	400879
350-ci 4-bbl	LM	401188	LU	400880	LM	401188	LW	400880
350-ci Firm Ride (1)	LM	401188	LU	400880	LM	40188	LW	400880
350-ci Firm Ride (2)	R5	402061	SC	400975	SC	400975	SF	400980
400-ci	LY	400881	SB	400882	LY	400881	SB	400882
400-ci Ram Air	SC	400975	SF	400980	SC	400975	SF	400980
400/428-ci (Grand Prix)	LT	400874	LA	400876	Body Style Not Available			
428 H.O. (Grand Prix)	LW	400880	SB	400882	Body Style Not Available			
400/428-ci Firm Ride GTO (1)	SC	400975	SF	400980	SC	400975	SF	400980
400/428-ci Firm Ride GTO (2)	SF	400980	SF	400980	SF	400980	SN	401174
400/428-ci Firm Ride Grand Prix (1)	LW	400880	SB	400882	Body Style Not Available			
400/428-ci Firm Ride Grand Prix (2)	SB	400882	SF	400980	Body Style Not Available			

(1) Without a/c (2) with a/c

1969 Tempest/Grand Prix Front Spring Identification

	Body Style							
					Convertible			
	Hardtop/Coupe							
	Spring ID Part Numbers							
Position	Right		Left		Right		Left	
Option	Code	Part Number	Code	Part Number	Code	Part Number	Code	Part Number
AUTOMATIC TRANSMISSIONS								
350-ci 2-bbl (1,3)	LS	400871	LT	400874	LS	400871	LT	400874
350-ci 2-bbl (1,4)	LM	401188	LW	400880	LM	401188	LW	400880
350-ci 2-bbl (2,3)	LW	400880	LY	400881	LY	400881	SF	400980
350-ci 2-bbl (2,4)	LW	400880	SB	400882	LY	400881	SF	400980
350-ci 4-bbl (1,)	LM	401188	LW	400880	LM	401188	LW	400880
350-ci 4-bbl (2)	LW	400880	SB	400882	LY	400881	SF	400980
350-ci H.D. Springs (1,3)	R5	402061	SC	400975	SC	400975	SF	400980
350-ci H.D. Springs (1,4)	SC	400975	SF	400980	SC	400975	SF	400980
350-ci H.D. Springs (2,3)	SF	400975	SN	401174	SF	400980	SK	401174
350-ci H.D. Springs (2,4)	SF	400975	SN	401174	SF	400980	SK	401174
350-ci Firm Ride (1,3)	LM	401188	LW	400880	LU		LY	408881
350-ci Firm Ride (1,4)	LM	401188	LW	400880	LU		LY	408881
350-ci Firm Ride (2,3)	R5	402061	SC	400975	SC	400975	SF	400980
350-ci Firm Ride (2,4)	SC	400975	SF	400980	SC	400975	SF	400980
400/428 GTO (1)	LY	400881	SB	400882	LY	400881	SB	400882
400/428 GTO (2)	SB	400882	SF	400980	SB	400882	SF	400980
400-ci Ram Air (1)	SC	400975	SF	400980	SC	400975	SF	400980
400-ci Ram Air (2)	SF	400980	SF	400980	SF	400980	SN	401174
400/428 Grand Prix (1)	LT	400872	LA	400876	Body Style Not Available			
400/428 Grand Prix (2)	LA	400876	LC	400877	Body Style Not avialbale			
400-ci Firm Ride GTO	SC	400975	SF	400980	SC	400975	SF	400980
440/428-ci Firm Ride Grand Prix	LW	400880	SB	400882	Body Style Not Available			
428-H.O. Grand Priix	SB	400882	SF	400980	Body Style Not Available			

(1) without a/c (2) with a/c (3) 2-speed automatic (4)- 3-speed automatic

1970 Tempest/Grand Prix Front Spring Identification

	Body Style							
	Hardtop				Convertible			
	Spring ID Part Numbers							
Position	Right		Left		Right		Left	
Option	Code	Part Number	Code	Part Number	Code	Part Number	Code	Part Number
MANUAL TRANSMISSION/AUTOMATIC TRANSMISSION								
350-ci	LT	400874	LX	400874	LT	400874	LX	400874
350-ci a/c	LY	400881	SF	400980	LY	400881	SF	400980
350-ci H.D. Springs (1)	SC	400975	SF	400980	SC	400975	SF	400980
350-ci H.D. Springs (2)	SF	400980	SK	401174	SF	400980	SK	401174
350-ci Firm Ride (1)	LU	400875	LY	400881	SC	400975	SF	400980
350-ci Firm Ride (2)	SC	400975	SF	400980	SC	400975	SF	400980
400-ci (1,5)	LT	400874	LX	400874	LT	400874	LX	400874
400-ci (2,5)	LY	400881	SF	400980	LY	400881	SF	400980
400-ci H.D. Springs (1,5)	SC	400975	SF	400980	SC	400975	SF	400980
400-ci H.D. Springs (2,5)	SF	400980	SK	401174	SN	401174	SK	400980
400-ci Firm Ride (1,5)	LU	400875	LY	400881	LU	400875	LY	400881
400-ci Firm Ride (2,5)	SC	400975	SF	400980	SC	400975	SF	400980
400-ci GTO (1)	LT	400872	LT	400872	LT	400872	LT	400872
400-ci GTO (2)	LT	400872	LA	400876	LT	400872	LA	400876
400-ci GTO H.D. Springs (1)	SF	400980	SN	401174	SF	400980	SN	401174
400-ci GTO H.D. Springs (2)	SN	401174	SK	401174	SN	401174	SK	401174
400-ci Ram Air (1)	SC	400975	SC	400975	SC	400975	SC	400975
455-ci Judge								
or with Firm Ride								
455-ci GTO (1,6)	LT	400872	LT	400872	LT	400872	LT	400872
455-ci GTO (2,6)	LT	400872	LA	400876	LT	400872	LA	400876
400/455-ci Grand Prix (1)	LX	400874	LA	400876	Body Style Not Available			
400/455-ci Grand Prix (3)	LA	400876	LC	400877	Body Style Not Available			
Grand Prix Firm Ride (1)	LY	400881	SF	400980	Body Style Not Available			
Grand Prix Firm Ride (2)	SF	400980	SF	400980	Body Style Not Available			

(1) Without a/c (2) with a/c 5- Except t GTO 6- Judge only

108

1971-72 Tempest/Grand Prix Front Spring Identification

	Body Style							
	Hardtop				Convertible			
	Spring ID Part Numbers							
Position	Right		Left		Right		Left	
Option	Code	Part Number	Code	Part Number	Code	Part Number	Code	Part Number
MANUAL OR AUTOMATIC TRANSMISSION								
350-ci (3)	LT	400874	LX	400874	LT	400874	LX	400874
350-ci a/c	LY	400881	SF	400980	LY	400881	SF	400980
350-ci H.D. Springs (1)	SC	400975	SF	400980	SC	400975	SF	400980
350-ci H.D. Springs (2)	SF	400980	SK	401174	SF	400980	SK	401174
350-ci Firm Ride (1)	LU	400875	LY	400881	SC	400975	SF	400980
350-ci Firm Ride (2)	SC	400975	SF	400980	SC	400975	SF	400980
400-ci (1,5)	LT	400874	LX	400874	LT	400874	LX	400874
400-ci (2,5)	LY	400881	SF	400980	LY	400881	SF	400980
400-ci H.D. Springs (1,5)	SC	400975	SF	400980	SC	400975	SF	400980
400-ci H.D. Springs (2,5)	SF	400980	SK	401174	SN	401174	SK	400980
400-ci Firm Ride (1,5)	LU	400875	LY	400881	LU	400875	LY	400881
400-ci Firm Ride (2,5)	SC	400975	SF	400980	SC	400975	SF	400980
400/455-ci GTO (1)	LX	400874	LA	400876	LT	400872	LA	400876
400/455-ci GTO (2)	LA	400872	LC	400877	LA	400872	LC	400877
400/455-ci GTO Firm Ride (1)	R5	402061	SC	400975	R5	402061	SC	400975
400/455-ci GTO Firm Ride (2)	SC	400975	SF	400980	SC	400975	SF	400980
400/455-ci GTO H.D. Springs (1)	SF	400980	SN	401174	SF	400980	SN	401174
400/455-ci GTO H.D. Springs (2)	SN	401174	R7	401174	SF	400980	R7	401174
400/455-ci Grand Prix (1)	LX	400874	LA	400876	Body Style Not Available			
400/455-ci Grand Prix (3)	LA	400876	LC	400877	Body Style Not Available			
Grand Prix Firm Ride (1)	LY	400881	SF	400980	Body Style Not Available			
Grand Prix Firm Ride (2)	SF	400980	SF	400980	Body Style Not Available			

(1) Without a/c (2) with a/c (5)- Except GTO

1964-65 Full-Size Pontiac Front Spring Identification

Option	Body Style		
	Hardtop/Coupe/Sedan	Convertible	Wagon
All Transmissions		**Spring ID Part Numbers**	
Standard or with a/c	9781177	9781177	9781181
Police	9781611	9781611	N/A
Trailer Or Firm Ride	9788467	9788467	9781811
H.D. Trailer	9781611	9781611	9781611-LH 9781612-RH
Firm Ride And Handling	9781611	9781611	N/A
2+2 package (1)	9781611	9781611	N/A
2+2 package (2)	9788467	9788467	N/A

(1)-Without a/c. (2)- with a/c

1966 Full-Size Pontiac Front Spring Identification

Option	Body Style		
	Hardtop/Coupe/Sedan	Convertible	Wagon
All Transmissions		**Spring ID Part Numbers**	
Standard	9781177	9781177	9781181
with a/c	9781177 (3)	9781177 (3)	-----------
Police	9781611	9781611	N/A
Trailer Or Firm Ride	9788467	9788467	9781811
H.D. Trailer	9781181	9781181	9781611-LH 9781612-RH
Firm Ride And Handling	9781611	9781611	N/A
2+2 package (1)	9781611	9781611	N/A
2+2 package (2)	9788467	9788467	N/A

(1)-Without a/c. (2)- with a/c (3) except 2+2

1967 Full-Size Pontiac Front Spring Identification

Option	Body Style		
	Hardtop/Coupe/Sedan	Convertible	Wagon
All Transmissions		**Spring ID Part Numbers**	
Standard	9781177	9781177	9781181
with a/c	9781177 (3)	9781177 (3)	-----------
Police	9781611	9781611	N/A
Trailer Or Firm Ride	9788467	9788467	9781811
H.D. Trailer	9781181	9781181	9781611-LH 9781612-RH
Firm Ride And Handling	9781611	9781611	N/A
2+2 package (1,5)	9781611	9781611	N/A
2+2 package (1,,4)	9781181	9781181	N/A
2+2 package (2, 5)	9781181	9781181	N/A
2+2 package (2, 4)	9788467	9788467	N/A
2+2 package H.D. Springs	9788467	9788467	N/A

(1)-Without a/c. (2)- with a/c (3) except 2+2 (4)- automatic only (5)- Manual trans. Only

FRONT SPRING INTERCHANGE

Firebird		*GTO/LeMans/Tempest*	
1967-1969	1	**1964-1967**	1
1970-1972	2	**1968-1972**	3
Grand Prix		*2+2*	
1969-1972	3	**1964-1967**	4

Interchange Number: 1
Part: Coil Spring
Usage: 1967-69 Firebird, Camaro; 1964-67 Tempest, Chevelle, Cutlass; 1968-72 Nova; 1971-72 Ventura II.

Interchange Number: 2
Part: Coil Spring
Usage: 1970-72 Firebird, Camaro

Interchange Number: 3
Part: Coil Spring
Usage: 1968-72 Tempest, Chevelle, Cutlass, Skylark, 1969-72 Grand Prix; 1970-72 Monte Carlo

Interchange Number: 4
Part: Coil Spring
Usage: 1958-70 full-size Pontiac, Buick, Oldsmobile
Notes: Chevrolet springs will *not* fit

Sway Bar

Commonly referred to as a stabilizer bar by Pontiac, these units were not standard items on some lesser-trimmed models, and different diameters were used according to suspension type and model. Models like GTO and Trans Am used special thick bars and smaller (less diameter) should never be used in their place, as the car's handling will be inefficiently hampered.

When inspecting the bar make sure that it is not damaged, and that the curves in the bar are smooth and the unit does not appear to be uneven, as if it as been in an accident or bent to fit a car it was not designed to fit. Also, check the condition of the ends, many time bushing ends will have to be replaced. This is acceptable in a used part, but the bores in the bar itself should not be worn.

Pontiac/GM Stabilizer Bar Usage and Identification

Part Number		Diameter		Models
Front	Rear	Front	Rear	
397704	Not used	7/8	Not used	1964-67 Tempest* 1964-65 Buick Sport wagons; 1966-67 Skylark; 1966 GTO w/ Soft-Ride Option.
397705	Not used	15/16	Not used	1964-67 GTO, 1966-67 Chevelle, 1964-66 Cutlass wagon or convertible; 1966-67 442; 1966-67 Tempest Firm Ride or 4-bbl 6-cyld.
9790916	Not used	7/8	Not used	1965-67 2+2 or full-size Pontiac with Firm Ride
9770959	Not used	-------	Not used	1964 full-size Pontiac H.D. Suspension
398499	Not used	15/16	Not used	1968-72 Tempest*
401194	394926	1.00	.875	1968-72 GTO, Tempest with Firm Ride; 1968-72 Skylark; 1968-72 Cutlass with Rally suspension; 1969-71 Chevelle except SS 396/454 or F41 suspension; 1970-71 Monte Carlo except SS 454
3955778	Not used	-----	Not used	1969 Firebird except Trans Am, Camaro 1969-72 Nova except F41 suspension.
3908373	Not used	11/16	Not used	1967-68 Firebird, Camaro (V-8 Camaro only); 1968 Nova except L79 or 396-ci
3958466				1969 Trans Am
9798922	Not used		Not used	1969-72 Grand Prix with Firm Ride
9795946	Not used	1.00	Not used	1969-72 Grand Prix except Firm Ride
3965651	Not used	15/16	Not used	1970-72 Firebird except Formula 400 or Trans Am
3975523	3983084	1-1/8	5/8	1970-72 Formula 400, Camaro with sport suspension except Z-28 (Camaro rear bar is slightly smaller in diameter but will fit.
3986480	482334	1-1/4	7/8	1970-72 Trans Am, 1970-71 Camaro Z-28 (Camaro rear bar is slightly smaller in diameter but will fit.

Rear Suspension

The components used in the rear suspension are dependent on the type of model. The Tempest, Grand Prix, and the full-size car line used a system of upper and lower control arms, which allowed the axle to travel up and down. Coil springs were also used with these models. The Firebird used a system of shackles and leaf springs to control the axle. Many components can be purchased used, so many it could fill a book on it own. To save space we will cover only the major components. This includes upper and lower control arms and the springs. Inspection of parts is much the same method that is used on their front suspension counter parts. There is one thing to note: on Tempest models with a rear sway bar special lower control arms were used. However, standard arms can be used and drilled in the proper location. When buying these arms, if the holes appear to have been drilled, but not by the manufacturer, make sure they are correct and the bar will line up properly.

Rear Control Arms

Grand Prix

1969

Upper	4
Lower	10

1970-1972

Except Firm Ride

Upper

Left	4
Right	4

Lower

USA built	10
Canadian Built	11

Firm Ride

Upper

Left	8
Right	4
Lower	11

GTO/LeMans/Tempest

1964

Upper	12
Lower	10

1965-1966

Upper	1
Lower	10

1967

Upper	1,2
Lower	10

1968-1969

Upper	3
Lower	

1968 | 10

1969

USA built	10
Canadian built	11

1970-1972

Except GTO or Firm Ride

Upper

Left	6
Right	5

Lower

USA built	10
Canadian built	11

GTO or Firm Ride

Left	7
Right	5
Lower	11

2+2

1964

Upper	9
Lower	13

1965-1966

Upper	1
Lower	14

1967

Upper	3
Lower	14

Interchange Number: 1
Part Number 9780959
Part: Upper Control arm
Usage: 1965-66 Tempest, full-size Pontiac;
1967 Tempest *
Notes: *Except 3.36, 4.33, 3.90 or 3.55
rear axle ratios

Interchange Number: 2
Part Number 9788993
Part: Upper Control arm
Usage: 1967 Tempest with 3.36, 4.33, 3.90 or 3.55
rear axle ratios

Interchange Number: 3
Part Number 9790152
Part: Upper Control arm
Usage: 1968-69 Tempest; 1967 full-size Pontiac

Interchange Number: 4
Part Number 9798473
Part: Upper Control arm
Usage: 1969-72 Grand Prix

Interchange Number: 5
Part Number 9790152-right hand
Part: Upper Control arm
Usage: 1970-72 Tempest

Interchange Number: 6
Part Number 9790152-left hand
Part: Upper Control arm
Usage: 1970-72 Tempest except Firm Ride or GTO

Interchange Number: 7
Part Number 478276-left hand
Part: Upper Control arm
Usage: 1970-72 GTO, Tempest with Firm Ride

Interchange Number: 8
Part Number 479848-left hand
Part: Upper Control arm
Usage: 1970-72 Grand Prix with Firm Ride

Interchange Number: 9
Part Number 538122
Part: Upper Control arm
Usage: 1961-64 full-size Pontiac

Interchange Number: 10
Part Number 9791773
Part: Lower Control arm
Usage: 1964-68 Tempest; 1969 Grand Prix,
Tempest USA built; 1970-72 full-size Pontiac
station wagon with 455-ci USA only.

Interchange Number: 11
Part Number 9790780
Part: Lower Control arm
Usage: 1969-1972 Tempest, Grand Prix. Canadian
built; 1970-72 Tempest, Grand Prix with Rim Ride
Notes: Has previsions for rear sway bar.

Interchange Number: 12
Part Number 9773166
Part: Upper Control arm
Usage: 1964 Tempest

Interchange Number: 13
Part Number 548806
Part: Lower Control arm
Usage: 1961-64 full-size Pontiac

Interchange Number: 14
Part Number 9791751
Part: Lower Control arm
Usage: 1965-68 full-size Pontiac

Rear Springs

All models covered in this guide, except one,
Firebird, used coil rear springs. Inspection and
selection is much the same as with front coil springs.
Firebird models utilized multiple rear leaf springs. The
part number is stamped on the rear leaf spring, and can
be used for identification. However, quick
identification can be done by counting the number of
leaves, and measuring the distance from eyelet to eyelet
at the center of each. When inspecting rear leaf springs,
inspect each leaf separately and look for broken or
sagging springs that can indicate over wear or
overloaded conditions. Reject any spring that has been
mended. Interchangeable range can be limited,
however; springs from a Camaro or 1968-72 Nova will
fit the 1967-69 models. Only Camaro springs will
interchange on 1970-72 Firebirds.

1968 Firebird Rear Leaf Springs

Options/Accessories	Body Style			
	Hardtop		Convertible	
All transmissions			Spring ID Part Numbers	
Springs	Part #	Leaf #	Part #	Leaf #
350-c 2-bbl	482548	6	9789635	6
350-ci 4-bbl	9789636	4	9789637	4
400-ci (1)	482548	6	9789635	6
400-ci (2)	9789636	4	9789637	4
Firm Ride and Handling	9789636	4	9789637	4

(1)- Except Ram Air or H.O. (2) Ram Air or H.O.

1969 Firebird Rear Leaf Springs

Options/Accessories	Body Style			
	Hardtop		Convertible	
All transmissions			Spring ID Part Numbers	
Springs	Part #	Leaf #	Part #	Leaf #
350-c 2-bbl	482548	6	9789635	6
350-ci 4-bbl	9789636	4	9789637	4
400-ci (1)	482548	6	9789635	6
400-ci (2)	9789636	4	9789637	4
Firm Ride and Handling	9789636	4	9789637	4

(1)- Except Ram Air or H.O. (2) Ram Air or H.O.

1970-71 Firebird Rear Leaf Springs

Options/Accessories	Body Style				
	Right		Left		
All transmissions			Spring ID Part Numbers		
Springs	Part #	Leaf #	Part #		Leaf #
350-ci	482545	5	480878		6
400-ci	482546	6	482548		6
Formula 400 (1)	482546	6	482548		6
Formula 400 (2)	481132	5	481132		5
Trans Am	481132	5	481132		5

(1)- Except F60x15 tires (2) F60x15 tires.

1972 Firebird Rear Leaf Springs

Options/Accessories	Body Style			
	Right		Left	
All transmissions			Spring ID Part Numbers	
Springs	Part #	Leaf #	Part #	Leaf #
350-ci	480878	6	480878	6
400-ci	482548	6	482548	6
Formula 350 400 (1)	482548	6	482548	6
Formula 350 400 (2)	481132	5	481132	5
Trans Am	481132	5	481132	5

(1)- Except F60x15 tires (2) F60x15 tires.

1964-65 Tempest Rear Coil Springs

Options/Accessories	Body Style	
	Coupe/Hardtop	Convertible
All transmissions		Spring ID Part Numbers
Springs	Part Number	Part Number
326-ci		
326-ci Trailer Package		
389-ci (1	9776201*	9776201*
389-ci Firm Ride 1965 only	9781727	9781728

*- part number 9776201 used with all appilcations in 1964

1966 Tempest Rear Coil Springs

Options/Accessories	Body Style	
	Coupe/Hardtop	Convertible
All transmissions		Spring ID Part Numbers
Springs	Part Number	Part Number
326-ci (1)		
326-ci (2)		
326-ci Trailer Package or Firm Ride		
389-ci (1)	9785487	9785487
389-ci (2)	9758487	9785488
389-ci Firm Ride	9781727	9773998

(1)- Without a/c (2) with a/c

1967 Tempest Rear Coil Springs

Options/Accessories	Body Style	
	Coupe/Hardtop	Convertible
All transmissions		Spring ID Part Numbers
Springs	Part Number	Part Number
326-ci	9777794	9777794
326-ci Trailer Package	9792855	9792855
400-ci	9788589	9788590

1968 Tempest Rear Coil Springs

Options/Accessories	Body Style	
	Coupe/Hardtop	Convertible
All transmissions		Spring ID Part Numbers
Springs	Part Number	Part Number
350-ci	9788447	9788447
350-ci Trailer pkg.	9792855	9792491
350-ci Firm Ride	9793101	9789814
400-ci all applications	9788447	9788447

1969 Tempest/Grand Prix Rear Coil Springs

	Body Style			
Options/Accessories	Coupe/Hardtop		Convertible	
All transmissions			Spring ID Part Numbers	
Springs	**Code**	**Part #**	**Code**	**Part #**
350-ci 2-bbl	PA	9788442	PU	9777794
350-CI 4-bbl	HI	9796937	HJ	9796937
350-ci Trailer pkg.	N5	9793156	NW	9792942
350-ci Firm Ride	HI	9796937	HJ	9796937
400-ci (1)	NL	9788447	NP	9688447
400-ci (2) or Firm Ride	P8	9793101	P8	9793101
Grand Prix	HF	9793819	Body Style not available	
Grand Prix Firm Ride	HY	9793819	Body Style not available	
Grand Prix auto level (3)	P8	9793101	Body Style not available	
Grand Prix auto level (4)	HY	9793819	Body Style not available	

(1) Without Ram Air (2) With Ram Air (3) without Firm Ride (4) with Firm Ride

1970 Tempest/Grand Prix Rear Coil Springs

Options/Accessories	Body Style							
	Coupe/Hardtop				Convertible			
All transmissions			Spring ID Part Numbers					
Springs	Right		Left		Right		Left	
	Code	Part #	Code	Part #	Code	Part #	Code	Part #
350/400-ci (1)	PU	9777794	NN	9777794	NN	9777794	NN	9777794
350/400-ci Firm Ride (1)	HJ	9796937	P8	9793101	P8	9793101	P8	9793101
400-ci Trailer Package (1)	NX	9792855	NX	9792855	NX	9792855	NX	9792855
400/455-ci (2)	NN	9777794	NN	9777794	NN	9777794	NN	9777794
400/455-ci Firm Ride (2)	P8	9793101	P8	9793101	P8	9793101	P8	9793101
400/455-ci Trailer Package (2,6)	NR	9792491	NR	9792491	NR	9792491	NR	9792491
400/455-ci Trailer Package (2,5)	NX	9792855	NX	9792855	NX	9792855	NX	9792855
400-ci Ram Air	NZ	9789814	NZ	9789814	NZ	9789814	NZ	9789814
455-ci H.O. (3,5)	NN	9777794	NN	9777794	NN	9777794	NN	9777794
455-ci H.O. (3,6)	PC	9777794	PC	9777794	PC	9777794	PC	9777794
455-ci H.O. (4,)	P8	9793101	P8	9793101	P8	9793101	P8	9793101
Grand Prix Trailer package	HZ	9789814	HZ	9789814	Body Style Not Available			
Grand Prix 455-ci H,O, (7)	HF	9793819	HF	9793819	Body Style Not Available			
Grand Prix 455-ci H,O, (8,)	H4	479866	H4	479866	Body Style Not Available			
Grand Prix 455-ci H,O, (9)	HY	546167	HY	546167	Body Style Not Available			
Grand Prix (10)	NZ	9789814	NZ	9789814	Body Style Not Available			
Grand Prix (11)	P8	9793101	P8	9793101	Body Style Not Available			

(1)   Except GTO (2) GTO   (3) Except Judge (4) Judge Only   (5) With Special Axle (codes XK XT, XV, XM) and 4-speed

(6) Except Special axle and 4-speed (7) Except Auto Level Control (8) Auto Level Control with Firm Ride except special axle and

4-speed (9) Auto Level Control With Frim Ride and Special Axle (codes XK XT, XV, XM) and 4-speed (10) With Auto Level

Control except special axle or Firm Ride (11) With Frim ride and Auto Level Control

1971 Tempest/Grand Prix Rear Coil Springs

Options/Accessories	Body Style							
	Coupe/Hardtop				Convertible			
All transmissions	Spring ID Part Numbers							
Springs	Right		Left		Right		Left	
	Code	Part #	Code	Part #	Code	Part #	Code	Part #
350/400-ci (1,2)	N2	9788447	NL	9788447	NL	9788447	NP	9788447
350/400-ci Firm Ride (1)	HJ	9796937	P8	9793101	P8	9793101	P8	9793101
350/400-ci Firm Ride (2)	HJ	9796937	HJ	9796937	HJ	9796937	P8	9793101
350/400-ci Trailer package (1)	NX	9788448	NX	9788448	NX	9788448	NX	9788448
350/400-ci Trailer package (2)	NX	9788448	NX	9788448	PL	9788448	PL	9788448
400-ci GTO	NL	9788447	NP	9788447	NL	9788447	NP	9788447
400-ci GTO Firm Ride	P8	9793101	P8	9793101	P8	9793101	P8	9793101
GTO Trailer Package (1,2)	NX	9792855	NX	9792855	NX	9792855	NX	9792855
Grand Prix (1,2)	NZ	9789814	HF	9793819	Body Style Not Available			
Grand Prix Firm Ride (1,2)	HZ	9792801	HZ	9792801	Body Style Not Available			
Grand Prix Auto Level Control	P8	9793101	P8	9793101	Body Style Not Available			
Grand Prix Firm Ride with Auto Lift Control (4)	HY	546167	HY	546167	Body Style Not Available			
Grand Prix Firm Ride with Auto Lift Control (3)	H4	479866	H4	479866	Body Style Not Available			

(1) without a/c (2) with a/c (3) -Pontiac axle only (4) K Axle only (Axle codes: XK,XT,XV,XM)

1972 Tempest/Grand Prix Rear Coil Springs

Options/Accessories	Body Style Coupe/Hardtop				Convertible			
All transmissions					Spring ID Part Numbers			
Springs	Right		Left		Right		Left	
	Code	Part #	Code	Part #	Code	Part #	Code	Part #
350/400-ci (1,2)	NL	9788447	NL	9788447	NL	9788447	NP	9788447
350/400-ci Firm Ride (1)	HJ	9796937	P8	9793101	P8	9793101	P8	9793101
350/400-ci Firm Ride (2)	HJ	9796937	HJ	9796937	HJ	9796937	P8	9793101
350/400-ci Trailer package (1)	NX	9788448	NX	9788448	NX	9788448	NX	9788448
350/400-ci Trailer package (2)	NX	9788448	NX	9788448	PL	9788448	PL	9788448
400-ci GTO	NL	9788447	NP	9788447	NL	9788447	NP	9788447
400-ci GTO Firm Ride	NP	9788447	NZ	9789814	NP	9788447	NZ	9789814
GTO Trailer Package (1,2)	NX	9792855	NX	9792855	NX	9792855	NX	9792855
Grand Prix 400-ci	PK	9793156	N5	9793156	Body Style Not Available			
Grand Prix 455-ci	HF	9793819	PK	9793156	Body Style Not Available			
Grand Prix 400-ci with Auto Lift Control	HF	9793819	NF	9787052	Body Style Not Available			
Grand Prix 400-ci Firm Ride with Auto Lift Control	N4	9792801	N4	9792801	Body Style Not Available			
Grand Prix 400-ci Firm Ride	HX	9798855	HX	9798855	Body Style Not Available			
Grand Prix 455-ci Firm Ride	HG		HG		Body Style Not Available			
Grand Prix 455-ci Firm Ride with Auto Lift Control	HZ	9792801	HZ	9792801	Body Style Not Available			

(1) without a/c (2) with a/c (3) -Pontiac axle only (4) K Axle only (Axle codes: WU, XU, WH, X,V, WH, WV

1967 Full-size Pontiac Rear Coil Springs

	Body Style	
Options/Accessories	Coupe/Hardtop	Convertible
All transmissions	Spring ID Part Numbers	
Springs	Part Number	Part Number
Standard (1)	485721	485721
2+2 Package	9777791	9777791
Trailer pkg Class II	9788483	9788483
Triler Pkg. Class III	540603	540603
Firm Ride	9788481* 9777792**	9788481
A/C (1)	9788474	9788474
	With A.I.R.	
Standard (1)	9788474	9788474
2+2 Package	9777792	9788481
Trailer pkg Class II	n/a	n/a
Triler Pkg. Class III	n/a	n/a
Firm Ride	9788481* 9777792**	9788481
A/C (1)	9788474	9788474

(1) Except 2+2 *-two door models only **-Sedans only

REAR SPRING INTERCHANGE

Firebird		*2+2*	
1967	6	1964	2
1968	7	1965-1966	4
1969	8	1967	5
1970-1972	9		

Grand Prix	
1969-1972	3

GTO/LeMans/Tempest	
1964-1966	1
1967-1972	3

Interchange Number: 1
  Part: Coil Spring
  Usage: 1964-66 Tempest, Chevelle, and Cutlass

Interchange Number: 2
  Part: Coil Spring
  Usage: 1961-64 full-size Pontiac, Oldsmobile

Interchange Number: 3
  Part: Coil Spring
  Usage: 1968-72 Tempest, Chevelle, Cutlass, Skylark,
    1969-72 Grand Prix; 1970-72 Monte Carlo

Interchange Number: 4
  Part: Coil Spring
  Usage: 1965-66 full-size Pontiac, Buick, Oldsmobile

Interchange Number: 5
  Part: Coil Spring
  Usage: 1967-70 full-size Pontiac, Buick, Oldsmobile
  Notes: Chevrolet springs will *not* fit.

Interchange Number: 6
  Part: Leaf Springs
  Usage: 1967 Firebird, Camaro

Interchange Number: 7
  Part: Leaf Spring
  Usage: 1968 Firebird Camaro, Nova.
  Notes: Nova has slightly more arch but will fit.

Interchange Number: 8
  Part: Leaf Spring
  Usage: 1969 Firebird, Camaro 1969-72 Nova.
  Notes: Nova has slightly more arch but will fit.

Interchange Number: 9
  Part: Leaf Spring
  Usage: 1970-72 Firebird, Camaro.

Front Spindles

A general inspection of the unit should include watching for rust frozen parts. And damaged spindle ends. The axle ends should be clean and not rusted beyond use.

Brake type will greatly affect the interchange. Those from a drum brake car will not fit a car with disc brakes. However, a very common swap is to place a disc brake set up on a Tempest model with drum brakes. This can be accomplished by using the spindles and brake rotors from a 1967-1969 Firebird, 1968-1974 Nova; 1971-1974 Ventura II, 1972-1974 Buick Apollo or Oldsmobile Omega,; 1967-1969 Chevelle or 1969-72 Grand Prix to your Tempest. However, in some cases it may at first appear that they won't fit, due to the location of the steering arm. To remedy this swap the steering arms (left to right and right to left) or better yet use the units that were use with your drum brake set-up.

Steering arms have to be switch or replaced to allow a disc brake conversation form 1967-69 Firebird

Firebird

1967-1969

Drum	4
Disc	1

1970-1972

Disc	5

Grand Prix

1969-1972

Drum 1969 only	4
Disc	1

GTO/LeMans/Tempest

1964

Drum	2

1965-1966

Drum	3

1967-1969

Drum	4
Disc	1

1970-1972

Drum	6

2+2

1964

Drum	7

1965-1966

Drum	8
1967	9

Interchange Number: 1
Brake Type: Disc
Usage: 1967-69 Tempest, Firebird, Camaro; 1969-72
Grand Prix; 1967-72 Chevelle; 1968-74 Nova;
1971-74 Ventura II; 1973-74 Omega;
1973-74 Apollo; 1971-72 Sprint; 1967-72 442.
Notes; See introduction for details.

Interchange Number: 2
Brake Type: Drum
Usage: 1964 Tempest; 1964-66 Skylark;
1964-66 Cutlass.

Interchange Number: 3
Brake Type: Drum
Usage: 1965-66 Tempest
Notes: Salvage yard owners say Interchange
number 2 will fit.

Interchange Number: 4
Brake Type: Drum
Usage: 1967-69 Tempest, Firebird, Camaro, 1967-72
Chevelle, Skylark;   1968-74 Nova; 1971-74
Ventura II; 1973-74 Omega; 1973-74 Apollo;
1971-72 Sprint; 1967-69 F85/Cutlass.

Interchange Number: 5
Brake Type: Disc
Usage: 1970-74 Firebird, Camaro; 1973-74 Chevelle,
Grand Prix, Monte Carlo, Cutlass, Tempest,
Skylark.

Interchange Number: 6
Brake Type: Drum
Usage: 1970-72 Tempest.

Interchange Number: 7
Brake Type: Drum
Usage: 1959-64 full-size Pontiac
Notes: Fit's either side. May require steering arms
be reversed or switched.

Interchange Number: 8
Brake Type: Drum
Usage: 1965-66 full-size Pontiac.
Notes: Fit's either side. May require steering arms
be reversed or switched.

Interchange Number: 9
Brake Type: Drum/Disc
Usage: 1967-68 full-size Pontiac
Notes: Spindles from a 1968-70 full-size Pontiac
will fit if you include the drum or discs. This can
make it easy for a disc brake conversion of this
model.

Chapter 7 Steering Systems

Steering Gear Box

Basically, three different types of steering gear assemblies were available on Pontiac that are covered in this guide. This includes the standard box, the quick steering ratio unit, and the power steering box. Of the three, the power steering unit is the most common. Early models will have the part number stamped on the end plate. It is harder to identify a later (1968 and up) steering gearbox by sight, however, you can determine it's model year usage by the date code which can be found stamped on a machined pad on the top inboard side of the unit.

This date code will consist of four digits, the first three digits are the day of the year 001-January 1 to 365 December 31, this is followed by the last digit of the manufacture year. Remember this is the manufacture year, not the model year. So the date 1539 would be in June and would be for a late built 1969 model but the code 3009 would be in October and would be for a 1970 model. Any gearbox built after August should be used for the next model year.

When inspecting a used gearbox, there should be no binding or grinding sounds when you turn the unit by hand, which can indicate inner gear damage, and should be avoided. Signs of roughness when turning the unit will indicate worn bearings.

PONTIAC STEERING GEAR BOX PART NUMBERS

Model	Model year	Steering Gear Box Part Numbers		Variable Ratio	
		Standard	Power		
Firebird	1967-69	5679271*	$7800713_{-1967-68}$	7805654_{-19-68}	*-w/o a/c **-with a/c
		7801592**	$7805654_{-1969\#}$		#-Except T/A ##-T/A only
			$7807056_{-1969\#\#}$		
	1970	N/A	7807742		
	1971-72	N/A	$7810872_{-(1)}$		(1)- Except Formula or T/A
			$7812711_{-(2)}$		(2) Formula or T/A
Grand Prix	1969	5679271	7807028		
	1970		7807742		
	1971-72		7810872		
Tempest	1964-65	5679271	5691673		
	1966-68	5679271	5696003		
	1969		$7807029_{-(3)}$		3- GTO only
			$5696003_{(4)}$		4- Except GTO
	1970	5679271	7807439		
	1971-72		7809529_{-0}		5- 14 INCH WHEELS
			$7813047_{-(6)}$		6- 15 INCH WHEELS
2+2	1964	5692342*	5691673		*-Without A/c
		5689683**			**-With a/c
	1965	5692342*	5696118		*-Without A/c
		5689683**			**-With a/c
	1966	5692342*	5696118*		
		5689683**	5696119**		
	1967	5679271	5699265*		
			5699271**		

Part number will sometimes appear on the end of the gear unit. And may only use the first five digits of the part number. Note the damage to this unit that makes it unusable

Typical date code location. On top inboard side. This code 012 6 means that was built on the 12th day of the year or January 12th, you have to cross reference the part number to find out the manufacture year.

.

Firebird

1967-1968

Standard steering	
Except A/C	1
A/C	2
Power steering	
Except variable ratio	3
Variable ratio	4

1969

Except Trans Am	4
Trans Am	5

1970

Power Steering	6

1971-1972

Power Steering	
Except Formula or Trans Am	7
Formula or Trans Am	8

Grand Prix

1969

Standard steering	1
Power Steering	9

1970

Power Steering	6

1971-1972

Power Steering	10

GTO/LeMans/Tempest

1964-1968

Standard steering	
Except quick ratio	1
Quick Ratio	11
Power Steering	3

1969

Standard Steering	1
Power Steering	
Except GTO	3

GTO	12

1970

Power Steering	13

1971-1972

14-inch wheels	14
15-inch wheels	15

2+2

1964

Standard Steering	1
Power Steering	3

1965

Standard Steering	1
Power Steering	16

1966

Standard Steering	1
Power Steering	
Without A/C	16
With A/C	17

1967

Standard Steering	1
Power Steering	
Without A/C	3
With A/C	18

Interchange Number: 1
Part: Standard Steering box
Usage: 1967-69 Fire bird without a/c; 1964-69 Tempest (except quick ratio); 1967-69 Camaro special steering; 1969 Grand Prix; 1968-69 Nova; 1964-69 Skylark, Cutlass, full-size Pontiac.

Interchange Number: 2
Part: Standard Steering box
Usage: 1967-69 Firebird with a/c; 1967-69 Camaro except special steering; 1968-69 Wildcat; 1969 LeSabre.

Interchange Number: 3
Part: Power Steering box
Usage: 1967-68 Firebird, Camaro; 1964-68 Tempest, Chevelle, Cutlass, Skylark; 1965-68 full-size Chevrolet, LeSabre; 1964 full-size Pontiac; 1967-68 full-size Pontiac; 1969 Tempest except GTO.
Notes: Will not fit variable ratio.

Interchange Number: 4
Part: Power Steering box
Usage: 1967-68 Firebird with variable ratio; 1969 Firebird, except Trans Am.

Interchange Number: 5
Part: Power Steering box
Usage: 1969 Firebird Trans Am.

Interchange Number: 6
Part: Power Steering box
Usage: 1970 Firebird, Grand Prix, full-size Pontiac without a/c.

Interchange Number: 7
Part: Power Steering box
Usage: 1971-72 Firebird except Formula or Trans Am.

Interchange Number: 8
Part: Power Steering box
Usage: 1971-73 Formula or Trans Am.

Interchange Number: 9
Part: Power Steering box
Usage: 1969 Grand Prix; 1968-69 Bonneville and Executive; 1969-70 Catalina with a/c.

Interchange Number: 10
Part: Power Steering box
Usage: 1971-72 Grand Prix

Interchange Number: 11
Part: Standard Steering box
Usage: 1965-67 Tempest quick ratio steering

Interchange Number: 12
Part: Power Steering box
Usage: 1969 GTO; 1968-69 Buick GS.

Interchange Number: 13
Part: Power Steering box
Usage: 1970 Tempest, Cutlass

Interchange Number: 14
Part: Power Steering box
Usage: 1971-72 Tempest with 14-inch wheels; 1971-72 Cutlass, Skylark except GS.

Interchange Number: 15
Part: Power Steering box
Usage: 1971-72 Tempest with 15-inch wheels

Interchange Number: 16
Part: Power Steering box
Usage: 1965 full-size Pontiac; 1966 Catalina 2+2, Ventura without a/c

Interchange Number: 17
Part: Power Steering box
Usage: 1966 Catalina 2+2, Ventura with a/c; 1966 Bonneville.

Interchange Number: 18
Part: Power Steering box
Usage: 1967-68 Catalina 2+2, Ventura with a/c

Steering Column

Used steering columns can be an excellent buy, and are usually the only choice when it comes to a classic car. However, before you buy a used column you should be aware of the factors that affect their usage. Transmission type, shifter location and steering type all greatly affect your selection.

Great savings can be had over a new column. You should carefully check over the column before you buy it. First, you should never buy a column out of a wrecked car. Due to the design of the column, which collapses during a crash, it makes them unusable after the crash. A mild rear end crash or passenger side collision might make be okay, but never take one from a car that has been hit head on or rolled over. For columns after 1966 and tilt telescopic columns this is even more vital. These columns are easily damaged, even if they are dropped so extra care when transporting these columns.

You should also check the condition of the joints of the column they should be free moving and not rusted or frozen, a common condition of columns in a salvage yard. Also check the teeth and threaded ends make sure they are clean a free of damage.

REMOVING THE COLUMN

Remove the nuts that secure half of the flex coupling together and retain nuts. Disconnect shift linkage from under hood, on manual transmission cars disconnect the clutch rod from the pedal. If the carpeting or cover pan is still in the car, remove that so that it is out of the way. If so equipped, disconnect the shift indictor pointer from the column. Next disconnect all electrical leads and harnesses from the column, if any vacuum hoses are present, disconnect them also. Now you can begin to lower the column. Remove any screws and brackets that hold the column to the underside of the instrument panel. While you do this, gently lower the column to the floor of the car. Next carefully pull forward on the column, watching for any wires or other parts that may block it from being removed. Once the column is free, pull free of car. Transport the column with the steering wheel still in place, and tape a paper cup over the other end. This provides protection for the threaded ends.

Avoid columns that have expose shafts. Be sure shaft is moveable. Unlike this rust frozen example that is unusable.

Firebird Steering Columns Part Numbers

Model Year	Transmission Type Shifter Location					Notes
	3-spd Manual		4-speed	Automatic		
	Column	Floor	Floor	Column	Floor	
1967-68	7805857	7805858*	7805858*	7805856*	7805858*	*Except tilt
		7805848**	7805848**	7805847**	7805848**	**-Tilt column
1969	7804324	7804325*	7804325*	7804323*	7804325*	*Except tilt
		7804366**	7804366**	7804365**	7804366**	**-Tilt column
1970	7807855	7807882*	7807882*	7807884	7807882*	*Except tilt
		7807883**	7807883**		7807883**	**-Tilt column
1971-72	7812228	7812229*	7812229*	7812225	7812229*	*Except tilt
		7812204**	7812204**		7812204**	**-Tilt column

Grand Prix Steering Columns Part Numbers

Model Year	Transmission Type Shifter Location					Notes
	3-spd Manual		4-speed	Automatic		
	Column	Floor	Floor	Column	Floor	
1969	NOT USED	7809798*	7809798*	7809794*	7809798*	*Except tilt
		7809989**	7809989**	7809985**	7809989**	**-Tilt column
1970		7809798*	7809798*	7809794*	7809798*	*Except tilt
		7809331**	7809331**	7809330**	7809331**	**-Tilt column
1971				7810648*	7810658*	*Except tilt
				7810269**	7810270**	**-Tilt column
1972				7813105**	7810658*	*Except tilt
				7810269**	7810306**	**-Tilt column

Tempest Steering Columns Part Numbers

Model Year	Transmission Type Shifter Location					Notes
	3-spd Manual		4-speed	Automatic		
	Column	Floor	Floor	Column	Floor	
1964						
1965						
1966						
1967	7802729	7802715*(1)	7802715*(1)	7802728*	7802715*(1)	*Except tilt
		7802704**(1)	7802704**(1)	7802703**	7802704**(1)	**-Tilt column
		7802713* (2)	7802713* (2)		7802713* (2)	(1)- Except 400 H.O. or Ram Air
		7802849** (2)	7802849** (2)		7802849** (2)	(2)-400 H.O. or Ram Air
1968	7803848	7803849*	7803849*	7803847* (3)	7803849*	*Except tilt
		7803852**(3)	7803852**(3)	7803851** (3)	7803852**(3)	**-Tilt column
		7801977** (4)	7801977** (4)	7801976** (4)	7801977** (4)	(3)-With Cornering lamps
						(4) Except Cornering lamps
1969	7804312	7804313*	7804313*	7804311*	7804313*	*Except tilt
		7804358**	7804358**	7804357**	7804358**	**-Tilt column
1970	7804312	7804313*	7804313*	7804311*	7804313*	*Except tilt
		7809327**	7809327**	7809326**	7809327**	**-Tilt column
1971	7810204	7810658*	7810658*	7810648*	7810658*	*Except tilt
		7810270**	7810270**	7810269**	7810270**	**-Tilt column
1972	7810204	7813105**	7813105**	7813105**	7810658*	
		7810269**	7810269**	7810269**	7810306**	

1972 Columns will fit 1971 models. Part number 7802715 can be found 1967 Skylark automatic long console. Part Number and 7902713 Can be found in 1967 Grand Sport with console.

Full-Size Pontiac Steering Columns Part Numbers						
Model Year	Transmission Type Shifter Location					Notes
	3-spd Manual		4-speed	Automatic		
	Column	Floor	Floor	Column	Floor	
1964						
1965						
1966						
1967	7805853	7805854*	7805854*	7805852*	7805854*	*Except tilt
		7805846**(3)	7805846**(3)	7805845**(3)	7805846**(3)	**-Tilt column
		7805844**(4)	7805844**(4)	7805843**(4)	7805844**(4)	(3)-With Cornering lamps
						(4) Except Cornering lamps

Steering Wheel

Steering wheels should be inspected carefully for cracks and discoloration before removal. Small cracks and chips can be repaired, but bent rims or large cracks should be rejected in a steering wheel. Discolored wheels, as long as it is not affecting the surface of the wheel, can be sanded and repainted. Since steering wheels were usually molded in a color to match the interior trim, this will mean you will most likely have to repaint the wheel to match your trim. Use some care in your selection; if your trim is light-colored, choose a light color steering wheel as light colored paint does not cover on a black steering wheel as well as it does a light color wheel. With a dark color interior, either a dark or light colored steering wheel can work.

A word about our interchange. Steering wheels came in two styles: standard and deluxe. Each of these types is listed in our interchange, where available. However, since the steering wheels are color keyed and it would take up too much space to list all the colors, we have based our interchange on the part number for the solid black steering wheel that number is given, but no other number is.

Note the large crack (arrow) in the hub this steering wheel. This crack cannot be safely and economically repaired. This wheel should be rejected.

With the horn cap removed. You next remove the retaining nut and the wheel is ready to pull.

REMOVAL OF STEERING WHEEL

Pry off ornament or remove horn shroud. Remove the two nuts from the steering column, remove spacer bushing which is held in place with three bolts. Remove the recover cup, or with the deluxe wheel, the horn ring. Next, remove the contact assembly. Now you are ready to remove the steering wheel it self, this can be done in two ways. First, by tapping on the steering shaft with a hammer and pulling the wheel off. This process can damage a steering column, especially the tilt telescopic kind. A better method is with a tool made for this purpose, a steering wheel puller.

Firebird

1967

Standard

16-inches	3
16-1/2 inches	4

Custom

16-inch diameter	12
16-1/2 inches in diameter	13
Wood	14

1968

Standard	3
Custom	15
Wood	16

1969

Standard	5
Custom	17
Trans Am	18
Wood	19

1970

Standard	5
Custom	17
Formula-style	18

1971-1972

Standard	6
Custom	12
Formula-style	18

Grand Prix

1969

Custom	17
Wood	19

1970

Custom	17
Formula-style	18

1971-1972

Custom	20
Formula-style	18

GTO/LeMans/Tempest

1964

Standard	22
Custom	7
Wood	8

1965-1966

Standard	1
Custom	11
Wood	10

1967

Standard	3
Custom	12
Wood	14

1968

Standard	3
Custom	12
Wood	

1969

Standard	5
Custom	17
Wood	19

1970

Standard	5
Custom	17
Formula-style	18
Wood	19

1971-1972

Standard	6
Custom	20
Formula-style	18

2+2

1964

Standard	24
Custom	23
Wood	8

1965-1966

Standard	2
Custom	9
Wood	10

1967

Standard	4
Custom	13
Wood	14

Interchange Number: 1
Part Number: 9743430
Type: Standard
Usage: 1965-66 Tempest

Interchange Number: 2
Part Number: 9743408
Type: Standard
Usage: 1965-66 Catalina

Interchange Number: 3
Part Number: 9746294
Type: Standard
Usage: 1967-68 Firebird; 1967-68 Tempest
Notes: Except early 16 ½-inch diameter wheel

Interchange Number: 4
Part Number: 9745779
Type: Standard
Usage: 1967 Firebird; 1967-68 Catalina
Notes 16 ½-inch diameter wheel

Interchange Number: 5
Part Number: 9751053
Type: Standard
Usage: 1969-70 Firebird; Tempest, Catalina

Interchange Number: 6
Part Number: 9756443
Type: Standard
Usage: 1971-72 Firebird; Tempest, Catalina

Interchange Number: 7
Part Number: 9740545
Type: Custom
Usage: 1964-65 Tempest

Interchange Number: 8
Part Number: 9741648
Type: Custom Sport wood
Usage: 1964 Tempest, full-size Pontiac.

Interchange Number: 9
Part Number: 9743415
Type: Custom
Usage: 1965-66 full-size Pontiac

Interchange Number: 10
Part Number: 9780784
Type: Custom Sport wood
Usage: 1965-66 Tempest, full-size Pontiac

Interchange Number: 11
Part Number: 9744322
Type: Custom
Usage: 1966 Tempest

Interchange Number: 12
Part Number: 9746314
Type: Custom
Usage: 1967 Firebird; 1967-68 Tempest
Notes: 16-inches in diameter

Interchange Number: 13
Part Number: 9746302
Type: Custom
Usage: 1967 Firebird; 1967-68 full-size Pontiac
Notes: 16-1/2 inches in diameter

Interchange Number: 14
Part Number: 9787429
Type: Custom Sport wood
Usage: 1967 Firebird, Tempest, full-size   Pontiac.

Interchange Number: 15
Part Number: 9748532
Type: Custom
Usage: 1968 Firebird

Interchange Number: 16
Part Number: 546470
Type: Custom Sport wood
Usage: 1968 Firebird, Tempest.
Notes: Full-size wheel will not interchange it is bigger in diameter.

Interchange Number: 17
Part Number: 9751059
Type: Custom
Usage: 1969-70 Firebird, Tempest, Grand Prix, full-size Pontiac.

Interchange Number: 18
Part Number: 546296
Type: Custom
Usage: 1969 Trans Am; 1970-72 Firebird, Tempest, Grand Prix, full-size Pontiac
Notes: Simulated leather rim

Interchange Number: 19
Part Number: 9795885
Type: Custom
Usage: 1969 Firebird, except Trans Am;   1969-70, Tempest, Grand Prix, full-size Pontiac.

Interchange Number: 20
Part Number: 9755928
Type: Custom
Usage: 1971-73 Tempest, Grand Prix, full-size Pontiac.

Interchange Number: 21
Part Number: 9755889
Type: Custom
Usage: 1971-72 Firebird, Ventura II

Interchange Number: 22
Part Number: 9741200
Type: Standard
Usage: 1964 Tempest

Interchange Number: 23
Part Number: 9774062*
Type: Custom
Usage: 1964 full-size Pontiac.
Notes: Part number for Yorktown blue

Interchange Number: 24
Type: Standard
Usage: 1964 Catalina

Power Steering Pumps

Firebird

1967

All	1

1968

Except variable ratio	1
Variable ratio	2

1969

All	2

1970-1972

All	3

Grand Prix

1969

All	5

1970

All	6

1971-1972

All	4

GTO/LeMans/Tempest

1964

All	8

1965

Early	9
Late	10

1966

All	10

1967-1969

All	1

1970

All	6

1971-1972

All	4,7

2+2

1964

All	8

1965

Without A/C

Early	9
Late	10
With A/C	10

1966

Without A/C	9
With A/C	10

1967

With A/C	11
Without A/C	1

Interchange Number: 1
Part Number: 5698070
Usage: 1967-68 Firebird, Tempest; 1967-68 Catalina,
2+2, Ventura without a/c. Except variable ratio.
Notes: Other full-size models will *not* fit.

Interchange Number: 2
Part Number: 7805161
Usage: 1968 Firebird variable ratio.; 1969 Firebird;
1969 Catalina, Ventura without a/c.
Notes: Other full-size models will *not* fit.

Interchange Number: 3
Part Number: 7808536
Usage: 1970 Firebird V-8

Interchange Number: 4
Part Number: 7811290
Usage: 1971-73 Firebird, Grand Prix, Tempest, full-size Pontiac; 1972-73 Ventura II.

Interchange Number: 5
Part Number: 7803762
Usage: 1968-69 Grand Prix; 1968-69 full- size Pontiac with air conditioning.

Interchange Number: 6
Part Number: 7808043
Usage: 1970 Grand Prix, Tempest; 1970 Catalina, or Ventura without air conditioning

Interchange Number: 7
Part Number: 7811290
Usage: 1971-73 Firebird, Grand Prix, Tempest, full-size Pontiac; 1972-73 Ventura II

Interchange Number: 8
Part Number: 5692613
Usage: 1964 Tempest, full-size Pontiac

Interchange Number: 9
Part Number: 5693871
Usage: Early 1965 Tempest, Catalina without a/c; 1966 full-size Pontiac with a/c
Notes: No grooves in head of orifice fitting.

Interchange Number: 10
Part Number: 5693861
Usage: Late 1965-1966 Tempest; Late 1965, Catalina without a/c; 1966 2+2 Catalina, Ventura without a/c
Notes: With grooves in head of orifice fitting.

Interchange Number: 11
Part Number: 7800002
Usage: 1967-68 full-size Pontiac with a/c.

Chapter 8 Rear Axles and Drive Shafts

Rear Axle Identification

The original ratio of the rear axle can be determined by a code that appears stamped in the axle tube assembly. For 1964-67 models, this code can be found stamped on the right-hand axle tube, and on 1968 and later models this code can be found stamped on the left-hand axle tube. For 1964 models the ratio itself is stamped on the axle tube (and a few early 1965 models), locking rear axles are identified by the letter L following the ratio. From 1965 on, the ratio, including locking rear axles, are indicated by a code that is the first two or three characters of the code on the axle. Following this is the axle manufacturer build date and the shift code.

Because ratios are often changed, it is likely that the ratio of the axle may not match the code. A method to determine the ratio in the axle can be determined two ways.

#1:If the axle has wheels, and can be rotated. Mark the top of the pinion with chalk. Next mark the top of the tire, and rotate the tire and count the revolutions the tire makes. With one complete revolution of the pinion, this will be your ratio. For example 3 - ½ revolutions will be 3.50 ratio. If no tires are on the axle or tires that different original sizes are used, then this method is inaccurate.

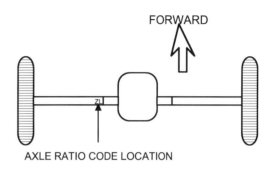

Axle code location for 1968-72 models

#2: By removing the axle cover and counting the teeth on the ring gear, and the pinion, and then dividing the numbers, you can get the ratio. For example: if a ring gear has 27 teeth and the pinion gear has 12, then the ratio would be 2.25.

AXLE HOUSING REMOVAL

Jack or lift the car up to provide sufficient room. Secure with jack stands.   Disconnect the drive shaft. Next remove the single bolt that holds the center support arm at the rear of the axle housing. Remove the wheel assemblies, disconnect the shock absorbers, and slowly lower axle assembly. Remove the bolt on each side which holds the torque arm to the rear axle, disconnect the parking brake, brake lines, the T-fitting over the rear axle and any other lines, such as with air shocks. Once the axle is free, slide it out from under the car.

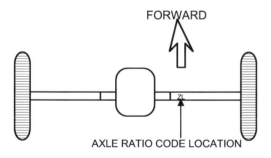

Location of axle code on 1964-67 models.

1967-68 Firebird Rear Axle Codes

AXLE RATIO	Codes Standard	Positraction	Teeth Number Ring Gear	Pinion
2.56	XB	UN	41	16
2.78	XC	UP	39	14
2.93	XD	UR	41	14
3.08	XE	US	40	13
3.23	XF	UT	42	13
3.36	XG	UV	37	11
3.55	XH	UW	39	11
3.90		UX	39	10
4.33		UY	39	9

1969 Firebird Rear Axle Codes

AXLE RATIO	Codes Standard	Positraction	Teeth Number Ring Gear	Pinion
2.56	YB	ZB	41	16
2.78	YC	ZC	39	14
2.93	YD	ZD	41	14
3.08	YE	ZE	40	13
3.23	YF	ZF	42	13
3.36	YG	ZG	37	11
3.55	YH	ZH	39	11
3.90		ZK	39	10
4.33		ZM	39	9

1970 Firebird Rear Axle Codes

AXLE RATIO	Codes Standard	Positraction	Teeth Number Ring Gear	Pinion
2.73	CRX	CRY	41	15
3.07	COS	COT	43	14
3.08	COE	COF	40	13
3.31	COU	COV	43	13
3.36	COK	COL	37	11
3.55	COW	COX	39	11
3.73		COZ	41	11

1971 Firebird Rear Axle Codes

AXLE RATIO	Codes Standard	Positraction	Teeth Number Ring Gear	Pinion
2.73	GZ	CA	41	15
3.08	GX	GY	40	13
3.42	CK	CJ	41	12
3.73		CG	37	11

1972 Firebird Rear Axle Codes

AXLE RATIO	Codes Standard	Positraction	Teeth Number Ring Gear	Pinion
2.73	GZ	CA	41	15
3.08	GX	GY	40	13
3.42	CL	CM	41	12

1965-66 Tempest Rear Axle Codes

AXLE RATIO	Codes Standard		Positraction		Teeth Number Ring Gear	Pinion
Brake Type	Std.	Metallic	Std.	Metallic		
2.56	WB		YB		41	16
2.78	WC		YC		39	14
2.93	WD	XD	YD	ZD	41	14
3.08	WE	XE	YE	ZE	40	13
3.23	WF	XF	YF	ZF	42	13
3.36	WG	XG	YG	ZG	37	11
3.55	WH	XH	YH	ZH	39	11
3.90	WK	XK	YK	ZK	39	10
4.33	WL	XL	YL	ZL	39	9

1967 Tempest Rear Axle Codes

AXLE RATIO	Codes Standard	Positraction	Teeth Number Ring Gear	Pinion
2.56	WB	YB	41	16
2.78	WC	YC	39	14
2.93	WD	YD	41	14
3.08	WE	YE	40	13
3.23	WF	YF	42	13
3.36	WG	YG	37	11
3.55	WH	YH	39	11
3.90	WK	YK	39	10
4.33		YL	39	9

1968 Tempest Rear Axle Codes

AXLE RATIO	Codes Standard	Positraction	Teeth Number	
			Ring Gear	Pinion
2.56	WB	YB	41	16
2.78	WC	YC	39	14
2.93	WD	YD	41	14
3.08	WE	YE	40	13
3.23	WF	YF	42	13
3.36	WG	ZG	37	11
3.55	WH	ZH	39	11
3.90	WK	ZK	39	10
4.33		ZL	39	9

1969 Tempest Rear Axle Codes

AXLE RATIO	Codes Standard	Positraction	Teeth Number Ring Gear	Pinion
2.56	WB	XB	41	16
2.78	WC	XC	39	14
2.93	WD	XD	41	14
3.08	WE	XE	40	13
3.23	WF	XF	42	13
3.36	WG	XG	37	11
3.55	WH	XH	39	11
3.90	WK	XK	39	10
4.33		XM	39	9

1970 Tempest Rear Axle Codes

AXLE RATIO	Codes Standard	Positraction	Teeth Number Ring Gear	Pinion
2.56	WB	XB	41	16
2.78	WC	XC	39	14
3.07	WT	XT	43	14
3.08	WE	XE	40	13
3.23	WF	XF	42	13
3.31	WU	XU	43	13
3.55	WH, WV	XH, XV	39	11
3.90	WK	XK	39	10
4.33		XM, 7N	39	9

1971 Tempest Rear Axle Codes

AXLE RATIO	Codes Standard	Positraction	Teeth Number Ring Gear	Pinion
2.56	WB	XB	41	16
2.78	WC	XC	39	14
3.07	WT	XT	43	14
3.08	WE	XE	40	13
3.23	WF	XF	42	13
3.31	WU	XU	43	13
3.55	WH, WV	XH, XV	39	11
3.90		XK	39	10
4.33		XM, 7N	39	9

1972 Tempest/ Grand Prix Rear Axle Codes

AXLE RATIO	Codes Standard	Positraction	Teeth Number Ring Gear	Pinion
2.56	WB	XB	41	16
2.78	WC	XC	39	14
3.07	WT	XT	43	14
3.08	WE, AE	XE, BE	40	13
3.23	WF, AF	XF, BF	42	13
3.31	WU	XU	43	13
3.55	WH, WV	XH, XV	39	11

1969 Grand Prix Rear Axle Codes

AXLE RATIO	Codes Standard	Positraction	Teeth Number Ring Gear	Pinion
2.93	SD, 4D	5D	41	14
3.08	4E	5E	40	13
3.23	2F,4F	5F	42	13
3.36	4G	7G	37	11
3.55	4H	7H	39	11
3.90		7K	39	10

1970 Grand Prix Rear Axle Codes

AXLE RATIO	Codes Standard	Positraction	Teeth Number Ring Gear	Pinion
2.78	AC	BC	39	14
2.93	AD	BD	41	14
3.07	WT	XT	43	14
3.23	AF	BF	42	13
3.31	WU	XU	43	13
3.55	WV	XV	39	11

1971-72 Grand Prix Rear Axle Codes

AXLE RATIO	Codes Standard	Positraction	Teeth Number Ring Gear	Pinion
3.07	WT	XT	43	14
3.08	AE	BE	43	13
3.23	AF	BF	42	13

1965 Full-Size Pontiac Rear Axle Codes

AXLE RATIO	Codes Standard	Positraction	Teeth Number Ring Gear	Pinion
2.41	UB	VB	41	17
2.56	UC	VC	41	16
2.73	UD	VD	41	15
2.93	UE	VE	41	14
3.08	UF	VF	40	13
3.23	UG	VG	42	13
3.42	UH	VH	41	12
3.55		VJ	39	11
3.73		VK	41	11
4.11		VM	37	9

1966 Full-Size Pontiac Rear Axle Codes

AXLE RATIO	Codes Standard	Positraction	Teeth Number Ring Gear	Pinion
2.41	UB	VB	41	17
2.56	UC	VC	41	16
2.73	UD	VD	41	15
2.93	UE	VE	41	14
3.08	UF	VF	40	13
3.23	UG	VG	42	13
3.42	UH	VH	41	12
3.55	UJ	VJ	39	11
3.73	VK	VK	41	11
4.11	UM	VM	37	9

1967 Full-Size Pontiac Rear Axle Codes

AXLE RATIO	Codes Standard	Positraction	Teeth Number Ring Gear	Pinion
2.29	UA	VA		
2.41	UB	VB	41	17
2.56	UC	VC	41	16
2.73	UD	VD	41	15
2.93	UE	VE	41	14
3.08	UF	VF	40	13
3.23	UG	VG	42	13
3.42	UH	VH	41	12
3.55		VJ	39	11
3.73		VK	41	11
4.11		VM	37	9

Rear Axle Housing Interchange

If you strip the axle of all its internal gears and axle shafts, a great deal of interchangeable parts become available that many times cross the GM lines. Listed below is the bare axle housing interchanges.

Firebird

1967

All	1

1968

All	2

1969

Ball bearings	3
Roller bearings	4

1970

10-bolt

Ball bearings	5
Roller Bearings	
12-bolt	6

1971-1972

All	7

Grand Prix

1969

All	8

1970-72

10-bolt	9
12-bolt	10

GTO/LeMans/Tempest

1964

All	11

1965

All	12
L.H.	11

1966

All	13

1967-1968

All	14

1969

All	15

1970

10-bolt

Ball Bearings	15
Roller Bearings	16
12-bolt	10

1971-1972

10-bolt	16
12-bolt	10

2+2

1964

All	17

1965 -1966

All	18

1967

All	19

Interchange Number: 1
Part Number: 9785843
Usage: 1967 Firebird

Interchange Number: 2
Part Number: 9793293
Usage: 1968 Firebird

Interchange Number: 3
Part Number: 9797902
Usage: 1969 Firebird with ball bearings.

Interchange Number: 4
Part Number: 546705
Usage: 1969 Firebird with roller bearings

Interchange Number: 5
Part Number: 3981971
Usage: 1970 Firebird, Camaro with 10-bolt rear axle.

Interchange Number: 6
Part Number: 3981972
Usage: 1970 Firebird, Camaro with 12-bolt rear axle.

Interchange Number: 7
Part Number: 3997573
Usage: 1971-73 Firebird, Camaro
Interchange Number: 8
Part Number: 9797901
Usage: 1969 Grand Prix
Interchange Number: 9
Part Number: 479725
Usage: 1970 Grand Prix 10-bolt rear axle.
Interchange Number: 10
Part Number: 3981669
Usage: 1970-72 Grand Prix, Tempest, Chevelle, Skylark, Cutlass, Monte Carlo, El Camino, Sprint.
Notes: All have 12-bolt rear axle.
Interchange Number: 11
Usage: 1964 Tempest
Interchange Number: 12
Part Number: 977604
Usage: 1965 Tempest
Notes: Will fit interchange number 11 if swapped with 1965 rear control arms.
Interchange Number: 13
Part Number: 9784925
Usage: 1966 Tempest; early 1966 Cutlass with Pontiac axle. Except wagon.
Notes: Has 2-3/4 outside diameter pinion seal.
Interchange Number: 14
Part Number: 9793453
Usage: 1967-68 Tempest
Interchange Number: 15
Part Number: 9797900
Usage: 1969-70 Tempest with 10-bolt axle and ball bearings.
Interchange Number: 16
Part Number: 479724
Usage: 1970 Tempest 10-bolt axle with roller bearings; 1971-72 Tempest 10-bolt axle.
Interchange Number: 17
Part Number: 543665
Usage: 1963-64 full-size Pontiac.
Interchange Number: 18
Part Number: 977625
Usage: 1965-66 full-size Pontiac.
Interchange Number: 19
Part Number: 9792645
Usage: 1967 full-size Pontiac.

Rear Axle Shafts

Highly interchangeable, axle shafts can cross model lines. However, you should note that axles with Positraction use a different shaft then those without this option. Also note that the below interchange is with the bearings, unless otherwise stated. Careful inspection of the axle must take place before you purchase it. Inspect the condition of the splines for wear, and look carefully for evidence of twisting. A twisted axle will show signs of stress that looks like lines in the metal; the lines will have a wrapped appearance. Any axle that has signs of twisting is unusable and should be scrapped. To check the axle for run out, place the axle in v-blocks and use a dial indicator, any axle that has run out beyond (.042 inch) the recommended limit should be rejected.. Also check the condition of the lug bolts. Never buy axle shaft from a car that has no wheels and is sitting on the ground. This position and the weight of the car can damage the axle.

To inspect an axle shaft it must be removed from its housing. Most Pontiacs covered in this guide used a flange type rear axle. To remove this type of axle, jack or lift the car up to provide sufficient room. Secure with jack stands. Remove the wheel and tire assembly and the brake drum. Note: if the brake drum is frozen in place this may require a puller. Remove nuts holding retainer plates to backing plate. Remove brake lines, and backing plate. Attach slide hammer puller to the axle flange and with quick sharp blows pull the axle bearing free of the housing, being careful of the splines. Wrap plastic, [a trash bag works excellently], around the splines to protect it while is being transported.

Firebird

1967-1968

Except Positraction	2
Positraction	1

1969

Except Positraction	
Ball bearings	2
Roller bearings	8
Positraction	
Except Ram Air IV	
Ball bearings	1
Roller Bearings	4
Ram Air IV	3

1970

10-bolt axle	5
12-bolt axle	6

1971-1972

10-bolt axle	5

Grand Prix

1969

Except Positraction	2
Positraction	1

1970-1972

10-bolt axle	8
12-bolt axle	7

GTO/LeMans/Tempest

1964-1965

All	8

1966

All	2

1967-1968

Except Positraction	2
Positraction	1

1969

Except Positraction	2
Positraction	
Except Ram Air IV	1
Ram Air IV	3

1970

Except Positraction	
Ball bearings	2
Roller bearings	8
Positraction	
Except Ram Air IV	
Ball bearings	1
Roller Bearings	4
Ram Air IV	3

1971-1972

10-bolt	
Except Positraction	8
Positraction	4
12-bolt	7

2+2

1964

All	9

1965-1967 | 10

Interchange Number: 1
Part Number: 9794671
Usage: 1967-69 Firebird; 1969 Grand Prix; 1967-70 Tempest with Positraction. Except Ram Air IV.

Interchange Number: 2
Part Number: 9794667
Usage: 1967-69 Firebird; 1969 Grand Prix; 1966-70 Tempest. Except Positraction.

Interchange Number: 3
Part Number: 9799118
Usage: 1969 Firebird; 1969-70 Tempest with Positraction and Ram Air IV

Interchange Number: 4
Part Number: 9799287
Usage: 1969 Firebird; 1970-72 Tempest with Positraction.
Notes: 10-bolt axle and roller bearings.

Interchange Number: 5
Part Number: 3969284
Usage: 1970-73 Firebird, Camaro, Chevelle; 1970-72 Monte Carlo; 1971-72 Sprint.
Notes: 10-bolt axle

Interchange Number: 6
Part Number: 3969285
Usage: 1970 Firebird, Camaro; 1968-72 Chevelle; 1970-72 Monte Carlo; 1971-72 Sprint.
Notes: 12-bolt axle

Interchange Number: 7
Part Number: 1234305
Usage: 1970-72 Grand Prix; 1971-72 Tempest; 1970 Skylark.
Notes: 12-bolt axle

Interchange Number: 8
Part Number: 546700
Usage: 1964-65 Tempest.
Notes: Salvage yard owners say 1964-65 Buick Skylark or Oldsmobile Cutlass axle will fit. Except Grand Sport or wagon.

Interchange Number: 7
Part Number: 1234305
Usage: 1970-72 Grand Prix; 1971-72 Tempest; 1970 Skylark.
Notes: 12-bolt axle

Interchange Number: 8
Part Number: 9799288
Usage: 1969 Firebird, 1970-72 Grand Prix, Tempest. Except Positraction.
Notes: 10-bolt roller bearings.

Interchange Number: 9
Part Number: 544925-R.H. 544926-L.H.
Usage: 1959-64 full-size Pontiac.

Interchange Number: 10
Part Number: 9783561
Usage: 1965-70 full-size Pontiac.

Drive Shafts

Drive shafts are usually identified by their length and diameter. General Motor drive shafts are measured from end to end. Sometimes, but not always the transmission type will affect the interchange and driveshaft usage. When inspecting a drive shaft, make sure that it is straight and undamaged, reject any warped or damaged shafts. Check the condition of all joints, they should be free-moving with no binding. To hold u-joints in place, bind them with a rubber band when transporting.

Firebird Drive Shafts

Model Year	Drive Shaft Part Numbers				Notes
	3-speed Manual	4-speed Manual	2-Speed Automatic Firebird	3-speed Automatic	
1967	7805686	7805686	7801322	7801899	
1968-69	7805686$_{(1)}$ 7805668$_{(2)}$ 7804661 $_{(3)}$	7805686	7801322	7805687	(1)- Std. Duty (2) H.D. insulated (3) H.D. non-insulted
1970	3891929$_{(4)}$	3981932$_{(5)}$	3891929$_{(4)}$	3891929$_{(4)}$ 3981930$_{(5)}$	(4) 350-ci (5) 400-ci
1971	7811094 $_{(6)}$ 3997539 $_{(7)}$	7811095 $_{(6)}$ 3981930 $_{(7)}$		3997539 $_{(4)}$ 3981930 $_{(8)}$ 7811095 $_{(9)}$	(6) 3.42 rear axle (7) except 3.42 rear axle (8) 400-ci except 3.42 rear axle (9) 400-ci 3.42 rear axle
1972	n/a	3891929$_{(4)}$ 3981930 $_{(10)}$	n/a	3891929$_{(4)}$ 3981930 $_{(10)}$	(10) 400 or 455-ci

Part number 3891929 found on 1970 Camaro 3-speed or P/G; 3981932 1970 Camaro 4-speed or 350-ci 4-bbl 3-speed automatic; 3981930 found on 197072 Camaro with 3-speed T.H. 400 automatic; 3997539 1971-72 Camaro 307,350-ci automatic, except Z-28; 7811095 1971 Camaro 396-ci 4-speed.

\

Grand Prix

Model Year	3-speed Manual	4-speed Manual	3-speed Automatic	Notes
	Drive Shaft Part Numbers			Notes
1969	7806533	7804896	7806534	
1970	7804896	7804896	7806534	
1971	7804896	7804896	7806534	
1972	Not used	Not Used	7813512	

Part Number 7804896 also found on 1968 GS 400; 1968-69 Skylark automatic; 1968 442 4-speed; 1968-69 Cutlass 2-speed automatic. Also used on Tempest models see Tempest Chart.

Tempest Drive Shafts

Model Year	3-speed Manual	4-speed Manual	2-Speed Automatic	3-speed Automatic	Notes
1964	7804895	7804895	5679502	Not Used	
1965	7804895 (1) 5697022 (2)	7804895	7804895	Not Used	(1) Std. Duty (2) H.D. Duty
1966	7804895 (1) 5697022 (2)	5697022	7804895	Not used	
1967	7804895 (1) 5697022 (2)	7804895	7804895	7801111	
1968-69	7804896 (3) 7806533 (4)	7804896	7804896 (5)	7804896 (5) 7806534 (6)	(3) Std Duty except GTO (4) H.D. Std. GTO (5) Except GTO (6) GTO only
1970-71	7804896	7806534	7804896	7806534	
1972	7804896	7804896 (7) 7813512 (8)	7804896	7813512	(7) 350-ci (8) 400-ci or 455-ci

Part Number 7804896 also found on 1968 GS 400; 1968-69 Skylark automatic; 1968 442 4-speed; 1968-69 Cutlass 2-speed automatic.
Part Number 5679502 used on 1964-65 Cutlass except wagon; 7804895 also on 1964-66 Skylark except wagon; 1965-66 Cutlass 3-speed manual or 2-speed automatic expect wagon; 5697022 on 1965-67 442 3-speed manual. Also used on Grand Prix see G.P Chart.

Catalina 2+2 Drive Shafts

Model Year	3-speed Manual	4-speed Manual	Hydra	3-speed Automatic	Notes
1964	5679993 (1) 5679954 (2)	5679954	5679737	Not Used	
1965-67	5679892	5695099	Not Used	569522	(1)

Chapter 9 Brakes

Master Cylinder

Because of the nature, master cylinders are hard to inspect unless the unit is operating on a functional model. When buying a used master cylinder, it is best to rebuild it or get a guarantee. When inspecting the master cylinder, look beneath the dust boot for signs of leakage past the secondary cup. Also, check the condition of the push rod and make sure it is not frozen in place. However, a push rod that is easy to push could show signs that the seals are no good. Some cylinders are stamped with identification letters.

Master Cylinder Casting Codes					
Model Year	Drum	Disc	Model Year	Drum	Disc
FIREBIRD			**TEMPEST**		
1967	BS	(1)	1964	(1)	(2)
1968	(1)	FR	1965	(1)	(2)
1969	(1)	FR	1966	(1)	(2)
1970	0084	(1)	1967	(1)	FR
1971-72	1344	(1)	1968	(1)	GD(3) DW (4)
GRAND PRIX			1969	(1)	CT
1969	(1)	CT	1970	(1)	0884
1970-72	(2)	BE	1971-72	(1)	BE
Full-size PONTIAC			(1) No Code Given		
1964-66	(1)	(2)	(2) Option Not used		
1967	HU (5)	(1)	(3) Except Power brakes (4)- Power Brakes (5) Moraine brakes		

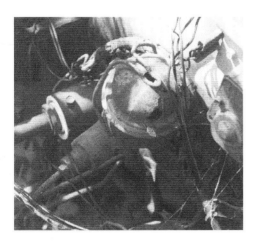

An example of unacceptable damage. The crack in the cover can allow moister to contaminate the master cylinder.

Firebird

1967

Drum	1
Disc	2

1968

Drum	4
Disc	3

1969

Drum	4
Disc	5

1970

Except Power Brakes	7
Power Brakes	6

1971-1972

Except Power Brakes	7
Power Brakes	8

Grand Prix

1969

Drum	4
Disc	9

1970

All	6

1971-1972

All	10

GTO/LeMans/Tempest

1964-1965

Except Power	11
Power Brakes	12

1966

Except Power	11
Power Brakes	13

1967

Drum	4
Disc	3

1968

Drum	4
Disc	
Except Power	14
Power Brakes	15

1969

Drum	4
Disc	9

1970

Drum	4
Disc	6

1971-1972

Drum Brakes	4
Disc Brakes	10

2+2

1964-1965

Except Power	16
Power Brakes	
Bendix	17
Moraine	18

1966

Except Power	16
Power Brakes	
Bendix	19
Moraine	20

1967

Drum	
Bendix	21
Moraine	22
Disc	23

Interchange Number: 1
Part Number: 545823
Usage: 1967 Firebird, Camaro, Chevelle, Chevy II, Corvair; 1968-69 Nova, Corvair. All with drum brakes, except metallic linings.

Interchange Number: 2
Part Number: 5463492
Usage: 1967 Firebird, Camaro, Chevelle, early full-size Chevrolet; 1968 Nova. All with disc brakes.

Interchange Number: 3
Part Number: 5459784
Usage: 1968 Firebird; 1967 Tempest, Cutlass, Skylark. All have disc brakes

Interchange Number: 4
Part Number: 541817
Usage: 1968-69 Firebird; 1969 Grand Prix; 1967-72 Tempest, Cutlass; 1967-70 Skylark. All have drum brakes.

Interchange Number: 5
Part Number: 5469357
Usage: 1969 Firebird

Interchange Number: 6
Part Number: 540664
Usage: 1970-73 Firebird, Camaro; 1970 Grand Prix, Tempest, Cutlass. All have power brakes.

Interchange Number: 7
Part Number: 540665
Usage: 1970 Firebird, Camaro. Except Power brakes.

Interchange Number: 8
Part Number: 5472652
Usage: 1971-73 Firebird, Camaro. Except Power brakes.

Interchange Number: 9
Part Number: 5468120
Usage: 1969 Grand Prix, Tempest, Skylark, Cutlass. All with disc brakes.

Interchange Number: 10
Part Number: 5471802
Usage: 1971-74 Grand Prix, Tempest, Skylark, Cutlass, Monte Carlo, full-size Pontiac, LeSabre, full-size Oldsmobile; 1973 Tornado. All with disc brakes and Moraine power booster.

Interchange Number: 11
Part Number: 5465180
Usage: 1964-66 Tempest. Except power brakes.
Notes: Cylinder from 1964-66 Skylark or Cutlass without power brakes is said to fit.

Interchange Number: 12
Part Number: 5465085
Usage: 1964-65 Tempest with power brakes.
Notes: Cylinder from 1964-66 Chevelle or G10 van with power brakes are said to fit.

Interchange Number: 13
Part Number: 5467025
Usage: 1966 Tempest; 1965-66 Gran Sport with metallic linings; 1965-66 Cutlass power brakes and manual transmission.

Interchange Number: 14
Part Number: 5468862
Usage: 1968 Tempest with disc brakes. Except power brakes.

Interchange Number: 15
Part Number: 5468774
Usage: 1968 Tempest, Skylark, Cutlass with power disc brakes.

Interchange Number: 16
Part Number: 5464284
Usage: 1964-65 full-size Pontiac. Except power brakes.

Interchange Number: 17
Part Number: 9785435
Usage: Late 1962-65 full-size Pontiac. Bendix power brakes.

Interchange Number: 18
Part Number: 5464325
Usage: 1963-65 full-size Pontiac. Moraine power brakes.

Interchange Number: 19
Part Number: 9785438
Usage: 1966 full-size Pontiac. Bendix power brakes.

Interchange Number: 20
Part Number: 5467345
Usage: 1966 full-size Pontiac. Moraine power brakes.
Notes: 1962-66 full-size Chevrolet; 1964-66 Chevelle. All with metallic linings will fit.

Interchange Number: 21
Part Number: 1489981
Usage: 1967-70 full-size Pontiac, Buick, Oldsmobile. Bendix drum brakes.

Interchange Number: 22
Part Number: 5458521
Usage: 1967-69 full-size Pontiac, Buick, Oldsmobile. Moraine drum brakes

Interchange Number: 23
Part Number: 9798957
Usage: 1967-69 full-size Pontiac. With disc brakes.
Notes: Built by Bendix.

Power Brake Chamber

Power brake booster chambers, like master cylinders, are hard to inspect if they are not on a running model, due to the fact that they need a supply of vacuum to work. Things to watch for are overall chamber condition. Watch for rusted or damaged chambers, which may affect their operable functions.

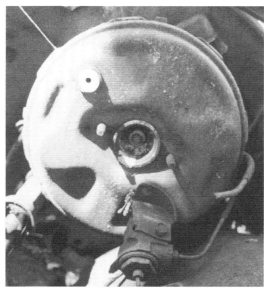

An example of a Delco Moraine chamber. Notice it's gold color.

Field-testing a chamber. By pressing down there should be some resistance and you should clearly hear the a vacuum sound.

Firebird

1967

Drum

Bendix	1
Moraine	2
Disc	3

1968

Drum	4
Disc	5

1969

Drum	6
Disc	
Except Trans Am	7
Trans Am	8

1970

All	9

1971-1972

All	10

Grand Prix

1969-1970

Drum	4
Disc	5

1971-1972

Disc	11

GTO/LeMans/Tempest

1964-1965	12
1966	13

1967

Drum	4
Disc	14

1968-1970

Drum	4
Disc	5

1971

Drum	15
Disc	16

1972

Drum	15
Disc	11

2+2

1964

Bendix	17
Moraine	18

1965

Bendix	17
Moraine	19

1966	20

1967

Drum	21
Disc	
Single Chamber	23
Tandem Chamber	22

Interchange Number: 1
Part Number: 3918715
Usage: 1967 Firebird; 1967-68 Camaro; 1968 Nova.
With Drum brakes.
Notes: Bendix Unit

Interchange Number: 2
Part Number: 5462049
Usage: 1967 Firebird; 1967-68 Camaro; 1968 Nova.
With Drum brakes.
Notes: Moraine Unit

Interchange Number: 3
Part Number: 5458828
Usage: 1967 Firebird; 1967-68 Camaro;   1968 Nova.
With Disc brakes.
Notes: Moraine Unit

Interchange Number: 4
Part Number: 5463666
Usage: 1968 Firebird; 1969-70 Grand Prix; 1967-70
Tempest. All with drum brakes.
Notes: Moraine Unit

Interchange Number: 5
Part Number: 5468817
Usage: 1968 Firebird; 1969-70 Grand Prix; 1968-70
Tempest. With Disc brakes.
Notes: Moraine Unit

Interchange Number: 6
Part Number: 5469210
Usage 1969 Firebird. Drum brakes
Notes: Moraine Unit

Interchange Number: 7
Part Number: 5469413
Usage 1969 Firebird with disc brakes. Except
Trans Am
Notes: Moraine Unit

Interchange Number: 8
Part Number: 5469345
Usage 1969 Firebird Trans Am.
Notes: Moraine Unit

Interchange Number: 9
Part Number: 5470735
Usage 1970 Firebird, Camaro.
Notes: Moraine Unit

Interchange Number: 10
Part Number: 5472354
Usage 1971-73 Firebird, Camaro.
Notes: Moraine Unit

Interchange Number: 11
Part Number: 5472379
Usage 1971-72 Grand Prix; 1972 Tempest;
1971-72 Cutlass.
Notes: Moraine Unit

Interchange Number: 12
Part Number: 5465080
Usage 1964-65 Tempest. Drum Brakes
Notes: Moraine Unit 1964-66 Cutlass,   Skylark
with drum brakes will fit.

Interchange Number: 13
Part Number: 5467917
Usage 1966 Tempest. Drum Brakes
Notes: Moraine Unit

Interchange Number: 14
Part Number: 5458513
Usage 1967 Tempest. Disc Brakes
Notes: Moraine Unit

Interchange Number: 15
Part Number: 5472358
Usage 1971-72 Tempest. Drum Brakes
Notes: Moraine Unit

Interchange Number: 16
Part Number: 5472357
Usage 1971 Tempest. Disc Brakes
Notes: Moraine Unit

Interchange Number: 17
Part Number: 2503276
Usage 1964-65 full-size Pontiac
Notes: Bendix unit. Interchanges 18 and 19 fit.

Interchange Number: 18
Part Number: 5467000 or 9771137
Usage 1964 full-size Pontiac
Notes: Interchanges 17 and 19 fit. 5467000 Moraine
9771137 Bendix

Interchange Number: 19
Part Number: 5465830 or 9779864
Usage 1965 full-size Pontiac
Notes: Interchanges 17 and 18 fit. 5465830 Moraine
9779864 Bendix

Interchange Number: 20
Part Number: 9784865 or 5467343
Usage 1966 full-size Pontiac
Notes: 9784865 Bendix 5465830 Moraine

Interchange Number: 21
Part Number: Varies see chart
Usage 1967-68 full-size Pontiac with drum brakes.

Interchange Number: 22
Part Number: 9778504
Usage 1967-68 full-size Pontiac with disc brakes.
Notes: Tandem chamber

Interchange Number: 23
Part Number: 9777751
Usage 1967-68 full-size Pontiac with disc brakes.
Notes: Single chamber

1967-68 Full-Size Pontiac Brake Boosters

Model Year	Bendix Std.	Bendix H.D.	Moraine
1967	9772994	9789760	5459551
1968	9793967	9789760	5459551

Calipers And Rotors

In 1967 General Motors introduced the disc brake system, Pontiac included. This system used special components that included a special master cylinder and booster chamber plus rotor plates and calipers. We have discussed the master cylinders and booster chambers in earlier sections. In this section we cover the rotor and the calipers.

CALIPERS

Calipers should be in good condition. Check the housings, inspect them for cracks or other signs of damage. Reject any housings that are damaged. Check the condition of the dust boots, torn or missing dust boots can allow foreign objects to enter and damage the pistons. Note: it is a good idea to rebuild all calipers that are purchase used.

ROTORS

The rotor should be free of excessive heavy rough scoring. Some scoring is okay as long as it is smooth. Rotors should also be free of rust. Check disc for sign of damage, especially along the lug nut opening. This area and the outer rim are easily damaged. Also check the rotor for run out. Run out should not exceed .003 inch of recommendations.

Firebird

1967-1968

Rotor	7
Caliper	1

1969

Rotor	8
Caliper	2

1970-1971

Rotor	9
Caliper	3

1972

Rotor	9
Caliper	4

Grand Prix

1969-1972

Rotor	8
Caliper	5

GTO/LeMans/Tempest

1967-1968

Rotor	7
Caliper	1

1969-1972

Rotor	8
Caliper	5

2+2

1967

Rotor	10
Caliper	6

Interchange Number: 1
Part Number: 5456076-outer
Part: Calipers
Usage 1967-68 Firebird, Tempest, Chevelle, Skylark, Cutlass.

Interchange Number: 2
Part Number: 5463806 left-hand
5463807-right-hand
Part: Calipers
Usage 1969 Firebird

Interchange Number: 3
Part Number: 5472532-L.H. 5472533-R.H.
Part: Calipers
Usage 1970-71 Firebird, Camaro; 1971 C10 Chevrolet pick up.

Interchange Number: 4
Part Number: 5474055-L.H. 5474056 R.H.
Part: Calipers
Usage 1972 Firebird, Camaro, C10 Chevrolet pick up.

Interchange Number: 5
Part Number: 5472161-L.H. 5472162-R.H.
Part: Calipers
Usage 1969-72 Grand Prix, Tempest, Chevelle; 1970-72 Monte Carlo; 1971-72 Skylark, Sprint, Cutlass.

Interchange Number: 6
Part Number: 5456479 outer
5468378-L.H. 5468379-R.H.
Part: Calipers
Usage 1967-68 full-size Pontiac, Oldsmobile

Interchange Number: 7
Part Number: 3901098
Part: Rotor
Usage 1967-68 Firebird, Tempest; 1967-69 Camaro, Cutlass; 1967-72 Chevelle; 1970-72 Monte Carlo; 1967-73 Chevy II/Nova; 1973-74 Omega; 1967-early 1971 Skylark.

Interchange Number: 8
Part Number: 405824
Part: Rotor
Usage 1969 Firebird; 1969-72 Grand Prix, Tempest; 1970-72 Cutlass; Late 1971-72 Skylark.

Interchange Number: 9
Part Number: 334348
Part: Rotor
Usage 1970-74 Firebird, Camaro; 1973-74 Tempest, Grand Prix, Chevelle, Monte Carlo, Cutlass, Skylark, Apollo.

Interchange Number: 10
Part Number: 9788421
Part: Rotor
Usage 1967-68 full-size Pontiac.

Brake Drums

Firebird

1967

Front	1
Rear	17

1968

Front	2
Rear	17

1969

Front	3
Rear	17

1970-1972

Rear	

Grand Prix

1969-1972

Front	3
Rear	17

GTO/LeMans/Tempest

1964

Front	
Except Metallic Linings	4
Metallic Linings	5
Rear	
Except metallic linings	17
Metallic linings	18

1965

Front	
Steel drum	
Except Metallic Linings	4
Metallic Linings	5
Aluminum Drum	6
Rear	
Except metallic linings	17
Metallic linings	18

1966

Front

2-bbl	4
4-bbl or 3x2-bbl	1
Aluminum drums	6

Rear

Except metallic linings	17
Metallic linings	18

1967

Front	1
Rear	17

1968

Front	2
Rear	17

1969

Front	3
Rear	17

1970

Front	7
Rear	17

1971-1972

Front	8
Rear	17

2+2

1964

Front

Cast Iron

Except Ribs	9
With Ribs	10
Aluminum	11

Rear

1965

Front

Steel

Standard	12

Special	13
Aluminum	14
Heavy Duty	16
Metallic	15

Rear

Except Aluminum or Metallic	20
Aluminum Drums	19
Metallic	21

1966-1967

Front

Steel

Standard	12
Special	13
Aluminum	14
Metallic	15

Rear

Except Aluminum or Metallic	20
Aluminum Drums	19
Metallic	21

Interchange Number: 1
Part Number: 9793677
Part: Front drum
Usage 1967 Firebird, Tempest; 1966 Tempest with 4-bbl or 3x2-bbl V-8. Except with disc Brakes
Notes: Has radial fins

Interchange Number: 2
Part Number: 3853799
Part: Front drum
Usage 1968 Firebird, Tempest; 1968-70, Camaro; 1969-72 Chevelle, Cutlass; 1968-73 Nova; 1973-74 Ventura II, Apollo. All have finned drums and are for front drums only; 1964-66 G10 Chevrolet van 12-bolt axle rear drums only.

Interchange Number: 3
Part Number: 9798690
Part: Front drum
Usage 1969 Firebird, Tempest, Grand Prix. Except with Disc Brakes

Interchange Number: 4
Part Number: 9776183
Part: Front drum
Usage 1964-65 Tempest, Chevelle, Cutlass, Skylark, Chevy II; 1964 Oldsmobile J88; 1966 Tempest 2-bbl V-8.   Except Metallic linings.
Notes: Steel drum with circumferential fins.

Interchange Number: 5
Part Number: 9776701
Part: Front drum
Usage 1964-65 Tempest, Chevelle, Chevy II with metallic linings.

Interchange Number: 6
Part Number: 9781513
Part: Front drum
Usage 1965-66 Tempest, Cutlass.
Notes: Aluminum brake drum

Interchange Number: 7
Part Number: 9798690
Part: Front drum
Usage 1970 Tempest. Except Disc Brakes

Interchange Number: 8
Part Number: 481832
Part: Front drum
Usage 1971 Tempest. Except Disc Brakes

Interchange Number: 9
Part Number: 541944
Part: Front drum
Usage 1964 full-size Pontiac except Police, trailer package, H.D. cooling or aluminum drums.
Notes: No ribs

Interchange Number: 10
Part Number: 9775689
Part: Front drum
Usage 1964 full-size Pontiac except Police, trailer package, H.D. cooling or aluminum drums.
Notes: With ribs

Interchange Number: 11
Part Number: 9776153
Part: Front drum
Usage 1964 full-size Pontiac except Police, trailer package, H.D. cooling with aluminum drums.
Notes: Stamped KH 49313

Interchange Number: 12
Part Number: 9785195
Part: Front drum
Usage 1965-68 full-size Pontiac except special drum brakes.
Notes: Steel drum

Interchange Number: 13
Part Number: 9785299
Part: Front drum
Usage 1965-68 full-size Pontiac with special drum brakes.
Notes: Steel drum

Interchange Number: 14
Part Number: 9778481
Part: Front drum
Usage 1965-68 full-size Pontiac with aluminum drum brakes.
Notes: Stamped 58154

Interchange Number: 15
Part Number: 9777202
Part: Front drum
Usage 1965-67 full-size Pontiac with metallic brakes.
Notes: Cast iron drum with 68 fins

Interchange Number: 16
Part Number: 9779302
Part: Front drum
Usage 1965 full-size Pontiac with Heavy duty brakes.
Notes: Aluminum drum with cast iron inner

Interchange Number: 17
Part Number: 9788681
Part: Rear drum
Usage 1967-69 Firebird; 1964-72 Tempest, Cutlass (except wagon), Skylark, 1969-72 Grand Prix. Except with metallic linings.

Interchange Number: 18
Part Number: 9788683
Part: Rear drum
Usage 1964-66 Tempest with metallic linings

Interchange Number: 19
Part Number: 9776152
Part: Rear drum
Usage 1964-68 full-size Pontiac with aluminum drums.

Interchange Number: 20
Part Number: 9794455
Part: Rear drum
Usage 1964-68 full-size Pontiac except metallic brakes or aluminum drums.
Notes: Cast Iron drums

Interchange Number: 21
Part Number: 9777204
Part: Rear drum
Usage 1964-67 full-size Pontiac with metallic brakes.

Chapter 10 Electrical

Due to their nature of high heat and high voltage, most electrical components are not a good buy as used parts. Electrical components are easily worn out and are hard to check. There are three that are favorable buys: the distributor, alternator, and starter. These units are sturdier and can be readily rebuilt. Distributors are keyed to engine size, output, and sometimes transmission. A ID number that is stamped on a band or stamped directly into the housing of the distributor identifies them. Without being on the car or using an expensive testing machine, it is hard to check a distributor. But things that you should watch out for are damage to the body, and check to see if the distributor will freely move, and that the shaft is not bent or frozen in place.

Their part number that is stamped on them can identify starters and alternators. To accurately check the unit, it must be disbarred and checked with various meters. A good check is to have the yard check the unit for you, and give you a guarantee that the unit is functioning. Note: this guarantee is not a warranty , but just a guarantee that the unit is in proper working order. It may fail in a short time, as is the case with most electrical components that are bought used, so it is always wise to rebuild all used electrical parts. As for interchangeable parts, check over the following charts and match part numbers. Note that many times the same engine will use the same parts regardless of the model. However, it common that the parts will only be used one year.

Alternator identification number is stamped on the housing here. Along with a build date and out rating.

. A simple field test. The alternator should rotate easily by hand. Reject any alternator that does not.

An example of a distributor identification band.

1964 Distributor Identification Numbers

326-ci

2-bbl		4-bbl	
W/O Trans. Ignition	With Trans. Ignition	W/O Trans. Ignition	With Trans. Ignition
1111052	1111040	1111052	1111040

389-ci

4-bbl		3x2-bbl
W/O Trans. Ignition	With Trans. Ignition	
TEMPEST		
1111175	1111047	Not Available

389-ci

8.6 C.R.		Except 8.6 C.R.	
W/O Trans. Ignition	With Trans. Ignition	W/O Trans Ignition	With Trans. Ignition
1111053	1111047	1111175	1111047

421-ci

All C.R.s		3x2-bbl
W/O Trans Ignition	With Trans. Ignition	
2+2		
1111052	1111040	Same as 4-bbl

1965 Distributor Identification Numbers

326-ci

2-bbl		4-bbl	
W/O Trans. Ignition	With Trans. Ignition	W/O Trans. Ignition	With Trans. Ignition
1111177*	1111081	1111177	1111081

389-ci

4-bbl		3x2-bbl
W/O Trans. Ignition	With Trans. Ignition	
TEMPEST		
1111078	1111080	1111175* 1111047**

389-ci/421-ci — 2+2

2-bbl		4-bbl		3x 2-bbl	
Reg. Fuel	Prem. Fuel	W/O Trans Ignition	With Trans. Ignition	W/O Trans Ignition	With Trans. Ignition
1111090	1111078* 1111080**	1111078	1111080	1111175	1111047

*- Without Transistor ignition **with Transistor ignition

1966 Distributor Identification Numbers

326-ci

2-bbl		4-bbl	
W/O A.I.R.	With A.I.R.	W/O Trans. Ignition	With Trans. Ignition
1111177*	1111102	1111175	1111081

389-ci

4-bbl					3x2-bbl
W/O A.I.R.		With A.I.R.			
TEMPEST					
MANUAL	AUTO.	MANUAL	AUTO.		
1111078* 1111080**	1111078* 1111080**	1111103*	Not Used		1111175* 1111047**

389-ci/421-ci — 2+2

2-bbl		4-bbl		3x 2-bbl	
Reg. Fuel	Prem. Fuel	W/O Trans Ignition	With Trans. Ignition	W/O Trans Ignition	With Trans. Ignition
1111090	1111078* 1111080**	1111078	1111080	1111175	1111047

*- Without Transistor ignition **with Transistor ignition

1967 Distributor Identification Numbers

326-ci				400-ci	
2-bbl		4-bbl		4-bbl	
W/O A.I.R.	With A.I.R.	W/O A.I.R.	With A.I.R.	W/O A.I.R.	With A.I.R.
FIREBIRD					
1111199	1111164	1111165	1111281	1111250	1111252
TEMPEST					
1111199	1111164	1111165 1111166*	1111281	1111250 1111242** 1111251*	1111252
2+2					

400-CI				428-CI	
8.6 C.R.		10.5			
W/O C.A.P.	With C.A.P.	W/O A.I.R.	With A.I.R.	W/O A.I.R.	With A.I.R.
1111242	1111261	$1111253_{(1)}$ $111268_{(2)}$ 1111255*	$1111300_{(1)}$ $1111269_{(2)}$	1111250 1111251*	1111252

(1) Early models (2) Late Models *- Transistor ignition **-2-bbl version

1968 Distributor Identification Numbers

350-ci				400-ci	
2-bbl		4-bbl		4-bbl	
Manual	Automatic	Manual	Automatic	Manual	Automatic
FIREBIRD					
1111281	$1111165_{(1)}$ $1111281_{(2)}$	1111447	1111282	1111449* 1111941**	1111270* 1111941**
TEMPEST					
1111281	$1111165_{(1)}$ $1111281_{(2)}$	1111447	1111282	1111449* 1111941**	1111270* 1111941**

(1) 3-vacuum hoses (2) 5-Vacuum hoses *-Without Ram Air **- With Ram Air

1969 Distributor Identification Numbers

350-ci				400-ci	
2-bbl		4-bbl		4-bbl	
Manual	Automatic	Manual	Automatic	Manual	Automatic
FIREBIRD/TEMPEST					
1111960	1111942	1111966	1111965	1111952* 1111941**	1111946* 1111941**
GRAND PRIX					

400-ci				428-ci	
2-bbl		4-bbl		4-bbl	
Manual	Automatic	Manual	Automatic	Manual	Automatic
1111253	1111253	1111952	1111253	1111952	1112009# 1111946##

*-Except Ram Air IV ** With Ram Air IV #-Except 390-hp ##-390- hp only

1970 Distributor Identification Numbers

FIREBIRD/TEMPEST

350-ci		400-ci		455-ci (Tempest Only) 4-bbl	
Manual	Automatic	Manual	Automatic	Manual	Automatic
1112008	1112008	1111176*	1111148*	1112012	1112012
		1112024**	1112009**		
		1112011#	1112011#		
			1112007$_{(1)}$		

GRAND PRIX

400-ci 2-bbl		4-bbl		455-ci 4-bbl	
Manual	Automatic	Manual	Automatic	Manual	Automatic
1112007	1112007	1111176	1111148	1112024	1112012

*-Except Ram Air **- Ram Air III #- Ram Air IV (1)- 2-bbl only

1971 Distributor Identification Numbers

FIREBIRD/TEMPEST

350-ci		400-ci		455-ci (Tempest Only) 4-bbl	
Manual	Automatic	Manual	Automatic	Manual	Automatic
1112083 $_{(1)}$	1112069 $_{(2)}$	1112070	1112089#	1112072*	1112072*
1112090 $_{(3)}$	1112090 $_{(3)}$		1112070	1112073**	1112073**

GRAND PRIX

400-ci 2-bbl		4-bbl		455-ci 4-bbl	
Manual	Automatic	Manual	Automatic	Manual	Automatic
		1112070	1112070	1112072	1112072

(1) Early On codes WR or WU only (2) Early codes YU or XR only (3) Late built codes WN, WP, YN or YP #- 2-bbl *-Except 335-hp **-335-hp only

1972 Distributor Identification Numbers

350-ci		400-ci		455-ci (Tempest Only) 4-bbl	
Manual	Automatic	Manual	Automatic	Manual	Automatic
			FIREBIRD/TEMPEST		
1112140	1111218[1]		1112119[1,3]	1112202 *	1112202*
			1112121 [4]	1112133**	1112133**

		GRAND PRIX			
400-ci 2-bbl		4-bbl		455 -ci 4-bbl	
Manual	Automatic	Manual	Automatic	Manual	Automatic
			1112121		1112127*
					1112133**

(1) Except California (3) California only (3) 2-bbl (4) 4-bbl *w/o transistor ignition ** with transistor ignition

The Delco Ramey starter is marked with the identification part number.
Along with the Manufactures name. And the build date.
It is best to rebuild a used starter.

Pontiac Alternator Identification and Usage

Alternator/Generator		Usage				
Alternator Number	Output Amp.	Firebird	Tempest	Grand Prix	2+2 (full-size Pontiac	Notes
1100549	55	55-amp	No	No	No	
1100627	52	No	1964 52-amp	No	1964 H.D.	
1100674	60	No	No	No	1964 60-amp	
1100676	37	No	64 (6)	No	No	
1100678	42	No	No	No	1964 (6)	
1100680	42	No	No	No	1964 (5)	
1100681	52	No	No	No	1964 (4)	
1100682	52	No	No	No	1964 H.D.	
1100683	37	No	1964 (5)	No	No	
1100697	60	No	No	No	1965 60-amp	
1100699	42	No	No	1969	66-67 V-8 (3,2) 68-69 42-amp	
1100699	42	No	No	No	1966-67 (1) 1968-69	
1100702	60	No	1965- 60 amp (5,8) 1966-60 amp (4,6)	No	1965-66 60-amp	
1100703	60	No	1965- 60-amp (6) 1966- 60 amp (4)	No	1965-66 60-amp	
1100713	52	No	1965 H.D.	No	No	
1100726	52	No	1965 (6)	No	1965 52-amp	
1100727	42	No	No	No	1965	
1100728	52	No	1965 (4,5)	No	1965 52-amp (6)	
1100729	37	No	1964 V-8	No	No	
1100736	42	No	1966 (1,3)	No	No	
1100737	55	No	1966 (3,6)	No	1966 (2,4, 5)	
1100738	55	No	1966 (4,5))	No	1966 (1,4)	
1100739	42	No	No	No	1966 (1)	
1100740	60	No	1966 (4,5,8)	No	1966 60-amp (1,4)	
1100769	42	No	No	No	1967 69 (2,3)	
1100895	61	No	70 61 amp	70 61 amp	70 61 amp	
1100903	55	55-amp	No	No	No	
1100904	61	61-amp	No	No	No	
1100927	37	71-73 V-8	71-74 V-8	71-74 V-8	71-74 v-8	
1100928	55	71-73 V-8	71-74 V-8	71-74 V-8	71-74 V-8	
1101015	80	71-73 V-8	71-74 V-8	71-74 V-8	71-74 V-8	
1100768	37	1967 V-8(1)	1967 V-8 (1,3)	No	No	(1)- with A.I.R.
1100770	55	67 V-8 (4)	1967 V-8 (1,4)	No	67 (4,5)	(2) -w/o A.I.R.
1100700	52	67 V-8 (4,6) 68 V-8 (4) 69 350-ci (7)	66 V-8 (4,6,8) 67 V-8 (2,4) 69-70 55-amp alt.	69 w/55-amp	66-67 (4,6) 68-70 55-amp	(3)-w/o a/c
1100704	32	67 V-8 (2, 3, 5) 68 V-8 (3) 69 350-ci	66 V-8 (1,3,6) 67 V-8 (2, 3) 68-70 V-8 (3)	1970	1970	(4)- with a./c
1100832	37	69 400-ci	No	No	No	(5)- w/o P/S
1100852	55	69 350-ci (9)	No	No	No	(6)- with P/S
1100854	61	NO	69 61-amp	69- 61 amp	69 61 amp	(7)- 350-ci w/o rear defroster
1100830	55	69 400-ci (9)	No	No	No	(8)- Trans. Ignition
1100902	37	yes	No	No	No	(9)- Rear Defroster
1117765	62	No	No	69-70 62-amp	63-70 62-amp	

Pontiac Starter Motor Identification

Starter Part Number	Firebird	Tempest	Grand Prix	2+2 Full-size Pontiac	Notes
1108328	1967 326-c 2-bbl 1968 350-ci 2-bbl	No	No	No	
1108495	1967-69 V-8 4-bbl 1970 (1) 1971 455-ci 335-hp 1972 455-ci	1967-70 (1, 2) 1971 455-ci 335-hp 1972 455-ci 300-hp.	No	No	(1) Ram Air (2)- H.O.
1107293	1969 350-ci 2-bbl	1964-67 326-ci 2-bbl 1968-69 350-ci 2-bbl	1969 400-ci 2-bbl	1965-66 (3, 4) 1967-69 (3)	(3)- Low Compression
1108434 1108445 1108498	1970-74 350-ci	1970-74 350-ci	No	1970-74 350-ci	(4)- Man. Transmission
1108435 1108446 1108495	1970-71 400-ci 1971 455-ci 325-hp.	1970-71 400-ci 1970 455-ci (5) 1971 455-ci 325-hp.	1970-71	1970-71 400-ci or 455-ci	(5) Except Ram Air or H.O.
1107355	No	1964-67 V-8 4-bbl or 3x2-bbl 1967-69 400-ci (5)	1969 400-ci or 428-ci 4-bbl	1965-66 (6) 1967-69 (7) 1967-69 428-ci	(6)- High Compression
1107791	No	No	No	1961-64 (3)	(7) 400-ci 10.5 C.R.
1107781	No	No	No	1961-64 (6)	

Chapter 11 Wheels and Wheel Covers

A used wheel is a good investment. Providing that you use care in inspecting the unit. Factors that greatly determine wheel usage is width and diameter. These two factors can be used to eliminate a majority of wheels. For an example if you are looking for 15-inch wheels for your 2+2, you can use a tap[e measure and eliminate the 14-inch diameter units. Next measure the width of the wheel. Avoid large changes in width, or diameter. The one plus rule is good to follow. Which simply means you can usually increase the size by one inch. For example, you can go from a 14-inch to a 15-inch wheel, or from a 14x6 to a 14x7 without any clearance problems.

Offset, or back spacing, should be checked next. This is the distance from the centerline of the rim to the inner side of the wheel hub. A smaller off set means that the wheel's face is deeper dished, set in further, while a larger off set means that the wheel face is set out more. Avoid large changes in offset than those that were originally on your car. For example going from a 3 ½ inches to a ¼ inch offset could cause braking and steering problems. While the reverses, going from a ¼ inch offset to a 3 ½ inches offset could result in tire clearance problems. However, if you do change an offset, diameter or width they must be replaced in pairs.

Note wheels from a full-size Pontiac will not fit a Tempest, Grand Prix (1969-72) or a Firebird due to the difference in the bolt circle diameter. The full-size models use a 5.00 diameter while the other models use a 4 ¾ inch diameter.

INSPECTING THE WHEEL

First, check the rim, it should be free of damage. A bent rim can make mounting a tire impossible and the wheel unusable.

Next check the condition of the inner area of the wheel. If the wheel is two piece unit make sure the mounting areas, where the two piece come together, are solid and not breaking loose. Slight rust can be okay, but rusted out areas should make you reject the wheel.

Check the condition of the lug nut and center hub holes in the wheel. Look for signs that they are out of round and oblong, which could indicate the wheel will not fit properly. On the subject of the center hub hole, make sure that is wide enough to mount the wheel. This is especially true if your are using different wheels than those that were designed to fit your car.

Wheel codes can be found stamped into the rim near the valve stem. The number correspond to a the wheel stamping date.

Pontiac Wheel Identification Codes				
Part Number	Diameter and Width	ID Code	Type	Models Use
9789327	14x5	HE	Space saver spare	1967 Firebird
9793125	14x6	HK	Stamped	1967-69 Firebird
9781246	14x6	KB	Rally wheel I	1965-68 Tempest; 1967 Firebird
9789329	14x6	KB	Rally wheel II	1967 Firebird
9787279	14x6	JA	Rally wheel II	1967-69 Firebird, Tempest w/D.B.; 1969 Grand Prix
9785955	14x6	HH	Stamped	1967 Firebird w/D.B.
9791450	14x6	HF	Stamped	1967-68 Tempest w/D.B.; 1969 Grand Prix
9792737	14x5	HI	Space saver spare	1968-69 Firebird
9789329	14x6	JC	Rally II	1968-69 Firebird, Tempest
9793592	14x6	KC	Space saver spare	1968-70 full-size Pontiac
3869457	14x5	B	Stamped	1968 Tempest
9792739	14x5	HJ	Stamped	1968-69 Tempest w/D.B.
9787860	14x6	JB	Rally II	1968 full-size
3966936	14x7	XT	Stamped	1969 Firebird w/F70x14 tires; 1969-72 Grand Prix
480723	14x7	JK	Rally	1969-70 Firebird, Grand Prix
3975660	14x6	AM	Stamped	1970-72 Firebird
3975667	14x7	CL	Stamped	1970-72 Firebird
525708	14x6	KT	Rally I	1972 Tempest, Grand Prix
409879	14x6	CZ HF	Stamped	1971-72 Tempest
334397	14x7	IF	Stamped	1969 Firebird, Tempest, Grand Prix
525709	14x7	KS	Rally II	1972 Tempest, Firebird; 1970-72 Grand Prix
D.B. Disc Brakes				

Firebird

1967

14x5	1
14x6	
Except Rally Wheel	
Drum brakes	2
Disc Brake	3
Rally I wheels	4
Rally II Wheels	
Drum Brakes	5
Disc Brakes	6

1968

14x5	7
14x6	
Except Rally	
Drum Brakes	
Disc Brake	2
Rally Wheel	5

1969

Space Saver Tire	
14x5	7
14x6	8
Except Rally wheel	
14x6	2
14x7	9

Rally Wheel	
14x6	5
14x7	10
1970	
Space Saver Tire	
14x5	7
14x6	8
Except Rally Wheel	
14x6	11
14x7	12
15x7	16
Rally Wheels	
14x6	13
14x7	14
15x7	15
1971-1972	
Space Saver Tire	
14x5	7
14x6	8
Except Rally Wheel	
14x6	11
14x7	12
15x7	16
Rally II wheels	
14x7	14
15x7	15
Honeycomb Wheels	
14x7	17
15x7	18

Grand Prix

1969	
Space Saver Tire	8
Except Rally Wheels	
14x6	19
14x7	9
Rally Wheel	
14x6	6
14x7	10
1970	
Space Saver Tire	8
Except Rally Wheels	
14x7	9
15x7	16
Rally Wheels	
14x7	14
1971	
Space Saver Tire	8
Except Rally Wheels	
14x7	9
15x7	16
Rally Wheels	
14x7	14
Honeycomb	
14x7	17
15x7	18
1972	
Space Saver Tire	8
Except Rally Wheels	
14x7	9
15x7	16
Rally Wheels	
14x7	14
15x7	15
Honeycomb	
14x7	17
15x7	18

GTO/LeMans/Tempest

1964	
14x5	20
14x6	21

1965-1966

Except Rally Wheel

14x5	20
14x6	21
Rally wheel	4

1967

14x5

Drum brakes	20
Disc Brakes	22

14x6

Drum brakes	21
Disc Brakes	19
Rally I Wheels	4
Rally II wheels	6

1968

14x5

Drum Brakes	23
Disc brakes	24

14x6

Space Saver Tire	8
Except Rally Wheels	19
Rally I wheels	4

Rally II wheels

Drum brakes	5
Disc Brakes	6

1969

14x5	24

14x6

Except Ralley Wheels	19
Rally Wheel	6
Space Saver Tire	8

1970

14x6

Except Rally	25
Space Saver Tire	8
Rally II	6

15x7	16

1971

14x6

Except Rally	19
Space Saver Tire	8
Rally II	6

14x7

Honeycomb	17

15x7

Except Rally	16
Rally II	15
Honeycomb	18

1972

14x6

Except Rally	19
Space Saver Tire	8
Rally II	6

14x7

Rally II	14
Honeycomb	17

15x7

Except Rally	16
Rally II	15
Honeycomb	18

2+2

1964-1967

14x6

Five-bolt	26
Eight-bolt	27
15x6	28

Interchange Number: 1
Part Number: 9789327
Size 14x5
Usage: 1967 Firebird
Notes: Space Saver spare tire

Interchange Number: 2
Part Number: 9793125
Size 14x6
Usage: 1967-69 Firebird drum brakes only in 1967.

Interchange Number: 3
Part Number: 9785955
Size 14x6
Usage: 1967 Firebird with disc brakes. Except Rally wheels.

Interchange Number: 4
Part Number: 9781246
Size 14x6
Usage: 1967 Firebird; 1965-68 Tempest
Notes: Rally I wheel

Interchange Number: 5
Part Number: 546495
Size 14x6
Usage: 1967-69 Firebird; 1968 Tempest with drum brakes
Notes: Rally II wheel

Interchange Number: 6
Part Number: 485456
Size 14x6
Usage: 1967 Firebird with disc brakes; 1967-68 Tempest with disc brakes; 1969 Grand Prix.
Notes: Rally II wheel

Interchange Number: 7
Part Number: 9792737
Size 14x5
Usage: 1968-71 Firebird; 1968-69 Camaro
Notes: Space Saver spare tire.

Interchange Number: 7
Part Number: 9792737
Size 14x5
Usage: 1968-71 Firebird; 1968-69 Camaro
Notes: Space Saver spare tire.

Interchange Number: 8
Part Number: 9793592
Size 14x6
Usage: 1969-72 Firebird, Grand Prix; 1968-72 Tempest; 1971-72 Ventura II.
Notes: Space Saver spare tire.

Interchange Number: 9
Part Number: 334397
Size 14x7
Usage: 1969 Firebird, Tempest, Grand Prix, Camaro; 1969-74 Nova; 1970-72 Cutlass

Interchange Number: 10
Part Number: 9798509
Size 14x7
Usage: 1969 Firebird, Grand Prix.
Notes: Rally wheels

Interchange Number: 11
Part Number: 3975660
Size 14x6
Usage: 1970-72 Firebird, Camaro; 1971-72 Ventura II. Except Rally wheels.

Interchange Number: 12
Part Number: 3975667
Size 14x7
Usage: 1970-72 Firebird, Camaro; 1971-72 Grand Prix, Ventura II. Except Rally wheels

Interchange Number: 13
Part Number: 492351
Size 14x6
Usage: 1970 Firebird; 1971-72 Ventura II; 1973-74 Tempest.
Notes: Rally II wheels

Interchange Number: 14
Part Number: 485455
Size 14x7
Usage: 1970-72 Firebird, Grand Prix; 1972-74 Tempest.
Notes: Rally II wheels

Interchange Number: 15
Part Number: 485454
Size 15x7
Usage: 1970-72 Firebird; 1972 Grand Prix; 1971-72 Tempest.
Notes: Rally II wheels

Interchange Number: 16
Part Number: 326875
Size 15x7
Usage: 1970-72 Firebird, Grand Prix, and Tempest; 1973-74 Skylark; 1971-74 Monte Carlo; 1973-74 Cutlass. Except with Rally wheels.

Interchange Number: 17
Part Number: 483084
Size 14x7
Usage: 1971-73 Firebird, Grand Prix, Tempest.
Notes: Honeycomb wheels

Interchange Number: 18
Part Number: 484425
Size 15x7
Usage: 1971-73 Firebird, Grand Prix, Tempest.
Notes: Honeycomb wheels

Interchange Number: 19
Part Number: 9791450
Size 14x6
Usage: 1969 Grand Prix,; 1967-72 Tempest; 1967-71 Cutlass; 1968-72 Skylark; 1970-72 Chevelle. All with Disc brakes
Notes: Without Rally wheels or Space saver tire

Interchange Number: 20
Part Number: 3872276
Size 14x5
Usage: 1964-67 Tempest, except GTO; 1964-68 Chevelle; 1964-69 Skylark; 1964-70 Cutlass.
Notes: All models have drum brakes and vented wheels.

Interchange Number: 21

Part Number: 3871919

Size 14x6

Usage: 1964-67 Tempest; 1964-68 Chevelle; 1964-69 Skylark; 1964-70 Cutlass.

Notes: All models have drum brakes and vented wheels.

Interchange Number: 22

Part Number: 9773689

Size 14x5

Usage: 1967 Tempest with disc brakes.

Without Rally wheels.

Interchange Number: 23

Part Number: 389423

Size 14x5

Usage: 1968-72 Tempest; 1971-72 Ventura II; 1967 Camaro; 1970-72 Chevelle; 1967-69 full-size Chevrolet; 1969-72 Nova.

Notes: All have drum brakes.

Interchange Number: 24

Part Number: 9792739

Size 14x5

Usage: 1968-69 Tempest with disc brakes.

Interchange Number: 25

Part Number: 3928297

Size 14x6

Usage: 1970 Tempest; 1968-69 Chevelle.

Notes: Except with Rally or wide oval tires.

Interchange Number: 26

Part Number: 9780855

Size 14x6

Usage: 1960-67 full-size Pontiac with five lug nut holes.

Interchange Number: 27

Part Number: 9787151

Size 14x6

Usage: 1960-68 full-size Pontiac with eight lug nut holes.

Note Integral wheel and hub.

Interchange Number: 28

Part Number: 1474185

Size 15x6

Usage: 1968 full-size Pontiac with heavy-duty wheels; 1958-1960 Cadillac.

1964-1972 Pontiac Wheel Cover Identification PART 1

Part Number	Type	Dia.	Description	Model Usage
9774609	(1)	10 ½	42 outer ribs imprinted "Pontiac Motor Division"	1964-69 all; 1970-72 Tempest and full-size Pontiac and
5738083	(1)	10 ½	Imprinted with Pontiac	some 1971-72 Firebird
9787697	(2)	15 13/32	6 holes three spinners	some 1971 Firebirds
9714055	(3)	14 ¼	26 holes no spinner	1967 Firebird, Tempest
9781478	(3)	N/A	Simulated wire	1967 Firebird
9791006	(2)	15 13/32	8 holes red back ground with black letters	1967-68 all models; 1969-72 Firebird, Grand Prix, Tempest
9714122	(3)	14 ¼	26 holes red background with black letters	1968 Firebird, Tempest
9795997	(2)	N/A	5 Spoke simulated mag wheel	1968 Firebird, Tempest
9718045	(3)	N/A	6-spoke simulated mag wheel	1969 Firebird, Tempest; 1970 Tempest
483426	(2)	N/A	36 spoke	1969-70 Firebird; 1969-70, Tempest, Grand Prix
486553	(2)	N/A	Finned cover for 14-inch wheels Pontiac logo in center	1971-72 Firebird
486554	(2)	N/A	Finned cover for 15-inch wheels Pontiac logo in center	1972-74 Firebird, Tempest; 1972 Grand Prix;
9890699	(3)	N/A	Firebird crest in the center	1972-74 Firebird, Tempest; 1972-74 Grand Prix; 1972 full-size Pontiac
9795959	(1)	N/A	Ribbed disc	1972-73 Firebird
9797019	(2)	N/A	Ribbed disc with slots	1969-72 Grand Prix stand. 1972 Tempest
481601	(2)	N/A	Ring disk Bright	1969-70 Grand Prix
9722915	(3)	N/A	Ringed disk for 15-inch wheels	1971 Grand Prix
9774611	(2)	15 3/8	8 elongated holes with tri spoke spinner	1972 Grand Prix, Full-size Pontiac
9774074	(3)	14 1/8	10 depression, half of each depression painted black	1964 Tempest, except GTO
9771087	(3)	N/A	Simulated wire wheel	1964 Tempest
				1964-66 Tempest, full-size Pontiac

169

1964-1972 Pontiac Wheel Cover Identification PART II

Part Number	Type	Dia.	Description	Model Usage
9780913	(3)	14 1/8	10 struts and slots	1965 Tempest
9780724	(2)	15 13/32	Three spinner six depression	1965 Tempest
9783624	(2)	15 15/32	6 holes and spokes	1966 Tempest
9783391	(3)	14 1/8	10 Holes	1966 Tempest
9786453	(3)	14 1/8	6 Holes no spinner	1967 Tempest
482538	(2)	N/A	Ribbed cover	1971-72 Tempest
9771228	(2)	15 7/16	Looks like standard wheel painted black Center hub	1963-64 full-size Pontiac
9771229	(2)	15 7/16	Looks like standard wheel painted black No center hub	1963-64 full-size Pontiac
5718810	(2)	15 7/16	60 ribs and tri-spoke spinner	1964 full-size Pontiac
9774560	(3)	14 1/8	3 large ribs with 36 smaller ribs	1964 full-size Pontiac
9780426	(2)	15 13.32	Tri-Spoke spinner with 72 ribs	1965 full-size Pontiac
9704036	(3)	14 1/8	16 Ribs	1965 full-size Pontiac
9784277	(2)	15 13/32	Tri-spoke spinner 24 holes	1966 full-size Pontiac
9707029	(3)	14 ¼	26 Holes no spinner	1966 full-size Pontiac
9787569	(2)	15 13/32	Solid disk with tri-spoke spinner	1967 full-size Pontiac
9710754	(3)	14 ¼	26 holes	1967 full-size Pontiac
9788773	(3)	15 1/8	10 Holes- for 15 inch wheels	1967 full-size Pontiac w/o D.B.
9788496	(3)	15 13/32	6 Holes imprinted PMD DISC BRAKES	1967 full-size Pontiac w/ D.B.

(1)- Standard Cover (2) Custom Cover (3) Deluxe Cover D.B. Disc Brakes

Salvage yards that helped with this guide:

CST Salvage
Ed Witte
Aurora, Mo 65605
417-678-6994 or 417-678-7305

R&R Auto Salvage
Aurora, MO 65605
417-678-2221

Henderson Auto Salvage
Monett, MO 65708
417-235-3719

!Get All the Information!
Order Body Trim and Glass
Chapter Include
Decoding
Front End Sheet Metal
Door and Outside Mirrors
Quarter Panel And Rear End Sheet Metal
Frame And Roof
Glass
Nameplates
Body Trim
Interior Hardware
Interior Trim And Accessories
Electrical Accessories

Order for Only $19.97 plus $4.95 S&H
Just fill out the form and mail with payment (check or money order) to:
PAH Publishing
Dept. SOPO101
711 Hillcrest St.
Monett, MO 65708

Name:			City:	State:		Zip:
Address:			City:	State:		Zip:
Your Car:			Each	Total		
Qty.	Item					
	Pontiac Muscle Cars Engine Drive Train and Suspension		$19.97			
	Firebird Body Trim And Glass (1967-75)		$19.97			
	Tempest/GTO Body Trim and Glass (1964-72)		$19.97			
	Shipping			$4.95		
	Total					

For A Free Catalog Write To:
PAH Publishing
Dept. Cat
711 Hillcrest St.
Monett, MO 65708
Or Call 417-236-0077
Fax 417-236-0850